I dedicate this to my wife, Judith ~
There was a time when we were close like the sea and sky,
sometimes calm, other times stormy.
Then the boundaries meld until we became one.
To some, this may seem my voice telling these stories
but it is in fact the two of us speaking as one.
Hand in hand we have crossed the continents of Earth,

Where Wild Winds Blow

but none as wide as my love for you.
Together we have voyaged across all oceans,
but none as deep as my love for you.

Jack Binder, master mariner and ship's engineer,
homebuilt *Banyandah* with his wife Judith in Sydney, Australia.
Launched in 1973, a year later, with two infant sons,
they embarked on a magical life encircling Earth in ever-increasing circles
taking sixteen years to visit more than eighty countries.
In 2007, Jack and Jude, then grandparents married forty years,
circumnavigated Australia aboard that very same craft.
Once back on dry land they wrote the inspirational book,
Two's a Crew detailing that adventurous journey.
A published writer since 1980, Jack is a regular contributor to international periodicals.

"Twenty years from now you will be more disappointed by the things that you didn't do than by the ones you did do. So throw off the bowlines. Sail away from the safe harbor. Catch the trade winds in your sails. Explore. Dream. Discover." ~ Mark Twain

Where Wild Winds Blow

The story of two modern day explorers deeply in love

Jack Binder

Tujays Publishing
Empire Vale P.O. NSW
Australia 2478
Email: capjack2j@gmail.com
Web: www.jackandjude.com

Copyright © Jack Binder 2011

All photographs and diagrams by Jack and Judith Binder

All rights reserved. No part of this book may be reproduced or transmitted in any form or by any means electronic or mechanical, including photocopying, recording or by any information storage and retrieval system, without prior permission in writing from the publishers or authors.

First published in Australia 2011
Second edition published 2012
Third edition published worldwide 2020

Papers used in the production of this book are natural, renewable and recyclable products sourced from sustainable forests.

Note: Both imperial and metric measurements used throughout.
1 nautical mile (NM) = 1.15 land miles (m) = 1.852 kilometres (km)
Australian dollars are shown
Australian spelling is used

National Library of Australia
Cataloguing-in-Publication entry:
Binder, Jack, 1944 -
    Where Wild Winds Blow / by Jack Binder ;
    photographs by Judith Binder ;
    edited by Judith Binder.
    ISBN 9780980872033 (Pbk.)
    1. Binder, Jack--Travel. 2. Binder, Judith--Travel. 3. Voyages and travels. 4. Yachting--Australia. 5. Offshore sailing--Australia. 6. Coastwise navigation-- Australia.

797.1246092

Contents

The Plan	1
We're Away	5
Little Geordie	16
Yet Another River Crossing	19
Christmas Afloat	25
No Christmas at Copenhagen	30
Now We Know Why	32
Black Man's House	38
A Few Tough Days	45
Friendship Is Why We Travel	54
The Nut	63
King Island Melody	71
Contradictions	83
Assault on Mount Sorell	97
One World to Another	109
Tears in Paradise	125
Hard at Work in Adelaide	134
Streaking Along to Streaky Bay	144
A Journey Much Feared	153
Chasing a Wild Goose	167
Feeling True Blue	175
Pirates at Esperance	181
Wild Stopover at Investigator	189
Too Many Choices	194
Bound For Tasmania	206
Perfection	214
Bibliography	226
Glossary	227

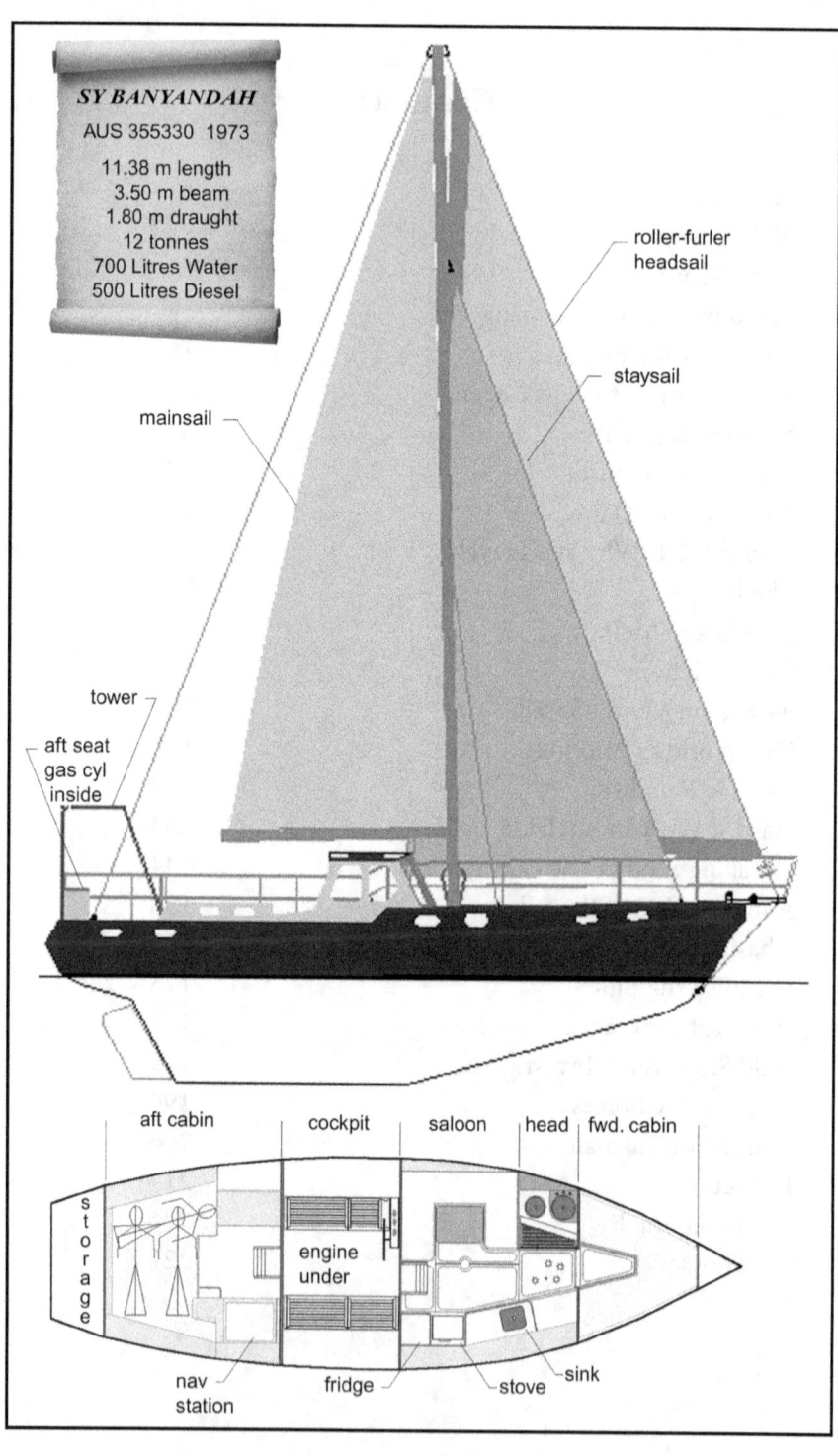

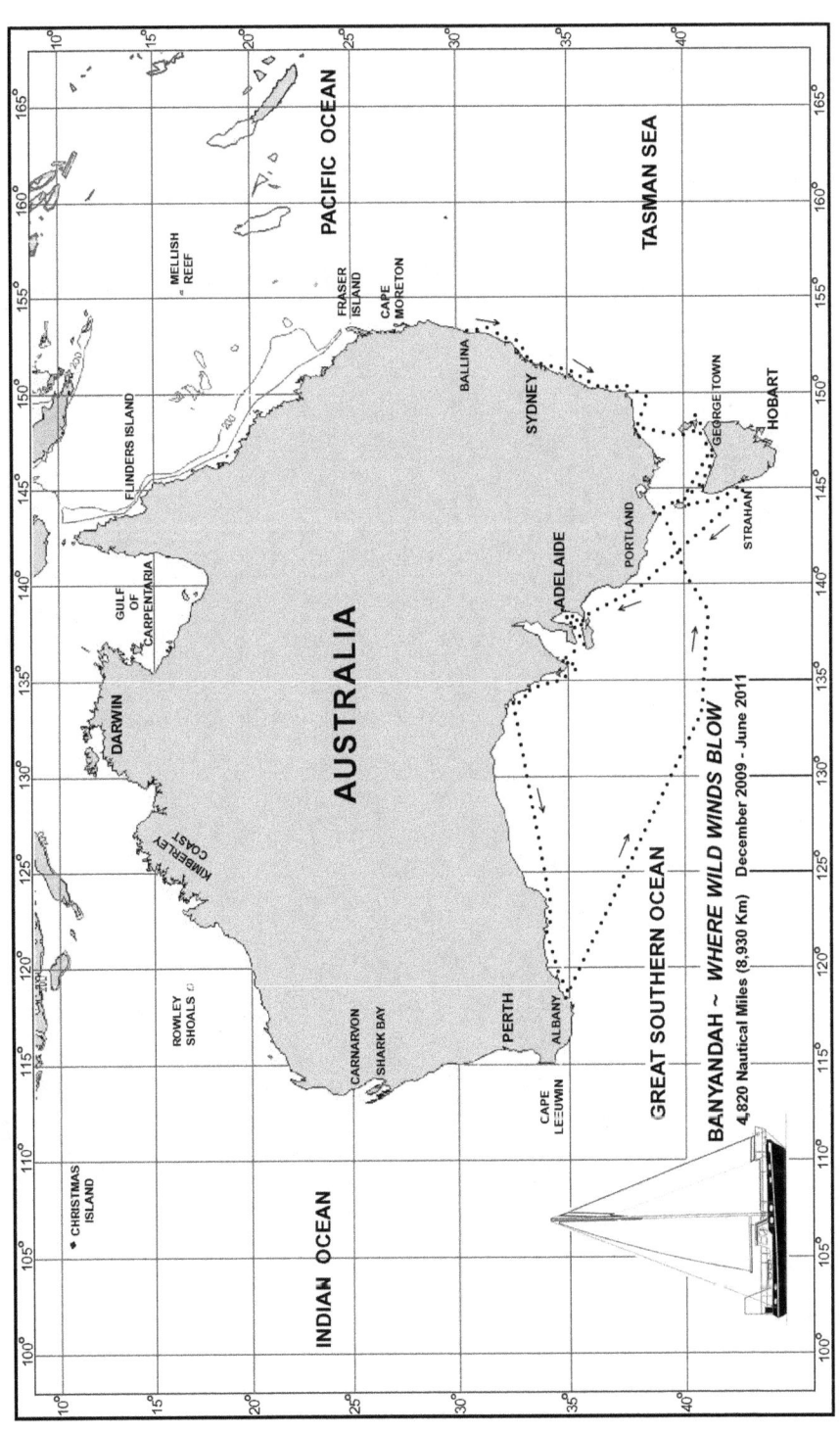

~ Chapter 1 ~

The Plan

I REMEMBER WALKING BACK FROM THE BEACH late one afternoon and passing an open hall where a lot of loud noise poured out. Looking in, a crowd of men stood around a man swinging a gavel, and I was intrigued by what might be happening. So, I cautiously snuck in hoping no one would notice a skinny 10-year-old boy. At the centre of everyone's attention, a tattered steamer trunk stood upon a table.

"How much for this mystery box," the ruddy fellow swinging the gavel suddenly yelled out, and the crowd in front of me shuffled about as if in a hurry to see what might come next.

"Do I hear $20 for this antique steamer chest and what it might contain?" the big bloke cried and winked to his assistant as if they shared an almighty secret.

"C'mon, someone here must feel lucky and want to risk a few dollars. How much for this mystery box?"

The crowd grew more restless, murmurs rose to laughter, and the bloke in front of me elbowed his mate. "What say we go lay a bet on the fifth at Belmont?"

Now I had seen boxes like this one in my storybooks and knew lost treasure could be in them. So when the man at the front called for bids, from the back, I blurted out, "A dollar! I'll give a dollar for that box."

Heads turned and searched the room. Those around me looked down and gave a chuckle. One slender old fellow ruffled my hair then called out, "The boy bids a dollar." And again, the room buzzed like a hornet's nest had been given a kick.

When I brought that trunk home and opened it up, it wasn't filled with old treasure - no pieces of eight, no gold. In fact, it contained nothing more than a loose roll of smelly stiff cloth, mottled off-white, with a rope sewn around its edge. But then as I pulled it out, I recognised it as a ship's sail.

Fingering the coarse cloth with my soft little fingers sent my mind reeling. Where had this sail been! Maybe to the far side of the ocean that stretched away from the end of my street. And in my mind, a ship sailed past the pyramids of Egypt. Maybe this sail had cruised along a coconut coast on wooden dhows manned by dusky men. Or had it sailed around the world and withstood vicious storms? Fingering a ragged hole in its corner, I felt sure that was so. Then and there, I decided to build my own little ship so my tarnished white sail could fly in the wind once again.

But I didn't know anything about building boats. So I started by looking through all my books, and from what I saw, figured that fibreglass material was the best stuff. With my father's hammer and some of his nails, a few burlap sacks and a big bag of plaster, I built myself a mould. But it had more ripples than there are swells on the sea. But that didn't matter. There were more problems to come. Like applying the fibreglass material, which proved kind of tricky. More than half ended up on our garage floor. But that didn't matter either. My pop never barked. He just watched over me with a great big smile. You see, he was just as keen, and knew just as little.

Jackie and his dad at Grand Canyon

Then the big day finally arrived. Father and son took their new boat to the beach, where surrounded by a big crowd, she was launched into the surf. Pity my poor pop, he couldn't swim a stroke, yet he stood up to his neck in the frothy stuff pushing his son and his lop-sided boat out to sea. A bit of a shame it didn't stay afloat.

The Plan

If there's one thing good about failure, it's that we learn what doesn't work. You see, from that first big failure, I realised I had never known why some things float. I didn't understand displacement. So, from that failure, I read more and learned heaps.

My next boating failure fell just short of outright success. On her launching, this new vessel not only stayed afloat, but she also took off like a rocket across the ocean. That was until she crashed into her first wave. I had wanted speed so had built her like a giant surfboard three times my own length. So when my new craft dipped her nose like a dolphin, she went underwater. Awash, she came to a halt. Then with a pop, she broke free to sail stop-start again and again.

Years quickly passed while I grew into a man trying and failing at many other things. Nevertheless, life was good. I found a loving wife, and we had two healthy sons. And from all those years of trying, I had learnt one important thing. That, if I kept plugging away and not quit, I'll mostly win. Then one day this bit of knowledge gave me the confidence to attempt building a proper, ocean-going sailing ship.

Well, it wasn't easy and took a lot longer than planned, and yes, on the way my lady and I failed at many new things. But we never gave up. After three years of tough, arduous work, on a lovely midwinter day, we launched our classy new craft, and for a change, everything went right. *Banyandah* took to the water like an elegant swan. Trouble was, straightaway we had to face a whole new wave of challenges we knew nothing about. You see, we'd never really learned how to sail.

First motor the day we launched

Now, I'm not as young or as wild as that any more. A gracious God and a whole bunch of good luck have given me a good life. Aboard our ship with my wife and sons, we travelled the world, eventually crossing just about every ocean. On the way, we visited those Egyptian pyramids, we watched volcanoes erupt and saw Africa's wild creatures. But I have failed and failed so many times I have learned a lot about what doesn't work. And that has made life a whole bunch easier.

Looking back over our life's experiences and the pain we endured to achieve our goals, I say this to the young: Give everything a go. By trying, you will learn, and gain an experience. By not trying, life passes quickly. Don't be a quitter. You never know, the next time you try might bring success.

These thoughts roamed through my head when back in our house watching the Richmond River taking rains from the ranges back to the sea. Our grandchildren were still quite young and madly running along their course of life. But Jude, my loving wife of forty-one years, and I weren't getting any younger.

Our circumnavigation of Australia after sixteen years of living on the land was a past event recorded in our logbooks. We had edited our videotapes into a DVD, written our first book *Twos A Crew*, and now wondered what lay ahead. Thinking back over our recent achievements brought into focus the few things we had failed to achieve while going around the vast island continent of Australia. We regretted not reaching the peak of Tasmania's Mount Sorell, and we never witnessed Black Man's Houses on Flinders Island, the site of one of Australia's greatest tragedies.

In plain sight just outside our front window, *Banyandah* stood ready to take us anywhere we command. We only needed a plan. Jude and I always function best with a destination fixed in our heads. But with so many choices, sometimes we can't decide and just take off to find one as we drift towards a first destination. We definitely wanted to go somewhere and be afloat while we still could. So we seized on the idea of sailing south down the New South Wales coast, something we hadn't done for many years. Probably nothing too exciting there. But we could then revisit Tasmania and get into those exciting things we missed. Who knows, after that, we might continue right around Australia again, this time clockwise, picking up all the things overlooked the first time.

~ Chapter 2 ~

We're Away

THE FAMILY CAME OVER FOR A BBQ ON DEPARTURE DAY and helped us shift out of the house. Then as our grandkids chased one another around the fire's dying embers, we locked up the house, said our fond farewells, then they drove away and we strolled down the jetty to move back aboard *Banyandah* full time.

That night, no longer in a stationary bed but floating somewhere between Heaven and Earth, both of us dreamt of past adventures until rising well-rested at dawn. Half-awake, after a last visual check of our house we shifted *Banyandah* off the jetty then proceeded downriver to check out the river bar.

The entire world seemed at peace at the river mouth. "Maybe we ought to just keep going," I jokingly suggested as Jude looked across the placid blue water to a crisp, empty horizon. With a pensive smile, she eventually shook her head then turned us about and within minutes, we'd pulled into in a small nook isolated by a low seawall. Breaking the silence, our anchor rumbling out of its locker startled a large flock of Crested Terns on the sandy beach engaged in a courtship ballet. It probably also awoke the only other yacht in sight.

Our journey had begun on a Sunday, a day we often take easy. But not this one. After six months of land-bound living, everything had changed in the blink of an eye, the time it had taken to cast free our mooring lines. Suddenly we were sailors again. We'd not been on the water since tying our lady to the jetty half a year earlier. Sure, we'd done some maintenance and improvements like new solar cells, but somewhere in that time, gone were our sea legs and a fair bit of physical fitness. Now we had soft hands, lily-white skin, and tender feet.

That cyclone hole near the river mouth was a weekend favourite for zooming speedboats towing screeching kiddies on inflatable rings. But before they arrived, Jude hesitated only a moment before diving in to scrape barnacles from our through-hull fittings. Meanwhile, I tried to coax our windvane steering device to work freely again. Winter westerlies had carried heaps of central Australian dust into Mr Aries innards, making him stiff. That dust had also seized up our poorly made Maxwell sheet winches, fizzing together too many dissimilar metals of alloy, stainless, and bronze into four mongrel non-moving lumps.

I usually use olive oil to lubricate the Aries, as it doesn't emulsify with water, but this time I tried light 3 in 1 oil hoping it would do the trick and not go claggy. That poor old gizmo has done thousands of miles since we first put it to work back in Malaysia in '78! Mr Nick Franklin, a genius, had designed a great device.

You may have noticed we don't give our gismos names. Maybe it would be apt to call the Aries Hercules because it toils mightily even in horrendous conditions. Our chart plotter would then be Einstein. But no. Only our lady, *Banyandah*, the lovely Miss B or Big Blue. Why? She's the magic, alive, part of the family.

All that first day, back to outside living, I was soon burnt pink. But as that hot sun's golden glow backlit the winking lights of Ballina, a cool evening breeze invigorated us, so we raised our glasses to toast our good fortunes. My arm slipped around my lady's waist. "Tomorrow," I said, clinking her glass. "We're off to the high seas at first light. That is if the wind comes as predicted." The wind had been somewhat lazy that day, just as we both felt right then. So, after a lingering cuddle in the lessening light, it was early to bed.

After another grand sleep, first light peeping through the portholes got me nudging Jude awake, and literally within minutes, we had slipped out the Richmond River into a zephyr stealing down out the north. My! For a calm morning, what a bumpy slide over the Ballina bar, it's getting more dangerous every year.

We're Away

For the first time in six months, we raised sail, then ran wing and wing, mainsail one side, headsail the other, as the northerly found its strength. Eight hours later and forty miles further south, under full main and far too much headsail poled out, *Banyandah* was proving rather hard to control just as the Clarence River breakwater came into sight. Rather than struggle to slab reef the main, Jude laboured harder at the helm while we closed in on white-water fronting the bar. Touching nine to ten knots, surely that must be our hull speed.

What amazed us was how well our first day back at work had gone after so many months of easy living. Earlier, while enjoying a blissfully empty ocean, we'd got talking why that is, and concluded it comes down to having systems in place. A system for raising the anchor - one for raising the mainsail - another for guiding the vessel in tricky situations - even one for flushing the dunny. In our first years, we hadn't a clue who should do what, or what should be done first. That confusion had caused so many panicky situations that we yelled at each other, which only made things worse. Now that we know and have systems in place, we hardly need to say a word.

It probably took twenty or thirty thousand miles to bed them down, so here's how Judith and I now manage *Banyandah*: Getting underway, Jude drives the boat while I get the anchor up and stowed. Then I'm free to look around, assess where best to go, and do the sail work. From the helm, Jude calls out the depth and anything extraordinary she sees. When the sails are raised, she tends the sheets until I can get there for the final trim.

Jerome & Jason hookah diving at 8 & 9

When we delivered vessels for a living, if we used a crew, training them was the first thing we'd do. Every manner of working the ship; tack, reef, hove to, even MOB (man overboard) would be practised. That way, the crew knew just what to expect and what was expected.

So, that first day as we raced into Iluka late, we automatically took up our positions. Jude driving, singing out the depth, watched for my hand signals while I stood on the dinghy, at the bow, or alongside her; wherever to see what lay ahead.

After the anchor took a bite, it being our first destination, we were whacked and ready to crash. Then we heard the next day's weather would be a duplicate of today, and as we never waste wind when there are miles to sail, that meant another early start for what would be a sixty-mile sail. We'd probably get to Coffs Harbour late, but no worries arriving there after dark, just anchor off the jetty. But this time we'll reef down early to make the passage a little less rocky-rollie. Gosh, wouldn't it be nice to catch a good fish? Goodnight.

While we slept, it blew strongly until the wee hours when a comforting silence finally sent us deeper into slumber. Greeting us at daybreak, a soothing coolness replaced the north wind's heat, bringing an invigorating stillness. And rising from the aft cabin, I found a bronze sky spread across low tide mudflats and little water under our keel. Muscle sore from tackling that first day's forty-mile sail in strong winds, I blew out my cheeks when thinking of the sixty miles of ocean separating us from our next anchorage, and looking below, thought of rejoining Jude in bed.

Electing to breakfast underway, with a cuppa in hand and mumbling directions we up anchored and very slowly eased *Banyandah* towards deeper water. Jude taking her out of gear several times to glide over the really skinny bits until the sounder stopped beeping its low water alarm. Once in the main river, deep water prevailed, as did a swift current rushing us towards the river mouth. Ahead, the rising orb turned the eddies into swirls of liquid gold which took hold of *Banyandah* and spun her off course, making Jude laugh as she worked the helm in a little game of spin the wheel as I scurried about raising the mainsail.

In a quick call to the coast guard, I inquired about leaving the river to the south. The chart showed a massive build-up of sand on that side, and with it now dead low tide, the sea might be breaking upon it. I also wanted to thank the duty officer for helping us the day before, by describing entry conditions as we approached with a bagful of wind in our sails.

Then in a rush, the last land slipped past, and a messy sea churned the open horizon. But we smashed through that, sending spray flying. Our heart rate slowed during the next half hour's easy motoring, and the backwash diminished, leaving a relatively calm sea warmed by a whispering north wind that we knew would soon start to roar. Another hour passed and its strength had sufficiently increased for us to silence the diesel and pole out the headsail. Rejoining Jude aft after that chore, the log read 3½ knots, a nice, smooth, jogging pace. Adding the south going current put our speed at a respectable 5 knots over the ground. Keep that up, and we'd make Coffs Harbour in 12 hours.

What a glorious day unfolded. Easy seas comfy enough just to read or once again get lost in gazing towards a shore that seemed veiled behind a silken scarf. Which in fact was smoke or heat haze. A bit disconcerting, the land so close and yet appearing far away, but never a worry while the current kept giving us free miles.

After lunch, the wind found its real teeth, subtly at first, increasing in gusts like the day before. With the wind aft and building seas that rushed down upon us, it was first noticed when our back end slewed round, and then the windvane had to work extra hard to bring us back on course. Several times in the worst sets, the mainsail went aback. That's when we slew around so far, the wind gets on the wrong side of the sail, and with a mini-explosion, it tries to fly across the ship. But cannot as it's held by a preventer, a block and tackle set to restrain the mainsail.

Yesterday, as sometimes happens when destinations are in sight, I'd been lazy to not shorten sail when the wind increased. Instead, we'd just tightened our grips and held on tight. Today, as soon as it started to huff, we double reefed the main knowing the wind would only get stronger. Initially, this slowed us a titch, but by the time we'd finished eating a cold lunch of salads, we were flying again.

When overpowered, especially with a following wind, *Banyandah* throws herself about like a tormented demon. And we've proved repeatedly that we gain little extra speed, and the poor windvane has to struggle to steer her.

Reducing sail made our journey far more relaxing as first North Solitary Island was passed then a strange yellow buoy. What was it doing out here in 50 metres of water?

Vague hills barely showed through the veil when just five miles off and this sent us further into our own private worlds and had me wondering how we ever navigated before the advent of the GPS satellite system.

Golly! We must have been lucky to find anything in days gone by, because, as we approached Coffs Harbour in a romper stomper second-day sail, we saw nothing but a thick curtain of haze. In fact, even though the GPS reported our destination only three miles away, we could barely see faint shadows of mountaintops.

Jerome (13) navigating across an ocean

In conditions like those, things happen fast. Suddenly the lump of Muttonbird Island jumped through, and seconds later, we were screaming into the harbour driven by short sail and a wicked wind of over thirty knots. We had flown, making the journey in less than ten hours, averaging more than six knots. Fast for a hefty lady like *Banyandah*.

Coffs Harbour, a man-made harbour situated about 440 kilometres north of Sydney, is the only deepwater, all-weather port between Port Stephens and Brisbane. Two rock walls jut out from shore, one each side of the town to encompass a bay with a historic timber jetty that once shipped timber harvested from the hinterland. Muttonbird Island, which is effectively one big hill, is a Nature Reserve protecting a significant Wedge-tailed Shearwater breeding site connected to the land via the northern breakwall that runs alongside an international marina.

When the area was settled in the late 1870s, the inshore islands of Muttonbird and South Coffs Island were all that provided shelter to ships in southerly gales. Then in 1892, with completion of the Coffs Harbour Jetty, an export timber trade and new fishing industry were established. That massive timber structure had to withstand huge storms unprotected until 1912 when work started on the formation of the harbour by first closing the gap between South Coffs Island and the mainland. The northern breakwater, over a 1000-metres long and joining Muttonbird Island to the mainland was constructed between 1914 and 1927. But the harbour was not completed until 1946 when the eastern breakwater, which extends 400 metres from South Coffs Island towards Muttonbird to narrow the opening, was finished. By the time *Banyandah* first visited Coffs Harbour in 1974, construction of new walls forming an inner boat harbour in the north-west corner had been completed.

Once inside the main harbour, in far easier conditions, our anchor went down next to the long jetty that runs towards a beautiful yellow sand beach, crowded with what looked a school sports day. An equal number were in the water paddling boards, swimming, or rowing canoes. And behind us, kids jumped from the jetty in loud yelps and big splashes, while next to them others madly paddled straight towards us. And when asked if we'd become their finishing line, their leader laughed. "Both the start and finish line." Then he yelled, "Go!" And they all rushed back towards the beach.

What fun to come from privacy and open space into a group of youths enjoying life. Short-lived though. To the south, black clouds were brewing. Silver lightning jagging through them. Then a cool zephyr replaced the hot north wind. Cold raindrops immediately followed a blast from the towering black anvil now directly above us. Fleeing youths paddled and swam ashore. And in seconds, our calm reverie was replaced by action stations. *Banyandah* was being blown towards the inner rock wall. Up anchor, motor back into open space and reset our plough anchor. What followed was typical of boat life. With every passage of cloud, a changing wind kept us looking about checking our position.

While keeping guard in our cockpit, we reminisced through previous visits to this historic harbour.

"Do you recall the time we sailed out to do a photoshoot for the Woman's Weekly Magazine, and our main halyard parted?" I said to Judith snuggled back under the protection of our dodger. A sheepish grin crept across her face as she sighed, "We must have been crazy."

In our early life wandering the world and raising our children aboard *Banyandah*, we sought any legal means to finance our travels. Once when

Where Wild Winds Blow

sailing back across the Pacific towards Australia, it had occurred to us that our recent spate of oceanic expeditions might interest Australian readers. So, from Norfolk Island, our last port of call before the Australian mainland, I mailed a letter to Australia's premier magazine outlining what we had just achieved and asking for payment in return for the story. Well, blow me down, when we arrived in Coffs Harbour a week later, a reporter and a photographer flew up from Sydney. The year was 1982, and we'd been sailing the high seas for eight years. The inner harbour was still under construction at the time, and we had tucked ourselves alongside a floating pontoon. As it happened, there was also a full gale blowing. We had no access to the shore other than a painter's plank to the northern rock wall, so picture this. The wind's howling, the water's active, spray and spume are being tossed over that immense rock wall, and on those rocks, a female reporter is standing getting wet while eye-balling our boat dancing about, with just a narrow plank joining us to shore.

"C'mon," we coaxed her. "Just look straight ahead. Or should we come ashore?"

Defiantly she shook her head, took off her pumps, and from what I recall, closed her eyes before setting off across that plank. Well, of course, she made it. So did the photographer who introduced himself as Kevin Brown. The reporter's hand was still shaking when she extended it, saying, "Hi, I'm Jill Bacon."

Well, that began an all-day session retelling stories of high seas dramas and about our educating Jason and Jerome afloat. What an event. The boys, just ten and eleven, captivated the photographer, showing him shells, souvenirs, and trinkets amassed from Asia and both sides of the Pacific. At the same time, he snapped photos pretty much non-stop. In the main cabin, school material was spread all over the place

Banyandah School circa 1980

while Jude explained to Jill how she had educated her children from first reading right through to grade six.

As dusk began to fall, the reporter became nervous, and although we offered to cook up dinner and bed them down, they preferred to take us out for dinner instead. For Jill, it was hands and knees over the surging plank, but before we knew it, we were up the road at the Chinese Restaurant downing two bottles of good Aussie red wine.

Another excellent storytelling session presided throughout a fabulous dinner and continued late into the night. After the last patron had departed, the restaurant owners pulled up chairs and joined us, adding two more bottles of red wine to replace the empties.

It was well after midnight when we pulled the plug. We probably would have continued if Kevin hadn't said he wanted a photo of *Banyandah* sailing across an empty horizon, to give the piece the feel of what we experience. We liked the idea. It's hard to get a good photo of your boat under sail, and to have one taken by a professional was a great opportunity. Problem was, outside that gale was still blowing. No worries, Kevin said. He'd charter the police launch if we agreed to go out. That clinched the deal, and we made tracks home to our beds.

Coffs has a deep water entry, but in severe weather, breakers can form right across its entrance. So, the next morning we weren't surprised to hear the police launch refused to go out. Would we still go out and just sail back and forwards near the end of the breakwater, the photographer had shouted, quickly adding that he would make the dash to the end of the eastern breakwall and grab the shots as we sailed past. In those days, we were supremely confident sailors. Hadn't we just notched up 65,000 miles in all sorts of weather? So we agreed, even though I had a terrible hangover.

What happened after that is an integral part of *Banyandah* folklore. The four of us untied our little ship and motored out into the main harbour to be bucked and tossed about as we raised our mainsail. We never attempt anything dangerous without the mainsail's steadying effect. Then we proceeded to motor out to sea. Of course, occasional swells were breaking clean across the opening, but no worse than those on some river bars. So, waiting for a calmer patch, we hit full power. Only, just as we were right amongst the big stuff between the rock groyne and Muttonbird Island, the main halyard parted. And the mainsail fluttered down. Or partly down. It got stuck halfway and began shaking us madly. So much so, I had no choice but to climb the mast with a new rope! Imagine poor me, hungover and queasy, climbing the mast with a big long rope in my teeth while hanging on for dear life as Jude drove *Banyandah* out into gale force seas. Well, of course, we got out all right. But then began the real drama.

With a small headsail raised, we started sailing back and forth in front of the seawall with a vacant horizon as backdrop just as instructed the night before. The sea is always much lumpier close to land, and some monsters were rearing up, forming massive walls of brute force as they approached the seawall. From our cockpit, we watched mesmerized as this tiny lone figure suddenly dashed from the safety of South Island, and ran helter-skelter along the seawall towards the scant protection of the light structure at its end, waves breaking over the seawall either in his footsteps or just in front of him. We were far safer on board *Banyandah*.

For the next ten or fifteen minutes, we sailed back and forth in front of this structure, and every now and then between the massive breaking waves, the lone photographer would jump out and snap photographs. At one point, the seventh wave of the seventh set reared up to a colossal height and crashed an avalanche of green water over the ten-metre high light structure. Oh my god, Kevin has been washed into the sea we thought, but a moment later relief poured through us as he reappeared above foaming seawater pouring off the structure.

Both made their flight home to Sydney. A few weeks later, when the Four J's had travelled to Sydney to pick up our cheque, we were shown into the Weekly's Assistant Editor's office where we met Sandra Funnell. Behind us, her well-appointed office had a connecting door that was slightly ajar.

Sandra was ever so sweet to our sons and asked them whether they liked their life afloat. "We love it," they replied. "Growing up on a sailboat and touring the world is exciting. We've got the wanderlust like mum and dad."

That's when I mentioned the pluses of our lifestyle had been independence, freedom of spirit, a close family relationship, a feeling of accomplishment. "Crossing an ocean of four and a half thousand miles is an accomplishment. We all work at it."

On her desk was a cheque, filled out for the amount agreed earlier I suppose. I was eyeing it lustfully when her desk phone rang. I thought I heard a female voice drifting through the interconnecting door, but kept my eyes on that cheque. When Sandra replaced the handset, she smiled even more broadly. "That was the editor. She admires what you're doing so much, she's doubling the amount we agreed to pay you."

We never actually met Dawn Swain, but through Sandra conveyed our appreciation.

Moments later a new cheque arrived and was handed to us along with a packet of photos taken by Kevin. Then as we gathered around, and oohed and aahed at those magical shots, Sandra told us that Kevin had lost both his cameras that stormy morning. His two beautiful Nikons had got drenched! And Kevin had had to scurry back to the motel to dump them into buckets of freshwater to save the film.

I was exhausted by the time Jude and I had re-lived that remarkable experience. Lightning was still flashing, but I was so whacked, I crashed straight into bed. Only once did I wake to see Jude up at the port checking our position against shore lights. Thinking, how lovely to have such a good crew, I turned over and went back to sleep.

~ Chapter 3 ~

Little Geordie

THE FOLLOWING SATURDAY'S VOYAGE SAW PRETTY scenery pass slowly until a collection of buildings signalled Port Macquarie. We'd not been there before, and its barred river entrance had a reputation for being dangerous, putting our apprehension levels several notches higher as we scurried around getting the boat ready for what could be heavy breaking seas.

The Coast Guard gave us some helpful guidance. They told us the bar had recently shifted so not to follow the leads in. Pretty obvious as we approached. Breakers rolled in across the opening, so we kept close along the north shore as advised. To a couple of old foxes like us, we still had a few adrenalin rushes while *Banyandah* sailed inside white water.

Once in, the shore was mad with Christmas holidaymakers. We waved back to some while searching where to go. It's always disconcerting entering a new place, especially when there is plenty of shoal water waiting for a moment's lapse of concentration.

To be safe, we just plopped the anchor down smack in the middle of the river and had a cuppa. Heaps of speedboats rushed past. Too busy there. And since we'd spied a quieter spot nearer the town, we picked up our hook and threaded more shallows to a pond filled with other yachts. Crikey, no room for us there either. Oh well! Finally, we picked up a mooring buoy with the thought that we'd hang there till morning, or until thrown off.

Little Geordie

As darkness came, a celebration began on the grass verge just a stone's throw from our door. How lovely. Carols by Candlelight filled the cabin until bedtime. But no sooner we were under bed covers then we had to get up. This time to watch a massive fireworks display. Nice first night.

Deathly still the following morning, we lay in bed, our floating home filled with unusual, yet familiar sounds. The slow, steady, finger drumming, drip, drip, drip of seawater seeping past the propeller shaft seal was vying with the irregular crackling-pop of shell creatures just below where we lay our heads. But there was also a sound that is always there, day or night, sunshine or gale. And that's the tolling of the half and whole hour from our constant friend Little Geordie. His smiling round face had joined our good ship when we first started on this sea roving life four decades ago. In the days when a dollar was a small fortune to us, he came as a gift from Judith's mum. Her kindly soul loved us so dearly she dug deep into her meagre savings and bought a timepiece to help manage our lives.

The quality set of Schatz ship's clock and barometer she purchased are two beauties still proudly mounted on our main cabin bulkhead next to where our sons did their schoolwork. In easy sight from where we steered *Banyandah* to thousands of destinations around this wonderful planet. Every seventh day one of us faithfully wound the clock twenty-seven turns with a silver key that had a special hook in the ship's galley. In return, rain, storm or shine, Geordie chimed the beginning of countless adventures and its ringing, a constant reminder of mum's love and best wishes.

From earliest times, shipboard work has been set to four-hour cycles. Our Geordie followed that routine, chiming once at the first half-hour following midnight. Then twice at one in the morning, thrice at one-thirty, four times on the second hour of the four-hour cycle. And so on until ending each cycle with eight commanding rings at four a.m., eight a.m., noon, four in the afternoon, eight o'clock at night, and the one I always eagerly awaited, eight bells announcing the change of watch at midnight.

For many years our faithful friend struck the time, never once missing a beat - not once. Not until our voyage around this island continent when Geordie started running slower, and slower, although his chime still sounded strong and hearty. Being the same frugal man, I removed Little Geordie from the wall and took off his back to be immediately impressed by a score of gleaming, beautifully cut, golden brass gears spinning round and round. Crowning this mechanical wonder was a perfectly shaped bell with twin strikers.

Hmm, I thought, a drop of oil must be required and lavished my friend with a splash before replacing him back on our wall. Well, alas, poor Geordie only got sicker and continued to run slower and slower till he stopped - dead. After that, our home seemed rather lonely, as though a family member had been lost. Geordie's chimes were especially missed in the long and lonely hours on watch.

When back home after our circumnavigation, I contacted a clock doctor, and his prognosis suggested a complete rebuild with an estimated cost upwards of a man's weekly wage. Now I realized labour costs had risen, but I was aghast by how much. I then thought about buying a new Geordie. Inquiries were made. But more astonishment followed when we heard that a new timepiece, now made in Asia, would cost ten times what my mother-in-law paid forty years earlier.

But there was one dealer who offered a glimmer of hope. An electronic gizmo was now available that would fit inside the old case. And we were told it would keep better time without the need to wind, and would electronically replicate the sounds we missed most. All at 10% replacement cost. What a quandary. Electronics can be good, but sometimes they are rubbish. Do we dig deep for an Asian look-a-like of olden day quality, or chance a little black box that had a mini-speaker attached? It's the same quandary facing all of us. Quality versus price.

And yet, in today's shopping mall mentality, quality seems a misbegotten term. It's often a word meaning a cut above rubbish with a better warranty. Why? Well, maybe because we live in such a rush. Pride in what we produce has been demoted down by necessity. And I'm wondering if that doesn't also apply to the way we live our lives. Quantity of rubbish versus less of the best.

~ Chapter 4 ~

Yet Another River Crossing

"HEY SWEETIE, WAKE UP, TIME TO GO," I gently nudged my sleeping beauty and placed a cup of tea at the bed head. She groaned, stretched, rubbed her eyes, then snapped awake. Listening intently, she asked, "Do I hear wind?"

Outside, the rain that had fallen sporadically throughout the night was again spitting fine mist in a bloom that shrouded darkened downtown buildings. Behind them, the rising sun created a golden archway, as if indicating the direction of treasure. But there was nothing rich about our departure in the dim light. Merely a silent routine, braving the wet while rolling up and storing the awning, followed by another wetting as the mainsail came out its cover accompanied by the deep rumble from our Perkins diesel warming.

The crisp, wet wind and throb of engine sharpened our bleary eyes as *Banyandah* gathered way to weave through the tight fleet of local vessels. Battling a rather fast incoming tide while retracing our path in, we eventually reached the sandbank fronting the Hasting River entrance and immediately felt relieved to see it placid and flat. Continuing along our incoming track, a breeze stinking of seaweed and fish from along the deserted beach heeled *Banyandah* as one lone white breaker swept past. A few minutes hard on the wind gained depth then we tacked all sails to head south, and straightaway began looking for our next destination.

Where Wild Winds Blow

Early morn, the isolation of sea lovely and nearly silent as tiny beetles rushed along the coast road, seemingly chasing one another towards darkened hives and another day at work. While on the horizon ahead, red perpendicular ramparts jutted out the quiet sea, followed by more golden beaches leading endlessly towards the ends of Earth.

Long before Europeans arrived on the NSW mid-coast, it was the traditional home of the Birpai Nation. Their Dreamtime legend describes how three brothers met their death at the hands of the Widjirriejuggi witch, and then they were buried where today the Three Brothers Mountains stand. These prominent coastal mountains, a feature of the Camden Haven Valley, were observed by Captain James Cook and named in his log, along with Perpendicular Point, which marks the mouth of the Camden Haven River.

A short easy sail took us to those red cliffs where yet another river mouth had to be negotiated. No matter how many we cross, I still get agitated, even in the fine conditions we had that day. Our tidal information said we were an hour too late. The incoming tide that would have calmed the bar should have finished. But we would have nearly full water in case a nasty one should jump out the flat sea.

Surprising us both, as the two triangles aligned points together to lead us in, we saw the water still making, taking us in with it. And with a whoosh, we crossed the skinny water, hailing a lone fisherman on the rocks as we flew past. Ahead, at the end of a laneway of still water bordered each side by rock groynes, stood North Brother dressed in verdant eucalypt forests under a grey cloud blanket.

Rain began again. This time in earnest. But we didn't care now that we floated along in smooth water. It only wrecked our 'photo opportunities.' But Jude mastered that by dashing out between showers to take quick snaps.

Welcome to Camden Haven, the sign read, and we thought, "This must be Tuesday." Our whirlwind tour since departing Ballina had taken us to yet another lovely spot, this one surrounded by lakes and waterways, and green mountains. Think we'll like this place.

Port Macquarie had been beautiful, but too busy. Touristy streets filled with cafes, restaurants, and souvenir shops are not why we travel. Besides, the sandflies had always been so hungry whenever we landed.

Yet Another River Crossing

Laurieton, the tiny town at Camden Haven, could be quite different. Unlike Port Macquarie, there are no crowded shopping malls, no multi-lanes of traffic. Plus, on our first sortie ashore, we found a friendly library just up the street, and a cosy coffee lounge filled with historical books and posters illuminating Camden River Valley's past.

Sandwiched between river and mountain are four quiet streets and one main drag making up the little known village of Laurieton. The area first explored by John Oxley, who named the inlet Camden Haven in 1818. Before that, the Gadang Aborigines had roamed the region for tens of thousands of years before Captain James Cook sailed up the coast in 1770.

Cook noted in his log:

> "At sunset were in 23 fathoms of water (65 m), and about a league and a half from the land (7 km), the northernmost part of which that we had in sight bore three remarkable large high hills lying continuance to each other... As these hills bore some resemblance to each other, we called them the Three Brothers. They lay in the latitude of 31°40' and are of a height sufficient to be seen 14 or 18 leagues (86 km)."

With *Banyandah* anchored in the river just off the Laurieton Services Club, each day at first light, the shadow of North Brother entered our lives. Even before that, it dominates with the earliest whistling of doves, repetitive and mixed with the laughing calls of kookaburra resident amongst its forested slopes. Sharp and cool in the mornings, North Brother becomes dark, and cloud draped when the afternoon sea breeze roughens the river and drives our anchored vessel into a tizzy. Charging first towards one bank then the other, or side on to slop, fighting wind against tide. That's when we look up to the mountain and yearn to be under its peaceful canopy.

For some peace and security, we shifted *Banyandah* to the Laurieton Service's Club dock after being caught too many times by the afternoon breeze and flung about like a cat by its tail. This made possible a trek up the 487 m North Brother mountainside the following morning.

Besides the usual food, water, and medical kit, we had a council printed map, which should have assured we'd find the trail without any hold-ups. Aah, but with Jack and Jude, that was not the case.

At the end of Laurie Street, under the first copse of trees, a green Park's sign welcomed us to the Dooragan National Park, further telling us that it supported some of the best old-growth Blackbutt forests in

NSW, along with pockets of sub-tropical rainforest providing habitat for gliders, koalas, and bats. It forgot to mention the unbeatable views up and down the coast.

At the end of the tarmac, our problems began when I spied a gate ahead and thought that must be the track. It wasn't. It leads to a quarry. Discovering this, I then lead Jude down another path, which I felt sure would take us up the mountain. It did, but for only a couple hundred metres before petering out into thick bush that descended into a thickly overgrown creek.

"Hey, blow this," I moaned after whacking my nose on some lantana, making it bleed profusely. "Let's just take the ridge where we know what we're doing." And I tramped off through low vegetation and up a hillside encumbered with some lovely trees.

Eucalyptus forests are usually quite open, the ground covered mostly with dead limbs draped in leaf, and if not hampered by vine or rock, they're normally easygoing. This ridge rose alongside a deep gully and went up at a rate that had us stopping every dozen steps to recover our breath.

But when taking these breaks, the morning breeze would rustle the trees and cool our sweaty shirts, and bring on a glorious feeling. It felt good to be off the boat, where the moments catching our breath gave many opportunities to observe the resident wildlife. Little golden skinks sunbaked on exposed rocks, parrots chattered on branches right above our heads, and some unseen critters rustled away, maybe a wombat or roo, but definitely not a fast-moving snake.

We were off track, but from our little map, we knew to reach the top would get us somewhere near one of the lookouts. But I never expected that we'd come out of the foliage and find the main viewing platform directly above us. Sometimes we're lucky.

From that viewpoint, the entire Camden Haven waterway was painted in cerulean blue, the coast and hinterland turning sepia and tawny as it stretched north as far as Smoky Cape, two day-sails behind us. Taking advantage of the stout posts to steady our cameras against the strong nor' easter blowing us about, we went to work zooming in on *Banyandah* lying peacefully alongside the town wharf.

We took a short circular walk through cool rainforest then headed back down, this time taking the approved track. Honestly, it was much harder The 880 steps down gave our well-worn knees a brutal work out.

The day after our mountain walk, we set off for another excursion, leaving *Banyandah* an hour after dawn. Jude and I first hitched a ride with a local boatie on his way to the Dunbogan boatshed and marina, a small piece of paradise – a quiet, serene river haven with bush surrounds where we wandered about the boats, taking a few photos before sticking our thumbs out a second time. Ten minutes later, another friendly local, a lad coming back from a morning of garage sales, dropped us at the entry to the Kattang Nature Reserve.

Jutting out to sea from the Kattang Nature Reserve are the lofty cliffs of Perpendicular Point named by Captain Cook. Filling the backdrop behind them are the Three Brother Mountains, with the beautiful blue waters of Camden Haven adding another splash of colour. As we strolled towards the cliffs, we passed through small pockets of sweetly perfumed flowering coastal heath that had us lingering with the sound of buzzing bees and rumble of the sea. The sounds of Nature.

A picture-perfect morning, with powerful swells dashing to white explosions against the red face, livened up the dreamy seascape. And making it even more dramatic, a lone humpback whale was chased by a pod of friendly porpoise that then raced off to frolic around the calm river mouth.

The rock formations at Point Perpendicular are absolutely astounding. They are a fining-upward sequence, meaning pebble and conglomerate at the base, getting finer through sandstone to siltstone to claystone near the top. The reddish-purple mudstone is unique to this formation, lying under a conglomerate that contains heaps of smooth red pebbles, with yet an additional layer of reddish sedimentary rock on top. Megaflora fossils have been found in the grey mudstone.

With socials at the club and on other boats, our climb up North Brother and walk to the point, it was very hectic at Camden Haven.

Who says retirees lead boring lives? The drumbeat continued, and we began looking forward to a relaxing overnight sail to Port Stephens, where we would celebrate Christmas with family before heading further south to Tasmania.

~ Chapter 5 ~

Christmas Afloat

THE BUREAU'S MECHANICAL VOICE DRONED ON, "Calm tomorrow till midday then increasing north winds with thunderstorms developing."

"Perfect," I told Judith. "Tomorrow we're off for Port Stephens." A voyage of 80 nautical miles (150km).

Poking my head up at dawn, Jim and Chris's *Twelfth Night* was just a reflection near the calm river mouth. I heard a noise and turned to watch Dennis and Barbara let go of their mooring lines behind us. Jude joined me in wishing them a safe journey while our video recorded their departure accompanied by songbirds greeting a new day.

Although each of us was heading to Port Stephens, probably a fifteen-hour journey, Jude and I were not in a hurry to join our fellow travellers. First off, we don't like calms, especially the ones common in early mornings. We'd rather wait than motor, even if that means staying out all night. Secondly, Jude needed to shop, and I had to return books to the library, which wouldn't open until ten.

At noon, the Alaskan boat with Mike, Elisha, and baby Eli, motored past on their way to join the others afloat on windless waters. Meanwhile, we were entertaining three giggling twelve-year-olds interested in joining our ship. On the jetty, two girls were blushing, frightened a bit, while next to them the boy was showing us his muscles.

Where Wild Winds Blow

Perpendicular Point

Exiting the Camden Haven River, we left our cocoon and were thrust into a blue world that had a thin line of cumulous stretched tightly where it met the sky. To our right rose the bold red headland, where the humpback whale had frolicked on his way south, and by the time we'd powered around it, a slight breeze rippled the glassy surface. Feeling its energizing caress was the signal to unroll our headsail to its max, and silence the donk then sit back and relax.

That ever-increasing wind drove *Banyandah* fast down the coast, and assisted by a fairly strong current, at one point our GPS said we were covering nine nautical miles an hour. We'd be in Port Stephens about midnight, so I hunkered down for a nap.

Relishing her time alone under the open blue heavens, Jude is not like me. She doesn't just sit back gazing at the passing horizon. No, she's checking the log and GPS, looking over the chart, calculating speed and drift, watching seabirds and looking them up in our library. So, by the time I got up for sundowners, she gave me such a complete rundown I felt I'd been right beside her the whole afternoon.

Nightfall brought black clouds over the land spitting silver flashes that had me fearing we'd not have the sweet northerly wind much longer. Jude's not fond of lightning. She gave me a quick peck then said, "I'm off to bed." I stayed topsides, entranced by Nature, even when cold raindrops started falling. And good that I did. Our steady wind suddenly went berserk. Roaring and shifting around like a dervish, before dropping to a whisper, overshadowed by my noisy rope work resetting sails. But to no avail. *Banyandah* either headed straight for a vast empty horizon hidden somewhere in the dark or land equally hidden.

With cars, you simply follow the road no matter the weather. But using Nature's power requires a bit more cleverness, and dare I say, a fair bit more patience. Especially on dark rainy nights.

We eventually got anchored at some ungodly hour. Not sure where. And I won't say we were up at the crack of dawn, but our first sight revealed *Banyandah* all alone atop a flat platter rippled by a pod of porpoise looking for breakfast. In the distance, minuscule tinnies raced along a yellow shore dotted with morning walkers, against a backdrop of those abrupt lumps we'd passed as shadows.

Captain James Cook had sighted the entrance to Port Stephens on May 11, 1770, naming the bay after the Secretary of the Admiralty. Twenty-one years later the British ship *Salamander* was the first to enter and found it as wide as Sydney Harbour. It is big and far too exposed to the Christmas Day gale that was being forecast by the weather bureau's mechanical voice droning over our radio.

Encircled by forested hills, Fame Cove is a cyclone anchorage with a lovely placid creek entering next to its narrow west-facing entrance. To our amazement, we found only the one boat sharing the serenity with a pair of brown and white kites soaring overhead. Their high pitch whistle seemed to welcome us, and quickly we took our choice of the remaining five free moorings. Once settled, up went the awning to save us from the stifling heat.

Next morning, the day before Christmas, with the gale imminent, I roused my crew early to brave the narrows in *Little Red*. "To the shops," I cried, "for food to feast." Then under my breath, I muttered, "That's if I can start this decrepit old thing." Our outboard hadn't been run since the Gordon River the previous year.

On our way out, we stopped at the two yachts now sharing our little cove, and in a short chat invited them over for Chrissie Eve refreshments. Warning them. "That's if we get back."

Around the headland, straightaway, we bucked into white caps with our destination, the pricey marina at Soldiers Point plainly in sight. In our heads was worry our trusty steed would not go the distance – never mind make it back.

Spray flew over the bows, Jude's rain gear dripped while my sunnies needed wipers and my going-ashore shirt got drenched. But our antique engine never missed a beat. Pulling in amongst those flash floating machines meticulously polished by uniformed workers, we felt a thousand eyes scrutinising our bedraggled attire and simple mode of transport. But did we care? Nah! We may not be young anymore, but we are free. All bills paid. We go where we like and do what we want, mostly. Like right then. That's if they let us tie up to their swank dock.

Which they did, then with a little swagger, heads held high, off we went to find the management to ask their prices. Their reply scrubbed the idea of spending Boxing Day in their swimming pool with our grandkids. Instead, we high tailed it for the front gate, trying to look like we belonged. Meeting a deliveryman outside we asked where we could catch a bus to the shopping centre. Minutes later we had senior's tickets in our hot hands riding on a very big, empty bus.

Being the last shopping day, our solo bus ride lasted just a block. After that, every stop gained several new folks. Each quite intriguing. It's amazing how buses lower the barriers, allowing conversations to flow across the aisle. And in no time we had a hot tip for Saturday's race, knew about the best Woolie's specials, and heard someone's granny tell us her troublesome tooth would be pulled that afternoon.

I won't waste much space on the shopping complex. Close your eyes and imagine the last shopping day before Christmas. Inside Woolworths seemed like WWIII had just started.

Taking the bus back, leaves were flying horizontally off treetops that shook like pom-poms. The storm was going to get us.

"No worries Honey." Big smile, patting her knee. "I can always row." And to reassure her, I flexed my arm muscles just like the boy on the Laurieton jetty. Not impressed, her eyes rolled back.

They needn't have. Expecting a great adventure, instead, our old outboard didn't let us down. Wetter than ever we finally rounded Fame Cove's slender point to enter a fairyland of calm water, now dotted with five yachts. Two's a gathering; five's a party. So we stopped by the others and invited them over.

Never expecting all would come, promptly at five arrived Ken and Karen from the smallest craft. Ken had suffered polio and dragged about a pair of useless limbs. But at 72, he's still got a good ticker and pulled himself aboard with little fuss. Next to arrive, big-boy Bob and his pretty lady Na, returning home after their first cruise aboard a magnificent 55 footer that just had to weigh 40 tonnes, although Bob claimed she weighed only 30. Next Craig and Karen with their three kids; Nicole, rather cute in pink wearing a Santa's hat, and twins Ethan and Tristan. Plenty to talk about with them. Irene and Dougy made up the tail, local folk brimming with all the gossip and provincial history.

Christmas Eve aboard *Banyandah* could not have been better. The northerly gale blew crazily above the hills, swaying the trees and occasionally lifting our awning. But it never disturbed our party. Almost every story a yachty can remember was told; we laughed till tears flowed over Karen's lost plastic bucket, then everyone grew serious when I described being shelled by the North Vietnamese. Bless him, our senior on board, Ken explained what it was like sitting on the weather rail of a superyacht running down to Hobart in the days following Christmas. He's made that trip not just once, but enough times to gain our admiration for a man who finds walking down a street a challenge.

Christmas morning got off to a slow start without high-pitched voices breaking our sleep. When we heard raindrops instead of little feet, we merely turned over for another forty winks. But then the phone rang with family calls taken in bed, lovely hearing the mayhem through the speakerphone and then be able to catch a bit more sleep!

We motored over to a popular town beach on Boxing Day morning. Jason and his brood were driving down, and we planned to spend the day playing on the magnificent beachfront. Their three little ones, all just toddlers, had never built sandcastles nor raced the water in and out. Joy and simple fun with loved ones.

The rain started in earnest the moment Jason and his lot pulled away for Sydney. Sad seeing them go, but oh so nice to be full of lovely memories. Also nice was filling our water tanks from the awning. There will be another day or two of rainy southerlies, and then we'll be ready to blast off for Tasmania with the next change.

~ Chapter 6 ~

No Christmas at Copenhagen

Dateline: 2009 UN Climate Change Conference Copenhagen

ONE CHRISTMAS EVE YEARS AGO, while on our honeymoon, my newly wedded wife and I sat upon the sands of the Sahara Desert fearing it might be our last night on the planet. Our only means of transport lay buried up to its doors in soft sand, while we sat sipping our last water under a multitude of constellations lighting the infinite heavens.

Searching for salvation, a comet streaked across the heavens, and pretending it was Santa Claus bringing goodwill to all mankind, I bowed my head and prayed we'd be set free and not perish.

Promising I'd be good reminded me of another Christmas many years before that, when I had promised to be very good if only Santa would bring me a new bike. And when the big morning arrived, when surrounded by torn wrappings, new socks, shirts and piles of toys, I had stomped my feet and yelled at my dad, "I wanted a new bike!" Then ran, tears flowing, out the house.

I had been good - as good as a young lad could, and should have been rewarded. Furious, I raced to the garage to hide. Passing last year's bike - before bumping into a brand new one festooned with a giant blue ribbon.

Today, the world is too much like that confused, spoiled little boy. Wishing for things and allowing greed to conceal what is right when we should be more like that young couple who didn't whinge or shout but struggled to survive in the real Earth. When the hot sun rose on them, they were still bogged to the axles and surrounded by an eternity of sand but found salvation by hard work, determination, and sacrifice.

This year's Climate Change Conference in Copenhagen clearly illustrated the failings of the 'me and mine' syndrome where each country only thinks of its needs.

Did you know that at the present time, Americans make up only 5% of the world's population, and yet consume 20% of its energy and generate 5 times the world average of CO^2 emissions?

In contrast to the almost 20 tons of CO^2 each person in the US produces per year, Europeans produce only 8 tons, and the developing countries only 2 tons. US greenhouse gas emissions rose by 15% from 1990 to 2006.

Time Magazine wrote, "The negotiations at Copenhagen were so contentious because of the very real impact the proposals will have, not only for the environment but also on national economies. China and the US played hardball."

Judith and I have come to believe, as many of you have, that we live in a global community. After all, the planet's air and our emissions can typically move halfway around the world in a week. So, America's large footprint places it front and centre to the world's changing climate. And yet emissions targets at Copenhagen were derailed once again by man's eloquence. Seems a pity so many more of Earth's creatures must perish simply because we won't, or cannot, control ourselves.

To us, it is the right time to start thinking outside the box for inspiration and direction and do something, besides talk, to change our impact on Earth.

~ Chapter 7 ~

Now We Know Why

OUR SAIL FROM PORT STEPHENS TO EDEN was nothing short of fantastic with a glorious fair breeze and heaps of current assisting us down the coast. *Banyandah* screamed past Sydney first seen glowing like a far-away fire. And with the morning star still bright, we spied the high rises at Sydney Cove then made fast miles for the next day and night. Even caught fish whenever we put the lure in the water.

A beautiful passage continued right till getting into port just as the predicted adverse change of weather struck. And although it then did blow strongly from the South Pole, we hunkered down across the bay from Eden in Boydtown, just off the historical Sea Horse Homestead that is now an inn.

Boydtown, 506 km south of Sydney, on the southern shore of Twofold Bay is a ghost town today. Little came of the grandiose plans of Mr Benjamin Boyd, the town's founder, and little remains at the site.

Benjamin Boyd was a London stockbroker who left Plymouth in his schooner *Wanderer* and arrived in Port Jackson on July 18 1842, ready to enhance his fortune after first persuading many British investors to financially participate in his schemes. Once here, he first established a coastal steamship service, and to control his investments Boyd floated the Royal Bank of Australia, with a nominal capital of one million pounds. He quickly purchased and put into service the *Seahorse* paddle steamer, which covered the southern route from Sydney to Hobart via

Twofold Bay. Within two years of his arrival, Boyd had become one of the largest landholders in the colony with nearly two and a half million acres in the Riverina and Monaro that carried 158,000 sheep and 21,000 cattle. Deciding that Twofold Bay would serve as the port for his enterprises, grandiose plans were made for the establishment of a township and construction of Boydtown commenced in 1843.

The huge expenditures to establish Boydtown soon began to weigh heavily against Boyd's assets. And in 1849, when he had overreached his investments, liquidators were called in. To make matters worse, the *Seahorse* had been irreparably damaged after striking a rock. All operations at Twofold Bay ceased, with most of the construction still incomplete.

After his spectacular failure, Boyd decided to try his luck on the Californian goldfields and late in October just seven years after his arrival, the *Wanderer* sailed from Australia. In America, he was unsuccessful at the diggings, and according to John Webster, his sailing companion, Boyd decided to cruise the Pacific Islands with the idea of establishing the Papuan Republic. In October of 1851, the *Wanderer* reached the island of Guadalcanal in the Solomon Islands, and early one morning Boyd went ashore with a native to shoot game. Two shots were heard. When Boyd failed to return, his companion searched, but his body was never found, and it was concluded that he had been killed and possibly eaten by cannibals.

With the *Seahorse* paddle steamer wrecked, the principal relic of Boyd's adventures is the Sea Horse Inn. Symbolic of Boydtown itself, the homestead was built by convict labour and never fully completed. Full transformation to a public Inn, with original detail such as hand-carved doors, stained-glass ornamentation, winding staircases, and large open grate fires occurred in the 1980s.

The completed Sea Horse Inn with its ambience of old world charm stood before us in full view as the wind increased towards late afternoon,

Where Wild Winds Blow

our bay filling up. One lone sailor laboriously beat his way in, dropped sail, anchored, and then immediately went below. We didn't see him for two days. Meanwhile, scudding clouds gave way to blue skies and sunshine. So Jude and I took several long walks, one to investigate the ruins of the church partially completed during the Boyd era.

A northerly arriving earlier than expected spurred us into action. Flinders Island lay only 200 miles away, and if the forecast held, the wind just might last the journey. I hurried Jude into finishing the repair of our red-trimmed furling headsail, and then, in increasing wind, we had a struggle getting it back onto the furler without repeatedly getting whacked in the face. Our lone sailor was also getting underway, and we thought we might have company going down the coast. He raised a headsail, but instead of heading out, *Carrion* drifted down to us, and this scraggy bearded fellow hailed us.

Now, most sailors are super social, so when Jude suggested a fresh brew of coffee, the old salt dropped sail again, and we were quickly catching his line to pull his engine-less craft up behind *Banyandah*. It seems David had just arrived from Tasmania after being in the Apple Isle a few years. Battling headwinds most of the way, he'd had a horror ride, taking more than five days from Hobart. But with a wide satisfied smile, he informed us, "I'm just one port away from my home in Bateman's Bay."

Sharing a coffee and heaps of information, all too soon we were hauling our dinghy aboard, getting ready to sail as Dave shouted some parting words of advice. "Don't forget Lake's Entrance, they've dredged the entrance."

"Don't think so," I yelled back. "We're going straight through with this wind."

Well, the run down the coast got better and better. The gods stayed by our side and helped get us good lifts, as first Green Cape then Gabo Island whizzed by. Come dark, we were entering Bass Strait with still heaps of wind up our backside. In fact, so much wind we were rolling along, robbing Jude, and then me, of a chance to sleep. Small sacrifice if we made the north end of Flinders.

But, a few hours after I hit the bed, the devil stepped in. Sucking big breaths, that nemesis swallowed the wind. And by 3 a.m. we were dead in the water, rolling madly about. Ugh!!

Now We Know Why

At dawn, it got worse, becoming still and hot. And our chance of making Flinders without at least another night in the firing line of the straits evaporated in the heat. Ships coming out of Bass Strait or heading there were becoming a real nuisance. So, throwing my hands up in capitulation, I started the engine, and, you guessed it, turned our nose for Lakes Entrance and hopefully a good night's rest.

David would have chuckled had he seen us wallowing along towards the empty heat haze above the Gippsland Lakes, which took the rest of that day to reach, arriving at nearly the bottom of the tide. David had informed us of the recent dredging of this notoriously bad channel, so I figured an hour before the low tide would be okay, and directed Jude to drive straight in.

Wow, suddenly we were battling an outpouring river with some heavy-duty overfalls trying to spin *Banyandah* about. Jude furiously worked the helm to keep us straight while ever so slowly we made headway. From her worried look, she didn't like the thought of an engine failure. Me? I was jumping about snapping photos, waving to the crowd gathered to watch us come in, and occasionally told Jude what a great job she was doing.

Lakes Entrance was full-speed-ahead. A tourist town along a narrow inlet next to that scary entrance, and since it was New Year, bulging with pleasure craft and fishing boats. We got thrown out of the first bay with a shouted, "you can't anchor there." But found a big barge alongside a jetty and thought, "why not." So we tied up alongside it, thinking we'd probably have to move when discovered. But no one objected to our middle of town, easy walk to everywhere spot. We were out of sight and out of earshot, so we stayed a full three days.

Outside, Bass Strait was either windless or headwinds for sailing to Flinders, so we finished our submissions to publishers, and when the mail went out, we went on holiday. Like all the rest of the folk in the lakes.

We took Miss B into the inner sanctum of the rich and not so rich, only touching our keel a few times when crossing the shallows. We managed to get a day's run up into the first lake where we lazed about, rather bored and anxious to be across Bass Strait. On sandy beaches and forest-clad hillsides, we stretched our legs and enjoyed the calm waters, quite possibly the last for a while.

Five days later, an exhilarating crossing of the Strait took us past brightly lit oilrigs and then into the paths of fast ships to find an anchorage behind Roydon Island in West Ann Bay, Flinders Island. It's just a nick in the sparsely populated main island of the remote Furneaux Group, but we haven't caught a single fish! And now we know why.

Meet Tom, pro fisherman, and Wade, his deckie, seventeen, slim and cute, except for a smile of bad teeth and a two-tone nose that is cherry red to a line of peeling flesh. Tom is weather-beaten differently. Dry skin and scaly spots from long exposure to salt poked out his flannel shirt. Friendly though. Honest smile slanted like an autumn moon under a nose that's suffered a whack. Likeable, both of them. Ordinary folks like you and I, working outdoors to pay the bills and get closer to their dreams.

Young Wade admitted not cottoning on to learning through books and instead has found a love for boats and the sea. Wants a yacht one-day, to travel free, he says.

All his youth, Tom worked trawlers. He'd scraped the seabed outside Lakes Entrance, took on the challenging seas, changeable weather, and commercial shipping. That was until the oilrigs took his best ground. That forced him further offshore, to drag a net amongst the bulk carriers and massive container ships that scare a trawlerman anchored to the bottom by his nets.

That life ended last year when Tom had scraped up enough to buy a Tasmanian net boat built in 1935 from good strong blue gum. A second mortgage on his house fitted her out, so now he fishes for live kelpie and red-banded morwong. Sitting in his big tinnie alongside *Banyandah*, he tells us, "The big ones live about ninety years and fetch the best price for overseas markets. Asian's love them. They see them swimming around a tank at the restaurant entrance and order them steamed with ginger, and thinly sliced carrot then placed centre table for all to pick at."

Candidly, Tom thinks their flesh too mushy, though he doesn't mind catching them so long as the buyers keep paying him thirty bucks a kilo. That's our world. Supply and demand. Tom gets what he wants and needs. The Asians get what they want too.

But it's all out of balance. Our poor world is askew on its axis. And the farther we tilt it, the faster we fall towards oblivion. You see, Tom fishes the very remote Flinders Island; both sides when the weather lets him, which isn't all that often. Spends a lot of time just holed up. Like we both were at that moment. The weather bad, listening to the wind, feeling the ocean's restlessness. But Tom doesn't just sit waiting. No, he's got to keep catching product to pay the bills, and his deckie has to earn a living too. So he goes out in his tinnie. In six months, Tom has annihilated these sheltered spots, which are now as barren as the bleak hills surrounding us. And when we ask, how long until the fish come back? Tom shrugs and admits he's no scientist.

We liked Tom and Wade. But too many humans on this planet take too much. All of Earth's creatures depend on the balance being just right. Just think of the other fish that hunt those same kelpies and red-banded morwong. They're now going hungry. And their young aren't growing up. Now, this doesn't just pertain to the sea. The white-winged gannets are hungry too, as are the red-billed pacific gulls that also rely on these fish.

All because Asian families and business groups like to marvel at ugly morwong swimming around a tank at a restaurant entrance. This has not happened before. We are now a global community who outgrew its limits. And that's why Jude and I keep saying, reducing our footprint will put Earth back in balance. Let's start now before we change so much we topple over into oblivion.

~ Chapter 8 ~

Black Man's Houses

EVER SINCE JUDE AND I FIRST WALKED the Needwonnee homelands of Southwest Tasmania, and then read of the destruction of the Aboriginal race by white settlers after they had lived in peaceful cohabitation with Earth for thousands of years, we had longed to witness Wybalenna, "Black Man's Houses," the final resting place for so many. Unable to make that visit during our voyage around Australia is one reason we returned to Tasmania this summer with Flinders Island our first destination.

Stormy weather kept us in hiding for four days at the West Ann anchorage, but when a high-pressure cell brought settled weather, I drew a rhumb line directly to Settlement Point. In 1642, when Abel Tasman first sighted the west coast of Tasmania, Aborigines had inhabited the island for 35,000 years and were the southernmost people in the world. During the ice age, they hunted giant marsupials on glacial plains, but when the planet warmed, and thick rainforest grew, they were forced onto the coastal plains. Often they travelled more than six-hundred kilometres every year to different food sources, trading red ochre along the way that held religious significances bonding them with the blood of the land. They wore it on their skin and in their hair mixed with animal fat and charcoal to keep warm and to disguise their scent when hunting. Despite the cold winds and rain, this was all they wore. When white man settled on the island of Tasmania, they found plenty of wildlife for their tables. Kangaroo was their favourite, which meant that after 1803, both the original Tasmanians and the newly-arrived British hunted kangaroo. With their guns, the British could hunt much more efficiently, and this rapidly pushed the animals towards extinction. Soon, the Tasmanians were starving. But the British kept shooting, sometimes for sport. It was this situation that started violent Tasmanian resistance, which rapidly escalated into the Black War, a sort of guerrilla warfare between settlers and Aborigines. Missionaries played their part. Quoting the Reverend Mr Horton, "They are a race of beings altogether distinct from ourselves… class them amongst the inferior species of irrational animals." From the lowliest convict to the highest official, all were utterly convinced of their superiority to the Tasmanian Aborigines, and this produced the spirit of the Black War of 1804 – 1830.

During the Black War, many Aborigines were captured and resettled on Bruny Island near Hobart. In March 1829, the authorities needed a "steady man of good character to affect intercourse with the natives." George Augustus Robinson was appointed and took the title, "The Protector of Aboriginal Tasmanians." During the year before the Black Line operation, the military action of 1830 to purge the Aboriginal people from the settled districts, Robinson travelled the island trying to convince the remaining Aborigines to join him and escape obliteration. Many did when promised they would be able to return to their homeland one day.

Robinson removed fifty-one Tasmanians to Swan Island, a tiny blot of land off the northeast coast. This proved too inhospitable, so in March 1831, Robinson shifted them to Vansittart Island, situated between Flinders and Cape Barren Island in Franklin Sound. This also proved unsuitable as it is another isolated barren place at the mercy of strong tides and winds. So, again they were moved. To *The Lagoons*, a fancy name for a very exposed peninsula at the base of the Strzelecki mountains on Flinders' west coast. After many deaths there, mostly by disease, Robinson was left with only 20 living Tasmanians. In January 1832, another shipment swelled his flock to 66. Badly treated during their capture, trouble erupted, and some were shipped to nearby Green Island, but a better solution was needed.

In October 1832, the decision was taken to build a new camp with more solid buildings at a more suitable location than the catastrophic

Lagoons site. Wybalenna, on paper a new Aboriginal reservation, was in fact, a prison colony and dumping ground. It was also badly managed. With or without their agreement, the Aboriginal captives were taken there, and then treated like prisoners or simply neglected. Any legal rights they might have had on paper or been promised, simply evaporated.

Moreover, Wybalenna camp was in a constant state of change with Robinson's continual stream of new groups sent there after capture or persuasion to follow him. Attempts were made to "civilize" the natives and exterminate aboriginal culture by replacing it with a sort of "Christian English peasant culture." Reading, writing and arithmetic were taught in English, along with religious instruction.

The population figures at Wybalenna fluctuated wildly. New captives were brought in; at the same time, the mortality rate was horrendous. Roughly, there were usually equal numbers of men and women and a few children. Child mortality was even higher than that of adults, very few survived infancy. When established in 1833, there were 111 Tasmanians, but when the camp closed in 1847, only 47 remained. Those last ones were shifted to unhealthy mudflats at Oyster Cove near Hobart where they could be paraded in fancy clothes on special occasions. Today, the bay next to Oyster Cove contains the Kettering Marina. But in 1855, the number of Tasmanians at Oyster Cove was down to 16. In 1869, there was only one. The last full-blood Tasmanian, Truganini, died in 1876. However, in 1889 Parliament recognised Fanny Cochrane Smith (d:1905) as the last surviving full-blood Tasmanian Aborigine, giving her a land grant of 300 acres (120 ha) and an annuity of £50.

Leaving our hideout behind Prime Seal Island after another strong westerly gale abated, we motored ten miles across an undulating cold blue sea. And then anchored *Banyandah* in Lillies Bay, in front of the dilapidated jetty once used to offload Aborigines and supplies. It lies in full view of the precipitous Strzelecki Mountains, within a beautiful sandy bay open to the south and bordered by polished granite outcrops at both ends. Wheat-yellow plains beyond the coastal dunes swept up a hillside speckled with black granite boulders and crowned by blue gum forests. On the point, a smaller hill rises upon which signals were once flown.

Floating on water so transparent we seemed to hover in air as we rowed *Little Red* above ribbon grass that grew right up to the extraordinarily coarse sand beach. With the tide falling, we pulled our transport up only a little, pulled on our boots then set off to find Wybalenna. Turning left past the old timber jetty after first placing our hands on it to absorb resident vibes, a dirt track was encountered which we walked along towards Settlement Point. Soon we found ourselves entering a private property that had been hidden amongst the twisted mallee scrub. Nevertheless, I lead on, thinking we could always ask the occupants for directions. But we saw no one, only a vacant house, its verandas facing a serene view over what can be troubled waters. All else was tangled windblown scrub kept company by a dull rumble of surf. When the track ended, Jude looked to me, quizzing where to go next. So I followed a vague animal track into the forest. I knew the old camp was now on private property and that the only remaining building, the chapel, had been last used as a shearing shed. From the map seen on the internet, it lay just beyond Signal Hill, which I thought we were now climbing.

Jack and Jude are not normal tourists. We'd not hired a car at the airport. Nor joined a bus tour. We were climbing up through tangled forest in the middle of no-where, excited, not worried. After one animal track vanished, we found another, and then breaching the hill, were stunned by a sparkling view over the blue bay, *Banyandah,* its only occupant. Climbing over a mass of fallen, twisted limbs, we reached an open hillside of yellow summer grass. And below on a small plain lay the remains of Black Man's Houses.

In my mind's eye, I saw a British flag right beside us on Signal Hill and could hear its fluttering. My imagination brought life to the lumps of overgrown rubble down below, which came alive with black figures clad in rags, collected in groups. Smoke drifted up from a chimney, weedy gardens darkened the slope, and as the present, no animals were about. Now I felt it to be a very depressing scene.

Of course, for Jack and Jude in warm sunshine with freedom almost unheard of even today, we were thrilled to have found the destination we had longed to witness since first standing upon Tasmania's stormy southwest shores. Minutes passed. We sat on a fallen log and gazed, letting our imaginations wander further. Then Jude snapped back to the present. Her framing photos prompted me to flick on the recorder, and together we strolled slowly down the open hillside while reviewing the history that had been Black Man's Houses. Near the bottom, our sharp eyes picked out unusual lumps that required further attention. The first provided a glimpse of those times. Bricks, made on this land more than a hundred and fifty years earlier by hunter-gatherers being civilized. Just touching them connected us to those poor souls who had had paradise on Earth, until discovered by a more 'advanced' race filled with the questionable ethics of that era.

Amongst a sparse glen of trees surrounded by a wooden picket fence, we discovered the chapel and headed directly towards it. Through its timber gate, dedicated to Aunty Ida West, we entered her "Healing Garden" and stopped in front of the tiny brick chapel that had at one time housed the first peoples of these islands. Its coarse bricks encased pebbles within the red clay. Touching one brought the warmth of a black man to my fingertips. Then running those sensitized tips along the flaking windowsills, a jumble of images rushed around my head. Visions of disgruntled souls awkwardly wearing heavy garments that hung like drooping blankets, intense unhappiness on their sullen faces and hatred in their childlike eyes. Why? I wondered. Why do we hurt harmless people? People aligned to mother-Earth, unsophisticated they may be, but connected to what is real and important for life to continue.

Inside, yes, the door was unlocked and beckoned us in; a plainly hewed floor marked by use took us under a charming roof of cross-battened rafters clad with thatch. Again, so easy to conjure up a hundred black folk being taught about our God. Jesus, who gave his life, so we may live. These people had their own beliefs. And who's to say either is better. Aborigine spiritual values are based upon reverence for the land and a belief in the Dreamtime, considered both the ancient time of creation and present-day reality. Our society's convictions seem more supernatural. One you can touch, the other requires belief without proof. To me, Earth is the closest thing to God. Its myriad creations can be seen and felt. And that's why Jack and Jude constantly say, *Put Earth First* in everything you do.

Where Wild Winds Blow

After we soaked up all we could hold within the chapel, we read the information on a noticeboard and looked upon the few old photos posted of Wybalenna just before it was abandoned. Sad faces stared back at us. They all seemed to be asking, "Why?"

Also known as Truganini / Trugernanner

Down a dirt track, in a fenced-off half-acre among tall, dry grass stood a few headstones. But none were for the hundred or so Aborigines buried within that hallowed ground. Buried they might have been, but their remains had long ago been dug up; sent around the world to different scientific facilities for study. How would you like that? Being so special you can never rest in peace, and yet, so little respected your head might be sent to Oslo while your torso sails off to Budapest.

~ Chapter 9 ~

A Few Tough Days

WE HAD TO MOVE. WE FELT LIKE A MOUSE TRAPPED IN A corner with a big shoe coming down. The weather dons were predicting gale force weather and exposed at Wybalenna, we thought we'd better high tail it for Lady Barron, the only seaport on Flinders Island.

When it had blown strongly at West Ann, we'd had a horror night dragging anchor across a weedy bottom and trying to reset it in cold, windy darkness with malevolent forces roaring like lions pushing us about. At the front of our ship in just a flimsy nightshirt, a torch in hand, shivering, I'm looking for a clear sandy patch amongst dark weed, hearing Jude yelling above all the noise, asking where to go. How would I know? Everywhere was black. It was terrible.

This time we thought the main port would be a far better place to find shelter. At least we might not lose so much sleep. Trouble was; Lady Barron was a beat upwind, threading the shallow Franklin Sound with its strong tidal streams that created overfalls where deeper water came upon shoals. Side slipping through the scary bits, it was a noisy motor-sail. Nevertheless, late in the day, a few houses broke through the hillside bushes and then a jetty emerged. First, we spied a single yacht, followed by others coming into view beyond treeless Great Dog Island. The ones we saw had not gone anywhere for a long time. Tattered sail covers and splotches of gull poo peppered their cabins. They looked a sorry mess.

Where Wild Winds Blow

Alongside the big timber jetty, a medium-sized purse seiner noisily disgorged twin columns of seawater out her side while gulls swooped and soared in the soupy greyness just above its structures. Further in lay a smaller trawler. Through binoculars, an empty space ahead of it closer to the shore came into focus.

"We might be able to tie up in front of that blue trawler," I mentioned to Jude, both of us watching a pair of triangles, points together, that were leading us past the last shoal into Lady Barron Harbour. A quick look about revealed what I had deduced from the chart. Lady Barron wasn't well protected from stormy west winds. The roadstead was open in that direction for a great extent of Franklin Sound.

Down here in the Roaring Forties, winds can come from any direction. Cold fronts and depressions are regular features; each bringing their own mix of winds. Today a feisty northeast wind blew straight onto those docks. Late tomorrow they would switch to the west, and the day after we'd be blasted from the south. But right then, the wind blowing onto the docks made going alongside a bit dicey, requiring good brakes or we might hit the trawler or run up the shore. Not wanting to look a fool or hear a bunch of yelling, after checking the rest of the anchorage, which was all rather weedy, we dropped anchor just off the jetty, thinking if the wind eased at sunset or dawn, we could slip in with less risk.

The northeast blew all night steadily, easing just before dawn. With the first hint of gold on the eastern horizon, I was peering through binoculars at those docks, my mind's eye moving *Banyandah* past the trawler, and then I'm hitting the brakes. While astern gear churned the water in my head, I'm praying our backend doesn't slew towards the shallow water seen from our dinghy the previous evening. The problem had come up, where to hook our ropes? Everything was too tall, built for bigger boats. Jude would never reach. Crikey! What to do?

The wind returning with renewed gusto made up my mind to stay put. Instead, I woke Jude and suggested we wander around the town to see if we even wanted to stay. In the back of my mind were thoughts to use the last of this good wind to sail to another spot.

Jude didn't take long to pull on her jerkin and thermal pants, and by half seven, we were rowing past the very spot we would have been pulling into. "I'd never get hold of that," Jude said, pointing to the huge piles.

"I thought you might have gotten a rope around that ladder." But soon saw it was set back more than her arm's length.

Landing in *Little Red*, we then wandered down the short dock finding the port and township of Lady Barron a tad unkempt. A deserted dirt road led past stacks of logs ready for shipment then a mess of shipping containers. Flaking paint on a factory showed cracks in its brickwork, and not much else we saw was in good repair. The lone resident we met summed it up. "It's quiet. Just the way we like it."

Lawns were mostly weeds; paint peeled off half the houses; windows were cracked; some doors off their jambs. Upon empty streets, we wandered, taking photos of *Banyandah* amongst the many islands surrounding the township. None of the islands had trees, only dry summer grass and buff granite rock with that orange lichen so typical of the area. The lichen is a Caloplaca, which means 'beautiful shield'. All were highlighted by aqua blue water showing an artistic mix of dark weedy splotches intermingled with lighter sand patches.

Two blocks from the harbour, the only shop stood forlorn and locked tight. Its twin petrol pumps holding a lone vigil until a nine o'clock start. There were no other businesses, except a pseudo pub offering cabin accommodation. And no other souls on empty streets. A gust whipping up dust returned my mind to the sailable northeast wind, and that had me wondering where we could get with it.

Back at the dock, we found two old fishers talking about nets and their catches, and I interrupted them with my problem.

"You can tie alongside me," the shorter, grizzly one said, indicating the blue trawler *First Pride*. I thanked him for the offer then asked whether Jamieson Bay would be good holding in the coming west winds.

"Good holding there. Pure sand. But those mountains make wind." His answer, I guessed, meant it was subject to bullets down a mountainside.

"Pretty?" I asked.

"Aye, quite the picture. Good flathead too. But I've never been able to stay. Maybe my cabin's too high," the fisherman replied.

That planted seeds of doubt. But I'd already judged Lady Barron a waste of time. I'd be bored waiting for the weather to clear with nothing to do, especially if we could sail another thirty miles to a pretty bay with good fishing.

So, in quick order, we packed up *Banyandah* and lifted our hook. Raising sail, we exited Lady Barron by continuing east, threading the gap between Little Green and Billy Goat Islands. Then we bumped about with swells rebounding off Pot Boil Shoals. And quite soon we were in a bit of strife while threading the needle between Vansittart Island and its off-lying shoals. Reminding us of what awaited careless sailors, half a mile distant stood the stranded, rusted remains of the *Farsund,* a 70 m barque driven onto the Vansittart Shoals in 1912.

Suddenly it became not a nice trip. Imagine milky green water. A spooky hulk little more than red iron lace just downwind and small white breakers suddenly appearing here then there before slipping back into oblivion. Jude was at the helm next to our depth gauge sounding a warning of skinny water, while I stood on the front rail peering ahead, trying to find a safe passage. An occasional ocean swell rippled through, making it not a place to run aground. And making the hour negotiating those shoals a heart-stopper and thumping adrenalin rush.

With the wind still out the nor-east, we continued to sail down the miles, running parallel along the lee shore of the large Cape Barren Island, admiring its severely fractionated granite outcrops surrounded by low scrub. Rounding Gull Island at its southeast tip, a crescent-shaped golden beach appeared at the base of Mount Kerford. And that's where we found peace, tucked away out of the swell in the NE corner of Jamieson Bay.

Nearly all the early explorers had some contact with the Aborigines. However, their visits were brief until the arrival of the French expedition of d'Entrecasteaux (1792) and Baudin (1802), both making proper scientific studies of the people and their customs. It is thought the Furneaux Group of Islands were uninhabited when first sighted by Captain Tobias Furneaux in 1773. This soon changed when European and American seal hunters began visiting the Bass Strait Islands from the late 1790s. By about 1800, sealers were regularly left on the uninhabited islands in Bass Strait during the sealing season (November to May). The sealers established semi-permanent camps, which were close enough for them to reach the Tasmanian mainland in small boats and so make contact with the Tasmanian Aborigines. Relationships developed and soon began a trade for Aboriginal women. Many Tasmanian Aboriginal women were highly skilled in hunting seals, as well as in obtaining other foods such as seabirds. Some women went willingly. Some were taken against their will.

The Cape Barren Island community can be traced back to the early 19th century when sealers brought Aboriginal women to that remote island. In the 1850s, muttonbirding replaced sealing as the main economic activity and the community-led a lifestyle based on a mix of both Aboriginal and European ways. Today, a few more than two-hundred Straitsmen inhabit Cape Barren Island.

Our very pretty anchorage soon got even better when the biggest Dusky Flathead we'd ever seen came wiggling over the railing hooked onto Jude's fishing line. Later on, while Jude talked to the kids during our free phone hour, I landed a second one and thought we'd found heaven.

We had just finished a scrumptious fish dinner when the nor' easter faded. And, as often happens in high latitudes, for a minute, Nature paused to catch her breath then the wind returned, shifted west, and got stronger.

Good, let's move we both agreed, and get settled in at the other end of the beach before dark. Easy to do, but the swell still attacked that end of the beach. Increasing blasts darkened the water as we motored the mile across the bay and set our hook in open, clean sand, taking the precaution of establishing a GPS position as it went down. Pulling it in brought wide smiles when our bow was sharply drawn in line with the full scope of our anchor chain. Then pitch-blackness closed in, leaving just a blinking icon on our GPS indicating where we were in the vastness.

Darkness also brought the first bullets down the mountainside and smacked by their blasts, *Banyandah* groaned as she slew round this way then that. The commotion made worse by the swell slapping her backside. All night we rock-n-rolled while the wind gods got angrier, screaming abuse. Of course, we couldn't sleep. We could only lay flat, listen, and wait, wondering if the next attack would send us into the black abyss. After a savage hit, one of us would get up to peer at the GPS to check if we had dragged. But all through the night, it kept saying .03 NM to our anchor. That relates to the 60 m of chain we'd laid out. It's strange, feeling a swell coming, the boat lifting, and imagining *Banyandah* crashing ashore with it.

Where Wild Winds Blow

Next morning at first light, the sea behind us was white and blown into spray. Worse yet, the wind had shifted past west and had begun to invade the bay with a bit of southing. In a few more hours, the sea could get nasty. We were being forced to move. But where? We didn't fancy going back round to the east side. Yesterday's swell would still be running there. Our only other choices; all the way back to Lady Barron, or further on, entering Banks Strait. Ten miles in that direction lay Clarke Island where our guidebook noted an all-weather anchorage. The current would be going our way, but the wind and chop would fight back. Could we punch ahead?

Winds are generally lighter at first light, so without stopping for breakfast, we pulled the hook, raised the mainsail, double-reefed it then ventured around the corner, keeping as close to the rocks as was safe. The first four miles were easy with windblasts still off the land. But then we came to Sea Lion Narrows, a tight opening between Passage and Cape Barren Island that the pilot says should only be used in case of necessity. Tidal streams can race though it at up to 10 knots! Further endangering vessels, partly submerged rocks restrict the opening.

Captain Delano, an American explorer aboard the *Perseverance*, wrote in 1817,

> "It would be folly to think of passing between... the tide ripples are so very dangerous that unless a person is well acquainted there is great danger of being lost in them."

Okay, you're the captain. Do you go back, or carry on for a look?

Passage Island provided some shelter for our approach, and it was there in its calm water we found a lone fishing boat laying what we thought was a net. A call on our VHF brought a laconic reply confirming the floats as just being cray pots.

"Clear water round 'em," was his short answer.

And when I asked about Sea Lion Narrows, wondering if our engine could get us through, he replied, "Current's going with you."

Nothing else was said. Sometimes bravado sinks a ship. Sometimes plain bad luck, mechanical failure or a change of wind does the same. Should we chance it? It's not like deciding whether to drive a car in bad weather. Here, the forces of Nature are truly immense, and unforeseen dangers are waiting to snuff out lives in a most horrible manner. In my mind, these thoughts swirled like the sea around us. Thrown into that mix, Jude and I have had several near misses, and scary as they have been, they have welded us into a capable team. Plus we know our vessel down to each nut and bolt.

So I gave the order to hug the calmer water behind Passage Island, pass the buoys, and then head towards the line of breakers. We expected some disturbance. Wind against tide will always cause overfalls, and we hoped we'd just barrel through them then continue our beat upwind. Well, in a few seconds, we were in the gap and from the GPS screen in the aft cabin, I was telling Jude to head more right.

"You sure?" she yells. "Straight for the rocks?"

Popping my head up, multi-storey granite boulders were just a boat length dead ahead. Alarmed, a bucket of adrenalin made me scream, "Turn hard left!"

Looking that way I saw what appeared a white avalanche, one wave after another for as far as we could see. In a flash, the first one crashed over us, sloshing water all around the wheelhouse. Our lady stopped dead in her tracks. The speedo sank to zero. That's when the next wave washed another avalanche over our decks. Between the howling wind and roar of the sea, the mayhem brought back Captain Delano's warning and a cold sweat shook my confidence. Jude gave the donk a big kick to regain steerage, and that added more noise to the mayhem as those twin rock monoliths seemed to loom even closer.

Ducking below I was instantly amazed to see a tiny dotted track going forward across the screen at nearly seven knots. Crash, we shuddered again, and more water came on board, sending spray up through the rigging. The speedo was not recording - the swells so frequent and deep, we weren't going through the sea. But we were going ahead carried by the current and leaving the obstructions behind.

"Just keep us pointing into them," I came up and said in my calmest voice to reassure Jude. And as she hurriedly spun the wheel back and forth, I further encouraged her by saying we were, in fact, getting through at an unbelievable rate of knots. Behind us, I think the fisherman must have been having a good chuckle watching us.

A nasty hour followed. The wind increased. And now on the weather side of the passage, the wind was full in our face. Drying sandbanks narrowed the safe water to a single roadway, and with the tide with us, we battled the wind in a steep, wet sea.

On the positive side, Clarke Island, as it got closer, offered a bit of lee. Then came a moment of bliss. Through a narrow passage between shoals, we entered Kangaroo Bay on Clarke Island's north side, feeling proud and more than just a bit buggered. Both of us were still drenched from the first wave we took in the narrows and quite ready for a sit down with a hot cup of tea.

Motoring in as far as depth would allow, we sent down our forty-five-pound plough. But do you think it would hold in that dark, weedy bottom? Nah! We were dragging with the first blast. So we tried another spot. That was just as bad. From high in the rigging, I searched the dark water for a lighter sand patch, but couldn't find any. After our third unsuccessful attempt, we hauled up the anchor now thickly covered in soft, gelatinous weed being blown across our deck in smelly lumps.

"Just drive about. I'm going to change to the Admiralty anchor," I said, before ducking below. That heavy monster had lived under our saloon floor for years. Getting it out was okay, but heaving it up the stairs, I wasn't feeling very confident. It had never proved very effective.

Knocked about by windblasts made the changeover heavy, dangerous work, but we had to find a solution before dark. At last, the monster was sent down, and for a while, it seemed to hold; the GPS showed .03 NM from the spot. Then a bigger blast sent us to .04, and then another pushed us nearer the shore. But it didn't just let go like the plough. Nevertheless, every big blast tore that hook through the weed until our keel was nearly touching bottom. Two other spots we tried, but still useless.

After so little sleep, with the difficulties we'd faced that day, finding ourselves in an anchorage from hell instead of what should have been a perfect spot for the stormy darkness an hour away, I felt angry and despondent.

"I'm going to hook up the Danforth." I said then responded to Jude's uncertainty, "Yes, I know it's only our lunch-hook and rather light, but something has to work. So cross your fingers."

Straightaway, with not even a hint of it taking hold, its big flukes harvested a whopping crop of gelatinous seaweed while at the same time sent us flying sideways towards the beach. Great!

A second attempt pulled us sharply around, and for several minutes we walked on eggshells not to loosen its grip. All the while, my mind's eye kept seeing us trapped in this tight little hole, in total blackness, side-on to the wind, being driven fast towards the shore. Fuzzy headed, unable to decide what to do next, my anxiety soared.

The plough was our best all-round anchor but clogged easily. The Admiralty dragged slowest but held poorest. And our lunch-hook, the Danforth, presently had a grip but would let fly if it moved an inch. How I hated boats right then. Why couldn't we just cuddle up in front of a television like normal folk?

Jude and I discussed laying two anchors in a vee, but that would be inviting disaster, especially if *Banyandah* should swing, they'd twist and become a mess in the night. With my brain frozen into an iceblock, I sat down to sip a beer. And just then, Poseidon's son took pity on us and had the wind demons suck in their breaths. Suddenly, only a gentle breeze breached the low shoreline, and that allowed *Banyandah* to settle into a slow waltz, instead of a mad samba. And so we slept holding our breaths with the angels that night.

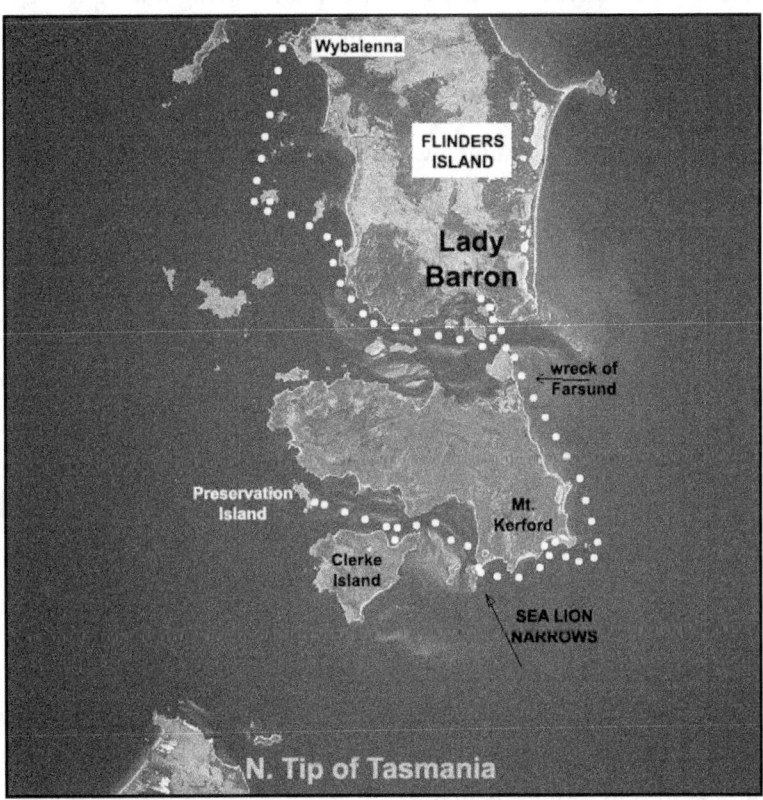

~ Chapter 10 ~

Friendship Is Why We Travel

WHEN THE SOUTH WIND ENDED AT CLARKE ISLAND, feeling exceedingly lazy after a deathly deep sleep and seeing our tight little bay reflecting droplets of cumulus clouds hanging in a cerulean blue heaven, even putting a fishing line over the side proved too much. Instead, we lazed on deck, listened to jazz, and watched seabirds soar above the bleak granite landscape dyed orange by lichen where it met the sea.

About the time the sun was bobbing red upon our silver mirror, our reverie was broken by the faint beat of machinery. A small, rather cute fishing vessel turned the far point, his fishing gear spread like a dragonfly about to land on water. Mesmerised we watched him drift up alongside until its wizened skipper hailed us. "How'd ya find the bottom?"

After Jude had snapped her first photo, her slow shake of head answered him across the water, then she shouted. "We tried three anchors yesterday, but none held."

On the open deck next to a stack of wicker cray pots, his beanpole deckie broke out a big grin while the weathered wizard backed *Jenny Sue* up to us. Then stepping out the cramped wheelhouse he called, "It's all weed hereabouts." Then he glanced up to the Mackerel sky. "There's another blow coming, so best get up to Preservation Island. In close, where it meets Rum Island."

Next morning, our pond was empty again. The wizard had gone as if he'd never been, but the wind was back. Simply amazing how winds around here gain strength so fast. From calm to gale in just a few minutes. Again, I'd left our move too late. Banks Strait was filled with whitewater. To our west by six miles, a flat, treeless island lay across its entrance. The merchant ship *Sydney Cove* had been driven ashore there on the 9th of February 1797, carrying a cargo of rum from India. The already seriously damaged ship had encountered yet more heavy weather the day

Small explosion when adding molten lead

before, which had caused the boat to take on water faster than her pumps and bailing could handle. Her captain spying an island ahead was forced to beach the waterlogged *Sydney Cove* at what is now known as Preservation Island.

Captain Hamilton ran the *Sydney Cove* aground at a well-protected location, in relatively shallow water. This allowed a large proportion of the ship's cargo of rum to be salvaged by the crew in the weeks following the disaster. Upon spotting crewmembers breaking open the casks of spirits, Captain Hamilton had all the barrels removed to an adjacent small island that subsequently became known as Rum Island.

While this was being done, the ship's carpenter modified the longboat to enable a small party to attempt the voyage to Sydney and summon help. Of the seventeen souls that boarded that longboat, only three survived the journey across Bass Strait and the long walk to Sydney Cove. After their arrival, several rescue attempts were made to salvage the valuable cargo, including a voyage by Matthew Flinders to survey the area, which led to his subsequent voyage aboard the *Norfolk* that proved Tasmania is an island. Preservation Island eventually became a sealers' den, then home for muttonbirders, finally a sheep station. Today it's as deserted as it began.

Approaching it through lumpy wet seas, two other craft sheltering from the west winds came into view; one a sailing catamaran, the other a large fishing craft. Both were in Horseshoe Bay, off the abandoned dwelling north of the wizard's spot. Between them and us ran a very large, dark blue weedy shoal. Preservation Island is low, so the wind deflects upwards as it crosses, and the closer we went, the less we felt the windblasts. And that pleased Jude, who as usual followed my hand signals, straight into the wind towards a Caribbean blue sand patch close off the beach. When she called out less than a metre under us, I released our anchor into clean white sand then we fell back over the ubiquitous black carpet of ribbon-weed. Looking at the beach so close, if the wind turned, we'd be blown onto it.

For two days, the wind pelted us; we read, listened to its howl, and waited. At high tide, slop rounding Rum Island rocked us, while just astern the sea was a white fluffy blanket so exquisite in its display of power and sharp colours. Being in close was pure heaven. At both ends of our pristine beach, granite poked up like lumps of butterscotch while virescent scrub ran between them just behind the sand.

When the weathermen predicted a change, we got edgy. The wind was going to turn south in the night, so at last light, we moved into the rougher water over weed to avoid being put on the beach. It worked out all right.

At first light was the silence we had yearned for days. Instead of a southerly, a zephyr out the north barely filled our sails as we motor-sailed at speed away from the Furneaux Group. We'd come, we'd witnessed, we were exhausted. What Jude and I wanted then was a mud bottom and something other than hostile, barren shores.

The northeast corner of Tasmania lacks good harbours, so we laid a course for the Tamar River, expecting an overnight sail. But the wind gods must have felt they'd whipped us enough, and bestowed upon us a fair wind from the northwest. And although that required our sails to be hauled in tight, all that day and into the evening, the miles slipped past. So, as the sun set, the lighthouse on Low Head could be seen flashing, and we had caught both a barracouta and believe it or not, a squid on our lure.

In 1798, George Bass and Matthew Flinders were the first white folk to enter the Tamar River. Those two adventurous lads were sailing in close, exploring the coastline aboard the thirty-four foot *Norfolk*. Their keen eyes would have spied the river's huge indentation, but for Jude and me, we had the sweep of the lighthouse piercing total blackness to guide us, plus a confusing array of winking red and green navigation lights. As we rounded Low Head, its light so bright, Jude's night vision kept being blinded.

The Tamar channel is wide and deep, but torturous. Its large tidal range creates swirls and eddies unseen by us, yet we felt them. In the darkness, it took care and teamwork to navigate the five miles up to George Town, which at the tightest corner was complicated by the confusing appearance of two non-blinking red and green lights. A cargo ship leaving at speed!

In 1804, six years after Bass and Flinders discovered the Tamar River, Terra Australis had just two settlements, Sydney and Hobart. With the French snooping about, the fear of a French invasion led the NSW Governor Philip Gidley King to establish a third settlement. And so, on the 3rd of November 1804, an aging Lieutenant Paterson with a party of 181 persons including 74 convicts entered Tamar Heads aboard a fleet of four ships to establish a third settlement near present-day George Town.

More than two centuries later, upon swirling waters in midnight's darkness when my torch found a mooring buoy at the entrance of the same nook used by Paterson, we immediately hooked onto it. What a stroke of luck, the waters all around were almost too deep to anchor.

Physically exhausted we were soon in bed, yet the tinkling of a running river coupled with the natural high from creeping into a mysterious new spot, kept us counting the ship's bells while wondering what lay beyond the darkness.

In the early light, I spied through the porthole above our bed, a large blue yacht nearby. Nearer the shore on a pontoon behind a locked gate was another named *Kidnap*. Out the other side window, a wide lake of foam-flecked water with few houses set on rising hills of dry summer grass. Later we posted our mobile phone number on a dodger window then set off to explore the town of little more than five thousand.

First known as Port Dalrymple when settled by Lieutenant Paterson, it later became York Cove, then when declared a town in 1811 that was changed to George Town. Almost immediately, it began falling into decline because of insufficient freshwater. Lieutenant Paterson had long since moved his main camp across the river, establishing Yorktown near swamps, which soon proved rather unhealthy. And so in 1806, the present city of Launceston was established much further upriver at the confluence of the two Esk Rivers.

Meanwhile, George Town continued to decline until mid-last century when the constant silting of the Tamar River forced the main port at Launceston to be shifted downstream to Bell Bay, which is around the corner from George Town. At the same time, a Commonwealth joint venture established a smelter there. The site was chosen because excess hydroelectric power was available alongside deep-water frontage. When Rio Tinto purchased the smelter in 1960, George Town grew bigger as it supplied an increased workforce to an enlarged smelter. And it became larger still with the subsequent BHP Ferro-steel plant and Gunns woodchip factory. Over the years, increased technology has reduced the workforce with automation. But presently the locals are hoping to be reinstated because Bell Bay has been chosen for a new wood pulp plant that is still seeking finance.

It's a little crazy really because there is no longer excess hydroelectric power. It now comes from gas-fired generators. Nevertheless, the huge tonnage of bauxite ore is still being shipped across vast oceans and then upriver, to be processed and shipped back out as aluminium billets.

Once onshore, we walked briskly in cool midday sun through a quiet neighbourhood dotted with historic houses. And after a quick look from the Pier Hotel revealed *Banyandah* safe on her mooring, I treated my lady to lunch at the Heritage Hotel, circa 1846, the oldest hotel still standing in Australia. Amongst its ornate façade and etched glass depicting sailing ships, we chatted with a few locals, hearing plenty of gossip about greenies blocking the latest development. From there it was on to the library and two more friendly helpful folks. Then more walking, poking into nearly every shop on the main street before meandering back for a libation enjoyed on the Pier Hotel's balcony looking out to *Banyandah* in York Cove. Cricket played on wall screens, but we were more engrossed in conversation with a pair of mature citizens of property. They quickly got us up to speed on farming life, the dry summer, the growing wine industry, and why the town's mayor was having so much trouble with his wife.

Sauntering home after excellent conversations with many folks, we discovered the tiny George Town Yacht Club open for business and stepped inside the simple white building to introduce ourselves. We met rotund Brian. His quick wit and warm smile straightaway had us feeling at home. Then we shook hands with Shane, a young-un of an old family who quickly proved helpful to a pair of newbies like us. In that short session, a ride with Shane to Launceston was arranged for the day after next, and we learnt some history of the Low Head Lighthouse and its unique foghorn.

"A volunteer group fires it up every Sunday at noon," Shane had told us, so we pencilled that into our heads. Brian then steered us to the owner of the mooring we were on, a ship's pilot. The big blue steel yacht next to us is crewed by a couple new to the sea, out on their first excursion. This we found out when Jo and John, a pair our age from Geelong sauntered in. After inviting them to *Banyandah* for morning coffee, we dragged our weary bones off for a quick snack before plopping into bed.

Next morning when John and Jo arrived, immediately I saw danger. Their dinghy 'string' wasn't very strong, nor would it float. Ropes that are sinkers foul props. Straightaway, we started talking boats; where to go and how to get there until we had talked ourselves hoarse. Quite pleasing really to offer good advice to a pair just starting out. Then, in a wink, there was trouble. Jo tried boarding her rubber dinghy facing outward, and her feet naturally pushed the dinghy away until her full weight was hanging off her seventy-one-year-old arms gripping our railing. In the kafuffle, her head was about to strike our deck on her way into swiftly running water. An easy mistake that could have been fatal.

It took two of us to rescue Jo, and by her grand smile, we guessed she must not have had enough of us when she insisted we come over for Sunday coffee.

Big boat theirs. Too big if you ask me, weighs thirty-six tonnes. It'd be quite a handful for a couple of strong-armed youths, although she does have bow-thrusters to help them get dockside. After being given the full tour, Jude gave Jo many more practical storage ideas and advice on how to relax by planning ahead. Meanwhile, I walked around with John pointing to things I thought might cause some bother. There's plenty of that without adding further surprises. We gabbed on and on, far too long before suddenly remembering the ancient foghorn at Low Head.

A fast row ashore and run to the main road, we promptly stuck out our thumbs. Yahoo. Would you believe we hitched a ride with a trio of youngsters?

"Do we trust them?" Jude whispered as we rushed towards the black sedan with a pair of dice swinging on the rear-view mirror.

"Let's have a look," I said, bending to see three seedy young fellows. "How goes?" I called. "We're off to hear the old foghorn."

"At Low Head?" The driver fired back. "Hop in, we'll take you there."

So we squeezed in, pushing aside a few discarded rum and coke cans and a red KFC box. Then, belting up, we put our daypacks on our knees at the ready. Right away, Mum Binder starts questioning them. Asking about school or did they work. With a chuckle and look at each other, the driver and offsider begin telling us about the local high school. Seems there are two, and they're nothing special, lots of kids quit after grade ten. That prompted me to ask what they did for excitement, and that got a better response. Drinking rated the highest. Great, I'm thinking just keep driving straight down the lonely road, and tried a different approach.

"We're on a sailboat," I said to no one in particular, but both in the front turned to face me. "Yeah," I nodded. "We sailed in Friday night from Flinders Island. Before that, we came down from near Byron Bay. Ever hear of that place."

Sure they had. Every kid has heard of Byron. Chicks and the world's best surfing. Well, I got a little wound up, and started talking about travelling the world when I was just a little older than them; how it changed my life, opened doors, awakened me to a universe of new ideas, and how I'd met the lady of my life hitch-hiking around Europe.

"You ought to try it. Of course, hitching is not done so much anymore. But you guys could team up with a cheap car, visit wowser historical sites, see the world, blow your mind away with something besides liquor."

Had I overstepped the mark? Would they turn into the next paddock and roll us for our few bucks? Nope. Their eyes lit up, wanting to hear more.

"Can you really just travel around the world as easy as that?"

So I told them, all that's required is a bit of gumption, a little money, and a lot of determination and willingness to work. That's about when the lighthouse popped into view and getting out, we extended an invitation to visit us. And then we looked at the time. We were there just two minutes before the first blast. Fantastic! Just enough to get the video camera rolling as the trio of boys disappeared down the road.

Hearing the type "G" diaphone foghorn was a booming experience we'll never forget. When the air blasted out the resonator facing Bass Strait, my eardrums vibrated as if bass drum skins being hammered. It evoked visions of frightful windy nights, and quiet ones lost to sight.

Putting our heads in to see the mass of green and red pumps, tanks and piping restored by two golden age brethren of machinery, one of them explained that it had been put there in 1929, then abandoned in 1979 after navigational aids made it redundant.

When they learned Jude and I were sailors who had relied on manned lighthouses, they took us over to their white-painted stone lighthouse and gave us the whole rundown. What a tale of drama through 200 years of evolution.

"Low Head Lighthouse started as a simple flagstaff in 1804 when first settled by Lieutenant Paterson," said the fellow with a salt and pepper beard like mine. The taller one then added, "When a sail was sighted at dusk, a fire was lit and kept burning all night to keep the vessel in touch with the port."

Putting a hand on the brickwork, the bearded fellow rattled off more details. "The first structure was erected in 1833 and constructed of local rubble with a coat of stucco to make it durable. It used sperm whale oil lamps." Then with a bit of pride. "This structure was built in 1888." Patting it affectionately, he added. "It's now completely automated with super bright LED lights, flashing 3 times every 30 seconds. But I remember a black windy night when……"

People are great. Young, old, doesn't matter. Listen to their story, share dreams and problems. We're all much the same. Stuck on Planet Earth, trying to get the most out of the short time we're here without getting hurt or going hungry.

~ Chapter 11 ~

The Nut

A WEEK LATER WHEN *BANYANDAH* CLEARED THE LEADS, a thick sea-fret erased not only George Town, it blanketed the entire north coast from sight. Nevertheless, we had a grand sail, wrapped in our own grey cocoon, while the miles swiftly slipped past. As far as we were concerned, we could have been crossing an ocean to a new continent because no-where on our journey was land in sight until our GPS heralded the town of Stanley at less than two miles ahead. That's when a strange monolith emerged from the mist. Followed by white breakers along its steep sides disappearing in the fog.

The strong easterly wind had raised a large swell that grew steeper and nastier as we rolled into the shallow bay. When we saw how they swept right across the harbour's narrow entrance, our hearts stopped. The opening was dangerous. All the more so as it's such a tiny harbour, with no room to manoeuvre, forcing us to drop sail outside.

Bobbing about as if a cork caught in a millrace, we measured each approaching wave, waiting for just the right moment to use horsepower coupled with a bit of bravado to shoot through the opening barely twice our width.

Stanley's tidal range is the greatest in Tasmania, up to four metres differential, so once inside and our pulse easing, we opted to lie alongside a cray boat at the dock. Our day's work done, we kicked back and cheered our success with a celebratory libation enjoyed under the

sheer basalt cliff now towering directly above us. It was indeed majestic and growing more glorious as the lowering sun pierced the mist, casting golden hues upon its craggy dark face.

Next day dawned calm and bursting with blue sky and hot sun, so I bundled up my lady for a tour of this historical town. It was named after Lord Stanley, the British Secretary of State in the 1830s and '40s, who later had three terms as British Prime Minister

The township of Stanley occupies one corner of a narrow peninsula jutting nine kilometres out into Bass Strait, and its 500 inhabitants enjoy the cleanest air in the world as reported by a nearby international sensor. Lying in the shadow of a gigantic monolith, the town also abounds with historical dwellings including the birthplace of the Right Honourable Joseph Lyons, Prime Minister of Australia from 1932 until he died in 1939. The only Prime Minister to come from Tasmania.

By far the most distinctive landmark in Stanley is the solidified lava plug first discovered by Flinders and Bass in 1798, who officially named it Circular Head. Before that, the Tommeginer Aborigines called it Moo-Nut-Re-Ker. But by 1851, sailors had come to know it simply as The Nut.

Although steep-sided and rising to 143 metres, it is possible to walk to the top via a steep track. But, as the day had clouded over, we enjoyed a fish and chip lunch instead. Then Jude wandered off with her sketchbook to the picturesque setting of the cemetery, its row upon row of headstones overlooking North Beach, while I went home to take care of some maintenance.

Our second full day began under a ceiling of mist, The Nut well hidden within cottonwool that muffled all sounds.

Tasmania's weather can change dramatically every few hours, and that day was no exception. By noon, a glorious sky had us scrambling to take a walk. Quickly packing lunch, we were soon panting up the steep path towards the Nut's top, calling out to other tourists riding the overhead chairlift and laughingly mocking us. But we like to stay fit and what better way than on a walk that would have lasted ten minutes had the ever-expanding vistas not enticed us to pause every few steps.

On top, our world became flooded in blue, except for the stretched-out turtle neck of parched fields, joining the orderly town at our feet to the rest of Tasmania. From our lofty viewpoint, that narrow neck looked under attack from both sides. Inlets, drying like desert sands as the tide retreated, stretched far into it. Meandering through these were aqua tendrils like arteries leading to the sea.

Oh, to be an artist with easel and palette in hand. To while away the days producing masterpieces confirming Nature's beauty was a fleeting dream when a band of cloud darkened the colours and brought a chill. Suddenly the seascape looked harsh and cruel. Then just as quickly that mood was quashed by brilliant yellow sunshine passing through Earth's cleanest air. High above, eagles soared effortlessly while on the flat volcanic rock a pademelon, which is a marsupial the size of a small dog, dashed away hip-pity-hop. Nearer at hand, scaly skinks scurried over rocks and out of sight into grasses. All around us, the sea was in action to the faraway horizon that only dimmed slightly where it blended into the sky.

Stanley's postmistress Sue and her husband Mick had invited us over for bon voyage drinks, and a short walk along a lane filled with cottages from the mid-1800s, the ubiquitous Nut towering above them, brought us to their modernized bungalow that stood a stone's throw from the town's scenically situated cemetery. They showed us to an area in full sun out the breeze commanding a view over North Beach and its row of

Norfolk Pines. The quiet wash of surf and whispering of tall trees made it even more serene.

We first met Sue when posting a letter. We saw a few old pictures on her counter, and that started us discussing Tasmanian Aborigines. Mentioning our visit to Wybalenna and our interest in Aboriginal history, she told us that she had been a teacher and had taught this subject at high school. Facts flew thick and fast after that as she replayed history in her quaint post office. She kept coming around her counter to first show us a poster filled with Aboriginal artefacts then again to point out a painting of Truganini, the last pureblood. In the course of our talk, we learnt that she had travelled not only to Wybalenna, enduring a scary single-engine air flight, but had also been to Oyster Bay, the black folk's final resting place.

The track up The Nut

One special joy of travelling by yacht is our ability to invite new friends to our home. And although Sue had mentioned several times her fear of scary things, in the past she had mastered those fears, so we weren't surprised when we heard her yoo-hoo from the dockside the morning after our first meeting. From that short visit and then others, was how we ended up at their place the night before our departure.

Pulling the cork on the red we'd taken, the four of us toasted our new friendship. And then, pointing across the isthmus to the rolling plains of grass, I asked whether that property raised lamb or beef.

"Some of the best wool came from this area," Mick began. "That's how the area was settled."

Leaning forward, Jude first looked to Mick as if to ask what he meant, when Sue said something about the British wanting a cheap supply of wool. And I must have looked confused because Mick then said, "Haven't you heard of the Van Diemen's Land Company?" And both Jude and I shook our heads.

Filling our glasses, Mick mentioned that before 1825 this had been unexplored territory when a group of London-based businessmen formed a company to establish a wool growing venture on the island to supply the needs of the British textile industry. The company was granted royal permission to select 250,000 acres in the far north-west, and Circular Head appeared to be the most promising place for the new settlement.

"Following that, British employees settled the area in October 1826," Sue added and laughed giving her blonde curls a cute shake. "Some refused to adapt to their new surroundings and wouldn't recognise that the seasons in the southern hemisphere were reversed. So, for many years, the costs of farming were only just recovered."

Then they both filled in the details of the port opening in 1827, the first school in 1841, and Sue's Post Office, first known as Circular Head, being opened on the 1st of July 1845.

"So does this company still exist?" I wanted to know.

"Oh, yes," Mick answered. "Changes to British law gave the Company greater flexibility, including the development of subsidiaries. After fifty years in the area, they formed the Emu Bay and Mount Bischoff Railway Companies, and then as Tasmania grew larger, they branched into timber and bricks in the early 1900s."

Sue then explained, "The Company remained British dominated right up until 1954 when an Australian became a director. Followed by a Victorian grazier who was succeeded by his son in '75. Then I think a Melbourne solicitor became Governor for a decade in the 80s. International influence followed when Italians joined the board. Finally, in the early 1990s, it was taken over by Tasman Agriculture of New Zealand."

"And today?" Jude asked.

"Today the company's main thrust is centred on dairy, sheep, beef, and tourism at Woolnorth. That's at the island's northwest tip. And it still controls one-seventh of the original quarter million acres." Her eyebrows went up, and dreaming of all that wealth, the four of us clinked our wine glasses again.

We had already seen our next destination when on our picnic at the top of The Nut. Strung away to the northwest was a necklace of islands; Robbins and Walker Islands lead onwards to Cape Grim, Hunter stretched north from there, and the last in sight was a flat triangle with conical hills in each corner.

Strong winds delayed our departure for the island Flinders had named Three Hummock that lay just twenty-four miles northwest of Stanley in the Hunter Group but is said to be one of the most isolated spots in this part of the world.

I had been ready to do battle with the boisterous conditions, but then Jude had taken me by the hand and walked me to the harbour entrance where mean ugly waves were washing across the narrow opening. Beyond, a nasty sea looked set to attack anyone setting out, and that made settling in for another day a much wiser alternative.

The following morning, although still lumpy, after lining *Banyandah* up with the narrow opening and giving her full power, once the sun had melted the early grey cumulus, we settled into an easy sail. Relaxing on the stern seat and looking back to North Beach thinking of Mick and Sue, I then turned to see the hummocks gain height and that's when our lure attracted one of those bony barracoutas. It was nice and small, so instead of chucking it back, I quickly cut off two small fillets for lunch.

The wind slowly eased through the day to hardly more than a light caressing breeze that smoothed the sea. All seemed perfect. And we looked forward to days of calm weather to explore what is reputed to be this area's prettiest island.

Then reality bit hard. Long before the island's shore break appeared, a buzzing was heard, followed by the landing of a pesky March fly. Those unacquainted with our Aussie March fly might know them as a Horse Fly. Large and strongly built with huge eyes - the male's eyes actually meet in the middle - but it's the females that seek meals of blood. The male feeds only on nectar and plant juices. After mating, the females disperse, travelling many kilometres in search of blood. Female tabanids are armed with two large blade-like mouthparts that can easily penetrate socks and trousers, piercing and slashing skin, inflicting a painful wound, which continues to ooze blood long after the mouthparts have been extracted. I have read that some animals can lose up to 300 ml of blood in a day due to attack by these flies. That's a serious loss.

First came one, then another, until our sunny cruise turned into a shipboard nightmare as a never-ending swarm invaded. How fortunate that Jude had recently purchased three new fly swatters, which were immediately put to work. Suddenly, it became very painful to manage our ship. So as soon as anchoring depth was reached, down went the hook and a serious battle began. My record during that stop was eight March flies with a single swot. But even though our cockpit gutters turned black with the dead, more kept coming. And the carnage never seemed to dent their numbers. It was dreadful because their bites stung too, and soon we couldn't stand it anymore. So, swotting as we worked, up went the sails, and still swotting, made our way to the anchorage off the homestead.

For many centuries, Three Hummock Island was the summer hunting ground for Aborigines of the North West who reached it by swimming across five kilometres of open water from nearby Hunter Island. Aboriginal people seasonally occupied all islands in the Hunter Group for hunting, fishing, and muttonbird harvesting. Shell middens provide evidence of a large presence in the prehistoric past. Again, the first European visitors were Bass and Flinders in the *Norfolk*, who made landfall during their circumnavigation of Tasmania in December 1798. Bass went ashore and reported the site as;

> "...impenetrable from the closeness of the tall brushwood, although it had been partially burnt not long before."

In 1889, the first recorded lease was issued to a small group of settlers who farmed until the early 1900s. The longest residents, from 1951 to 1976, Commander John Alliston and his wife Eleanor farmed dune land adjacent to the small settlement at Chimney Corner. Eleanor Alliston wrote two books about her family's island life: *Escape to an Island* and *Island Affair*.

In 1976, the Parks and Wildlife Service proclaimed Three Hummock Island a Nature Reserve and took on its management including destocking. The small settlement area around Chimney Corner remained privately leased and was only recently sold to new managers.

Wildfires in 1982 and 1984 destroyed much of the island's vegetation, which has reverted to scrub/short forest. Here are a few more details we learned in Stanley. South Hummock, the highest point at 237 metres high takes in views of nearby Hunter Island and Tasmania as far as the wind farm on Cape Grim. The stunning beaches and coves, with rolling surf breaks, are punctuated by rocky granite outcrops. Fish, crayfish, and abalone are plentiful. Birdlife abounds, with over 90 species recorded. Eagles, wild ducks, and black swans frequent the small lakes behind the sand dunes lining the beaches. Fairy penguins can be observed making their nightly trip up the beach to their nests, and a wide variety of seabirds can be seen around the coast, including international visitors that stop there to breed.

It all sounded delightful, but how much we would enjoy depended on those pesky March flies that now blackened our decks, forcing us below behind tight netting.

In fact, although the weather remained placid over the next several days, with bright sunshine followed by a cloudy one, we ventured ashore just once. And that once was enough. Dressed head to toe in thick safari garb, we had to continuously swat those nasty buggers from our faces as we strolled empty beaches and rock hopped some spectacular granite formations. We would have loved to have done more; the interior tempted us with hints of wild creatures, as did the beach profusely dotted with multiple animal tracks, and at sundown came the plaintive cries of penguins. But those troublesome March flies just wouldn't release us from our netted prison. Anytime we went out, to fish, watch a sunset, or even catch a refreshing cool breeze, they would swarm in, no matter how many we swatted dead.

It's no wonder we chucked in the towel when the first serious sailing breeze stirred our fourth dawn at the Three Hummock. It came in the night, and by first light was strong enough to warrant double reefing the mainsail and letting out only a small portion of our headsail. So strong in fact, maybe we should have stayed put another day. But we'd had it with being imprisoned on our own ship. So we sailed, preferring to face an angry ocean than endure another moment with those pesky, irksome, horrible March flies.

~ Chapter 12 ~

King Island Melody

CAN YOU REMEMBER A WARM BALMY DAY driving through the countryside with the heady sweetness of summer scenting the air and the car almost finding its own way? Well, sailing between islands can sometimes be like that. But, on the midsummer's day of February 12, it was not.

Under menacing grey clouds, *Banyandah* made her way out of Coulomb Bay on the island of Three Hummock, happily leaving behind the marauding army of March flies as she swung wide of Hunter's northern tip to clear a mass of white overfalls piling up there. These islands off Tasmanian's north-west coast are renowned for rough conditions brought about by swift currents through the channels leading into Bass Strait. History recites a long requiem of ships lost on their rocky shores, and that grey morning typified the horror conditions that have taken so many human lives. Clearing Hunter exposed us to the full strength of a south wind that was driving hard against a determined sea being pulled in the opposite direction by the sun and moon. Caught in the middle of an almighty tussle, *Banyandah* bashed her head against short heavy seas, and though under double-reefed main, she made fast ground towards King Island some forty miles away.

In 1798, when Bass and Flinders discovered Tasmania was an island instead of what was thought to be the most southern tip of Terra Australis, their discovery prompted many sea captains to risk these dangerous straits to shorten the time to the new colony at Sydney Cove. But what Bass and Flinders hadn't seen is that the western entrance to Bass Strait is blocked by a very large obstruction. Situated midway between the mainland and Tasmania is an island 64 km long by 24 km wide. Its gently rolling hills rising to 213 metres at Mount Stanley were sighted later that same year by Captain John Black. Claimed for Great Britain in 1802 to prevent the French from taking possession, it was named to honour Philip Gidley King, the third governor of New South Wales.

Lying directly in the path of the Roaring Forties, the tourist pamphlets say King Island is a land of long, empty beaches and clean, fresh air, with rocky coasts, lighthouses, and shipwrecks. While its treacherous shores may have claimed hundreds of ships and far more than a thousand souls, today it is more renowned for award-winning cheeses, succulent beef, and fresh seafood.

But all that seemed on the far side of the moon as *Banyandah* yawed and pitched wildly in conditions so severe her faithful windvane could only steer as if a drunken sailor three sheets to the wind. The lowest moment of the passage, my being doused by a sneaky wave as I ran aft to tinker with it. And then after an hour's drying in the sun, my beautiful ship laid over so far, her cockpit seat took a deluge, drenching my bum yet again. By the time the smudge of King Island appeared, Jude and I were sick and tired of clinging to our wild ship. So when we surfed in past Omagh (Oh My God) Reef to enter the tiny sanctuary called Grassy Harbour on King Island's southeast corner, we were greatly relieved.

Immediately calm conditions surrounded us, as did a dozen moored vessels scattered just off a noisy wharf that distracted us while I tried to direct Jude to a mooring closest the shore. Our mate Trevor, from the charter yacht *Stormbreaker* in Strahan, had already given us the goss on where to park. So it took only minutes to travel from battling high seas to sitting quietly in the heart of Grassy Harbour.

There wasn't much in sight. Only two cargo sheds and a rather rough metal shack that had 'King Island Boat Club' brushed on a piece of tin above what we presumed was its entrance. Rising high beyond them was a black cliff of blasted rock, the old mine face of Scheelite (tungsten ore), mined sporadically since 1917.

Ashore to explore early next morning, immediately we saw a woman walking two white Silky Terriers. Well, she was actually driving her car holding the leash while her white terrors ran alongside. But after she stopped, Pat welcomed us enthusiastically to her isle of birth then gave us directions to the town located six kilometres up a steep road. Our dismay must have shown because the old lady asked with a pert smile that made her white hair seem even whiter, "would we like a ride?"

Old mine open pit with manmade Grassy Harbour in distance

"Thanks, but we really need to stretch our sea legs." With that, she told us about the shortcut through the abandoned mine site.

The dirt track wound around the island's fuel depot then ascended through bushland littered with roo poo. In fact, a dozen times or more, furry marsupials bolted out, only to skid to a stop in front of us before scampering back into the security of the bush. A thirty-minute climb brought us in front of Grassy's 'supermarket' with the gourmet butcher we'd read about next door, the community hall opposite needing a lick of paint. The only thing missing was a sign welcoming us to the Grassy community, population 100.

In days gone by, mainly during wars, Grassy had been a bustling community of several thousand. Scheelite is used for hardening armament. Today, Chinese labour digs up what mineral is needed much more economically than Aussie lads. Therefore Grassy is now just one notch up from a ghost town. On the west coast is Currie, the island's main town where a few hundred live. Scattered around are quite a few more folks, so all up, King Island boasts a population of about twelve hundred. But, at any one time, tourists can increase this number by half again.

After perusing the supermarket's two lanes, we met Dimitri, the young lass in charge. And when we asked if King Island had a bus service, sweet, shy Dimitri offered us a ride to 'town' on the following Monday morning when she goes to pick up stock. Next door, John from northern Italy makes his own sausage and salami. Everything he showed us seemed enticing and cheap. Not that Jude eats red meat, but the vacuum-packed prosciutto, capocollo, and salami looked so yummy, I nudged my lady with the idea of taking some home for my lunches.

From John, we heard that the township of Grassy had been built by the mining company, and when it closed in 1990, someone proposed bulldozing all the housing into the open pit. Instead, it seems a local entrepreneurial lad offered a pittance for the whole place, and after building his own power, water, and sewage grids, sold the houses back to those who wanted to stay. Many have grand views over the mighty Southern Ocean, heaps of the freshest air, and a pretty laid back existence.

Of course, everybody knows everyone's business. In our short walk around the community's three streets, from her doorstep, we were sighted by Pat and her neighbour Nance, and they insisted we come in for tea. If you want to know local history, have tea with Nance and Pat. One hundred and sixty years of King Island life is stored in their heads. They recited chapter and verse the entire history of the mine, farming, fishing, births and deaths, as well as extremes of weather, pausing only to pour more lovely cups of tea and top up a big plate of homemade vanilla fruit cake. Yum. This was capped by a trip around their garden, which yielded a fistful of glossy silver-beet. Well, that took care of our Saturday morning.

Deep that night, rain fell heavily, gusting in from the South Pole. Although we were attached to a stout mooring, uneasiness stirred me awake early the next morning because the weekly container ship was due to dock. Now, Grassy Harbour is minute when it comes to docking a good-sized ship when stormy conditions could severely complicate turning the big vessel around. Any muck-up and we could see *Banyandah* splashed across the six o'clock news.

At first grey light, I was in the cockpit, my teeth chattering, the video camera on, recording two brave lads in a line boat working in sheets of rain. Then through the thickness emerged two faint red and green navigational lights on a huge, dull green thing that further darkened our already dim environment.

In dress circle row, Jude and I watched the leviathan perform an impressive ballet, and pirouette without the aid of tugs, while sets of lines were stretched across to pull the monster into its spot. In a well-practised routine, tiny figures in yellow slickers raced about securing it then stood clear as the ship's large rear door lowered to the wharf. Immediately following, our morning became a cacophony of machinery unloading the monster's innards.

Just after noon, a rush of bodies going in and out of the Boat Club motivated us to don wet-weather gear and row in to meet the locals. In a corner, a cheery fire increased the warmth of their hospitality that had us feeling right at home, and after greeting all, Jude and I parted to mingle with our male and female counterparts. Jude said later that she'd had a wonderful discussion comparing isolated island life with life afloat; particularly how women cope, as well as educating children. But the men's prime topic was beef; cartage costs, vet charges, and occasionally a few words on fishing. And I felt more like a fly on the wall until a tallish fellow stuck out his paw, and said, "I'm John, which boat's yours?"

After pointing to our dark blue hull nearest the container ship, John remarked, "Oh, you're just behind me, mine's the double-ender." It was the yacht Jude and I had especially noticed because one side had 'King Island' in fresh paint, while the other side said, 'New Haven Ct.' in faded letters. From that moment on, John and I settled into an easy, rainy afternoon chat covering the saga of buying his boat in Queensland then sailing it to King Island. It seems *Serenity* had numerous problems, the biggest, saltwater getting into her engine oil.

In a voice inviting comment, John said, "The experts round here think it gets in through the engine exhaust."

But that didn't quite gel; too much water I thought, which would have caused greater damage. So I offered to take a look.

Meanwhile, the ladies were getting along famously, resulting in John's wife Lyn offering us the use of her car the following day.

Lyn does Yoga Monday mornings, and afterwards, she came to the harbour to pick us up in her burgundy coloured Land Rover. In the bright sunshine, her blue eyes sparkled, and her chestnut hair danced when she handed across an island map then encouraged us to, "use the car all you want, and don't worry about fuel, we have an account."

Our first stop was Currie to return books due back at the library. Tasmania has a great system. It's all one region. We've been borrowing from one library then returning them at the next port. Perfect for us.

Currie Harbour - one low wall stopping the Great Southern Ocean

Currie is a small cosy village just up the hill from the harbour with its one main shopping street adjoining the road leading down to it. We whizzed through its two small supermarkets just for a look then grabbed a 'crayfish pie' from the fabulous bakery before pricing wine and beer at the two pubs. Oh, and Jude mailed postcards to the grandkids.

Everything in Curry is scenically placed on a bold rocky shore dotted with green forest surrounded by lush pastureland. But their small harbour we felt is very exposed being on the winter weather coast.

King Island Melody

Looking to sea from the headland, we saw a tiny breakwall and rocky reef, and imagined Southern Ocean winter waves crashing over. Even in mild conditions, there could be difficulties bringing *Banyandah* in. There's no room to anchor. All the boats were either on moorings or alongside the jetty.

Dominating the hill was a white, steel lattice light structure built fifty years after the island's main lighthouse at Cape Wickham. The reason according to the local curator is it seems after weeks without sight of land, early shipmasters got confused, thinking the Cape Wickham light was the one on the mainland, and so they sailed south, colliding with King Island with disastrous results. More on that later, but first we're off to the King Island Dairy.

King Island has developed an enviable reputation as a producer of some of the world's finest dairy products. Several types of Cheddar, Brie, Camembert, Washed Rind, Blue, Crème Fraiche, Pure Cream, Triple Cream, Ricotta and Mascarpone are made. Phew! That's a lot.

And King Island cows are famous for their unique quality of milk. It is one of the few areas in Australia, and indeed the world, where cows graze all year round. Hard to imagine, but a steady, reliable rainfall is one reason.

The award-winning King Island Dairy's *Fromagerie* has a sampling room open every day. Cunning little foxes, we'd not eaten much lunch thinking about sampling their wonderful cheeses. So the first destination was to satisfy our taste buds. Driving north out of Currie, we began noticing 'the raised-finger hello' from just about every car going the other way. A feature of a small community, everyone knows each other's car. We laughed thinking Lyn's phone would be ringing off the hook, being told strangers had her car. We needed have worried, she later explained, "There's no car theft on KI. Everything has to go out on that green ship."

The flat road north from Currie first passed their small airfield, as well as the ever-present cows and pastures for about twenty kilometres until we drove over a rise and found the cheese factory. Having made sure we were really hungry, we weren't disappointed when shown their tasting room. A long table we could walk right around was covered in all varieties of cheeses supported by an assortment of water biscuits. Mind, I think we easily paid for our glut of samples by purchasing sixty dollars of their products.

Bulging when we got outside, a bright sun high in a crystal clear sky begged us to explore further and looking at the island map brought a hankering to see the southern hemisphere's tallest lighthouse located on the island's northern tip. On the way, a sign declaring Yellow Rock Beach veered us left along a dirt sidetrack to a lonely coastal spot where we found the *Shannon's* boiler still resting on an empty sand beach. Just offshore, forming a glorious background, upon a shimmering blue sea lay Christmas and New Year Islands.

On a sign we read another harrowing story of fair weather quickly turned foul, degenerating into gale-force winds and driving rain. Too much for the 21 horsepower *Shannon*. "Tossing and twisting as she rode the storm behind Christmas Island, her Red Gum planks began to spring, and she began to take water at an alarming rate….."

King Island lighthouse keepers must have lived a Spartan life. And those at Cape Wickham, operating its forty-eight-metre tall structure had to climb eleven flights of stairs at the start of every shift. Each flight has twenty steps!

Keeper Col Cotter put it succinctly, "People seem to have romantic notions about lighthouse keepers, but I've found nothing romantic about it. It's a long way up that light at 2 a.m."

One of the worst shipwrecks occurred on some rather nasty looking black rocks that we could see sending white breakers high into the air from our vantage point on the sparsely vegetated bluff. You just got to love those informative signs. This one had a line drawing of a square-rigged ship on its side, sails and lines quite a clutter, with boats nearby, filled with desperate people. The *Neva*, a 104 ft long barque of 327 tons sailing from Ireland, bound for Sydney in 1835, had onboard 150 female convicts with their 33 children, 9 free women and their 22 children, plus a crew of 26 under the command of Captain Benjamin Peck. The voyage, which had been almost completely free of illness or incident, ended in early winter fog on the 13th of May when the *Neva* crashed onto these reefs within cooee of King Island, horrendously ending 224 lives. When the lookout called the dreaded warning "breakers ahead!" the helm was put over hard to starboard, but when she struck rocks, her rudder carried away. Huge Southern Ocean seas breaking over her, the *Neva* soon filled with water and the straining of the hull caused the prison stanchions to collapse. There were quickly 200 panic-stricken women and children on deck. In the stillness, as we read this, we closed our eyes and could hear the women's screams and wailing of frightened children.

Authorities may have been unmoved by the death of convict women and children on the *Neva*, but a decade later, when the *Cataraqui* lost 402 emigrants, the colonies combined to fund a giant light structure that would be seen for 20 miles.

Late that day, exhausted yet still carrying the day's excitement, we pulled into 'Orchard Farm,' where from behind a line of pines, John and Lyn's stylish house enfolded with commanding views over large acreage. Typical farmhouse, boots on the porch, overcoats on hooks, broken mechanical bits nearly blocking our access, and then a huge Grey Ghost Weimaraner tried kissing me as we entered their lovely house that was filled with timber features. "Down girl." I pushed her away. "I never kiss on the first date."

The King Islanders exhibit the very best traits of humanity. From Pat and Nance, we saw how folk in smaller communities tend to look after each other; and from John and Lyn, we were lavished with genuine hospitality. These traits are what separate humans from the other creatures, and maybe if they became more widespread, then we would be better able to cohabit peacefully with each other, and with the other animals. What we saw at King Island reinforced our belief that a reduced world population could bring that about. Fewer inhabitants mean less pollution, and more space leads to less stressful lives and more room for the wild creatures.

We also believe the ancient hunter-gatherer instincts still exist within most of us. Even city folk love to fish. And on an island like King with prolific wildlife, it's an intrinsic part of life. So, the next day when John suggested we toddle off to pop a few abalones on the west coast, Jude immediately said she's into that. And when Lyn and I said we'd act as shore support, in next to no time we were in John's Ute, raising a dust trail across the island, towing a trailer filled with lucerne for his beef cattle.

Not that long ago, huge forests of eucalypts, blackwoods, and tree ferns covered this island. But these were devastated by wildfires, land clearing and milling, their place taken by undulating green pasture with pockets of paperbark and tea-tree. With no foxes or rabbits, and a larder of excellent feed, an amazing variety of native and introduced animals roam the island.

Tagging along with 'rancher John' brought the essentials of existence to the fore. He pointed out, we all must eat, and to do that food must be farmed. This concentration of sustenance attracts and increases the numbers of wild creatures, which creates the dilemma of how to maintain the balance – cull, fence, or poison. Then there are the weeds. All this ensured we had a lively discussion en-route.

John didn't need to go out of his way to show us huge mobs of marsupials feeding on the island's lush grasses. Nor did he sidetrack to show us the stack of dead ones his neighbour had just shot. To keep control on his property, John uses a higher, tighter mesh fencing that he says keeps the critters out of the pastures. But, where they roam free, we saw bare earth, the grass nearly gone.

From atop an open hilltop that was once forested, we faced the infinity of the blue Southern Ocean and felt our spirits soar. Next to us, John needn't have called his cattle for they came running at first sight of the lucerne rolling out. But, he did holler, simply to get them to associate his call with food, saying it'd make rounding them up easier.

Across the open grassy paddock with that blue sea in sight, down a slope to pools of aquamarine occasionally fluffed in white, we found a flat patch to put on wetsuits. Moments later, John and Jude were braving icy water.

Sitting on the surrounding rocks, Lyn and I heard Jude squeal, not from the chill up her spine, but the underwater beauty. John, the hunter, took little time to harvest some beautiful black lip abalones well covered in burgundy moss. All measured the legal size.

Earlier that morning, while having brekkie on *Banyandah*, a returning cray fisherman had come alongside in his tender. "Can't market this one," he had said with a twinkle in his eye then he plopped down a lobster minus a few legs. "Ocky got in the cray pot," he explained. Now, with the abs, a feast was in the making.

None too early next morning, Jude and I packed our rucksacks to trek to the island's south coast. We needed some training for our second attempt at reaching Mount Sorell's summit in Macquarie Harbour, and the night before, John had suggested a route.

"There's a shack down the coast where the views and fishing are special," he had advised while quickly cooking the thinly sliced abalone on his barbeque. So, about noon, carrying full weight kits, we rowed ashore and set off down the golden beach leading away from Grassy Harbour.

Walking in soft sand is heavy work. Even though flat, our legs soon knew they had a chore before them. Augmented by glorious views, having laboured several hours we'd raised a heavy sweat when a loud cooee stopped us in our tracks. John, coming from the opposite direction, was on the rise, waving.

"Just thought I'd take a walk," John commented when we met. Then indicating the far point. "The Ute's up there, a couple of litres of freshwater for your use in the back." Now, how about that!

On our journey, although the sky remained clouded, we browned then burned while glorying in unparalleled views of Nature's kingdom, and it felt grand to feel so free with faraway vistas. Flocks of golden-headed gannets vied with crested terns, and brown muttonbirds, all diving for school fish pooled just below the turbulent waters. From vacant hilltops, black rocks strewn near and offshore renewed our visions of tragic shipwrecks. And these made our stomachs churn and had us promising to be extra careful when sailing from these shores.

We trudged an honest forty kilometres over three days and saw no other person before taking up John's offer of a lift back home. Quite surprising us, at the island's lonely southern tip, our mobile phone made the connection.

Cray & Abs, a feast in the making

All good things come to an end. That's a sad truism. But for us, the end of our King Island melody arrived upon the caressing hand of a warm north wind that actually brought a new beginning. Northerly winds are rare around those parts. So, when one's forecast, anyone sailing south had better grab it.

Early that Saturday, as the rising sun chased away the chill, we raised sail and waved goodbye to no one in particular. Except perhaps the little Fairy Penguins diving off the harbour wall to go fishing. Maybe Pat and Nance spied us, looking down from Grassy Hill, and John and Lyn from their lookout on the coast road. Didn't matter, we were bidding adieu to King Island but already thinking of calling in again.

~ Chapter 13 ~

Contradictions

THIS STORY BEGINS SEVERAL LIFETIMES AGO when three old codgers were scratching for gold on the forested slopes behind Macquarie Harbour on Tasmania's remote west coast. All of a sudden, their spades brought up some sparkling golden stuff along with lumps of a green mineral. It was the year 1883 when those gold diggers pegged out fifty acres of what later became known as Linda Valley, and their claim included a large ironstone outcrop that eventually became 'The Iron Blow' in the Mount Lyell fields.

So began The Mt Lyell Mining Company, an icon in Australian mining, spanning nearly a hundred years. In those early days, roads were few and far away, so supplies were brought by ship to Strahan in Macquarie Harbour then up the King River to Teepookana. From there they were taken by punts up through some 26 rapids to Sailor Jack's Creek, and after that, lugged by professional packers through four miles of thick forest above the King River Gorge, for a penny a pound, to the 'Fifteen Mile Store' where it was sorted and taken to the fields.

I'll come to our little adventure in a moment, but there's a bit more history that's important. In 1888, five years after first pegged, the Mt Lyell Gold Mining Company was formed by a syndicate of six; the original three claimants, plus Bill Dixon, James Crotty, and F.O. Henry. Unfortunately, their mine made little profit. But then four years later in

1892, two Adelaide financiers, who realised a fortune in copper was being washed out the sluice boxes, bought in.

Following a feud with these new people, James Crotty decided to leave the Company and was bought out with 3000 Mt Lyell shares, plus a small lease at North Mt Lyell. More about him later.

To get ore out and supplies in, a railway was proposed, and The Mt Lyell Mining & Railway Company was formed in March 1893. In a glorious testament to man's ability to overcome immense difficulties, an army of young men hacked down the thick virgin rainforest, and then sometimes working in waist-deep freezing water, they built a twenty-kilometre railroad. Their motto, *Labour Conquers All*.

Many surveyors said it wasn't possible; the land too harsh, the weather extreme and thirty-nine timber bridges had to be built over cold creeks, and raging rivers, plus the trains had to climb one metre in sixteen (6.25%). But in three labour intensive years, the railway was completed between Teepookana on the King River to Penghana, which was soon renamed Queenstown after the Queen River that flows through it.

The new township of Queenstown flourished as the mine grew rapidly in size. The ore was crushed and processed on-site, and the tailings were discharged directly into the Queen River, which, flowing into the King River silted it so badly, ships started finding it impossible to reach Teepookana. So, in 1901, government funding was sought to extend the railroad to Regatta Point in Strahan.

Mount Lyell's brilliant metallurgist, Robert Sticht, built a smelting plant that had eleven blast furnaces. Short and stocky, with a baldpate and fair moustache, Sticht had perfected a system called Pyritic Smelting, which utilised sulphides locked within the ore to generate heat. His system revolutionised smelting throughout the world, resulting in a drastic cut in the fuel required for smelting. But it produced such noxious fumes; the surrounding forests in a thirty-kilometre circle around Queenstown were killed. However, this suited a company needing timbers to fuel smelters and shore up mine shafts. Guess they thought, what's one giant bald patch when surrounded by miles of virgin forests?

Unfortunately, that patch was just the first visible sign, because the mine tailings, the left behind processed earth containing toxic chemicals and heavy metals, started killing vegetation and critters as it drained down the King River. Not for a month or a year, but even today it is still polluting what was once pristine rainforest. It's amazing what humans will do for jobs and profits.

Mt Lyell Company smelter at Queenstown c.1900.

In August 1963, after 67 years of operation, the railway was closed because along with increased financial costs, many bridges needed rebuilding and the rolling stock required replacement; besides there was then a road straight through to Hobart. Despite various proposals post-1963, it was not until the late 1990s, that this railway was rebuilt using Federal and State money as part of the Gordon below Franklin Dam agreement to increase tourism. During the reconstruction, the rail line was given various names. A common one was the 'ABT Railway' because Swiss Engineer Dr Roman Abt developed the system using cogs on a third central rail to assist the engines up the steep incline on the part into Queenstown.

In 2002, it recommenced operations as the ABT Wilderness Railway, but after Federal Hotels took it over the name was changed to the West Coast Wilderness Railway. In summer, the tourist train trip lasts four hours and runs twice a day in each direction between Queenstown and Strahan. The two trains cross at Dubbil Barril Station ('double barrel'). Here, the special ABT steam loco turns around on the turntable and returns to Queenstown taking the ascending carriages up, while the diesel loco takes the descending wagons to Strahan.

It's been estimated 100 million tonnes of tailings have been dumped into the Queen River. So it shouldn't have surprised us that during our six-week stay in Macquarie Harbour the previous year, the excessive acidity and toxic heavy metals in its muddy bottom ate the galvanising off our brand new anchor chain, and we left with raw steel that soon started to rust.

Since that happened, we have wanted to witness the contradiction of heavy pollution alongside pristine forests and madly rushing river gorges. Here's a further paradox that came in 1998. When the mine was sold into foreign hands, to guarantee it would continue and protect five hundred jobs, a Federal exemption was requested and granted, allowing the continued dumping of tailing's acid into the river.

Jude and I just had to see this, but a four-hour train ride was no way enough to gather a true image. So, we decided to walk the tracks.

My planning discovered an emergency access road leading from the main highway down a mountain spine to the Rinadeena Station at the track's highest point. Generally, the King flows at a gentle pace, except below Rinadeena where it madly crashes through a massive rock gorge. The Mount Lyell engineers first proposed blasting a tunnel through the mountain, but that would have taken too long. Remember James Crotty? Well, back in 1898, after discovering rich copper deposits in the tract of land he was given, he gathered up a bevy of wealthy English investors and began his own company. His North Mount Lyell Mine started, in a hurry, laying its own tracks down the Bird River, a much easier route, to carry their higher-grade ore to market. So, a fierce race to supply copper was started. To save time, The Mount Lyell Directors chose the newly invented ABT.

Before setting out, I studied the train schedules to determine just when they'd be on the track and obtained a topographical map to help find suitable campsites. On the morning of our departure, with packed rucksacks we're standing alongside the road just beyond Strahan's only servo, thumbs extended soliciting rides, with little idea of what lay ahead. Then a 4WD pulled in, and a bespectacled, goofy type jumped out and starting re-arranging the mess on his seats. Climbing in, I still had to push jars of something rather heavy aside. Jars full of coins.

"We're on our way to the Rinadeena Lookout," I said, and Mr Goofy smiled wider, causing his short red hair to stand erect.

"Used to ride that train lots when a boy," Mr Goofy said. "Dad used to take us to the coast for holidays."

"Oh, you're a local then!"

"Yep, born and raised in Queenstown."

The so-called highway, twisting and turning like a wiggling worm, is much loved by bikies, but I'm not a fan, and concerned for our safety I asked how often Mr Goofy drove between the two towns.

"This road. At least once every day, sometimes twice. It used to be three round trips daily before we moved to Strahan."

"Crikey, what do you do?"

"Oh, I'm Strahan's general manager. Every day I bank the parking meter money and sometimes attend meetings." A light chuckle then, "You thinking of walking the train track?"

Oops. Not sure that was allowed, I thought honesty the better policy than trying to fool him. "Yeah, I've read there's an access road from the lookout, so we're off to see what a hundred years of mining have done to the King River."

Well, this started a long dissertation on the destruction predicated on the once majestic King River and how funds had once been set aside to begin cleaning it up, only to have them reallocated to other needs. Our driver then elaborated on the scheme agreed to when the mine went to foreign owners and gave us considerably more detail on just how the ore is processed. It's a Catch-22. The area needs the jobs, but the company can't afford to clean up the process or rejuvenate previous companies' environmental destruction. So it's all in limbo. Except for Nature. It's still being hammered. But hey, you have to take a four-hour train ride just to see a tiny bit of that destruction.

Jumping out at the lookout, with the bare hills of Queenstown before us, and two groups of tourists madly snapping photos of the orange-yellow hills and plumes of white smoke, Mr Goofy winked. "The tourists love it. Queenstown council once voted to pluck out the regrowth, so the place would stay barren. But Nature's winning. You can just see the green tinge of new growth." Then with a wave, he wished us good luck and drove off down the highway.

Where Wild Winds Blow

Loading up, Jude and I slipped around a metal boom gate. On a well-formed dirt track, we headed steeply downhill. In the distance, we heard the puffing of a steam engine labouring up a rise. Then slowly, the sound and we started coming together. Walking around a thickly forested bend, we saw a metal walkway over the railway tracks, and then came a shrill whistle and whoosh of hissing steam as the morning train out of Queenstown slowed into Rinadeena Station. Jude and I quickly chucked our sacks into the understorey, and then like little elves, scampered to snap photographs without being seen.

After a short ten minutes, there came the cry of, "All aboard." And when No. 5 Engine started huffing and puffing great clouds of steam, I stepped out with my video camera to record her leaving the station.

Cautiously we peeked up and down the tracks - our motto is low profile – it's no use ruffling feathers. But there were no feathers in sight. So, strolling along the platform with our big rucksacks on our backs, we were quite alone surrounded by Nature's beauty. Small, leathery leaf myrtles were casting deep shadows, and the glossy, toothed leaves of native laurels shone bright red and yellow. And rather quaintly among them was a replica of the original Rinadeena Station. We had a quick look through the windows then it was time for us to walk those very same historic tracks. As no signs were declaring we shouldn't, we took off along the side.

It was gloriously surrounded by dense forest, smelling sweet leatherwoods and being showered by their white, round petalled blossoms while walking down the gently sloping line. Freshets rushed out of gullies along the three-kilometre stretch cut into the mountainside above Sailor Jack's Creek, many spanned by new steel bridges. Every crossing had non-slip grating along one side, and each exposed a magnificent bird's eye view over the Tasmanian rainforest. Imaginary hints of smoky campfires seemed to waft up into the stillness above rushing streams, and we often stopped, swearing we could hear punters singing while poling their cargo towards the Fifteen Mile Store. What surprised us was how many fallen limbs littered the gravel bed and sleepers. In fact, every so often we'd come to a big stack of sawn wood, ready for someone's fireplace.

Just when we thought the small valley would never end, coming round a sweeping bend, we beheld the colossal chasm of the King River

Gorge and instantly understood how those sheer rock sides would have diverted man's best efforts, forcing the company to try a new invention. Above its distant roar, a fine mist from rushing water filled the chasm, partly hiding its dull grey jagged face. Primeval Earth, unmeant to be conquered found its way onto to my recording tape as I spoke of man's will and the environmental destruction that still lay ahead.

Not far ahead was Dubbil Barril Station, where the two trains meet and transfer locos while the passengers enjoy lunch during an hour-long stop. As we approached grimacing under our loads, we heard the familiar, "All Aboard." And we ducked into the forest in time to film the puffing steam engine start-up the rise in a scene that would have brought glee to any child's eyes. Thomas the Tank Engine passed, hissing clouds of steam from its green livery.

After it disappeared, boldly we strode into the now-abandoned station carved out of a hillside, finding two sets of tracks and a hand-powered turntable at the uphill end. Again, the station reproduced the era, except this one had a collection of lunch benches, mostly big Huon planks, separated by pictorial placards enlivening the story of the men who had created this huge undertaking. Walking from one to another, we were moved by old stills of denuded hills littered with fallen trees and young lads in bowlers and vests struggling to push logs through what looked freezing cold mud. Their hard life illustrated in a story of a labour strike when the men downed tools to shorten their eighteen-hour workday down to fifteen for a bit more money. No dole in those days, no medical insurance or retirement funds, just employment if lucky. And if not, kind relatives hopefully.

There were also a few pictorial placards depicting some of the early families who had lived thereabouts, and we read that the Kerrison dairy had been a mile into the hills and that their ten children had taken the train to school each day, few of them wearing shoes.

Surrounded by the station, water tower, and mountain rock giving way to green forest, Jude and I had lunch with a view down to the King River after first reading and photographing each of those information signs. In doing that, the true magnitude of this achievement started to have its impact. Man can conquer huge tasks when we all pull together; be it for a dream or for money. Both relate to our survival. But now planet Earth is struggling to survive, and witnessing these great achievements encourages us to think that mankind can rise to the task to save her. We just need a vision we can all strive to achieve.

Leaving Dubbil Barril, we had several hours before the afternoon trains started their second run, so heaving backpacks in place, we set a slower pace with the track now following the King River. Immediately on the first bend, and then along wider stretches, were banks of pulverized, lacklustre ruby rock that trapped river pools coloured yellow as if watered down honey with streaks of lurid red where the sun penetrated.

West Tasmanian rivers aren't normally clear. Everywhere in this region, rain passes through button grass or tea-tree, picking up tannin that stains it to look like weak tea or good whisky. But this river also had dirty foam floating down, and mud banks coated bright sulphur-yellow. Seemed unearthly. A total contradiction when our eyes rose up to the thousand greens of lush rainforest just above.

After walking the tracks for nearly ten kilometres, the sun would soon be casting dark shadows down the western hills when we heard the toot of dear Thomas chugging his way up for the second time that day. Off to our left, the map showed river flats leading to the 'Quarter Mile' steel bridge crossing the King River, so we plunged into the bush to search for a campsite.

Contradictions

Finding our first camp proved really easy. The thick bush quickly gave way to a wide flood plain of mine overburden barren of trees. Over patches of it grew thick, soft moss, with a double column of saplings hiding the river. In other places lay piles of rotting trunks and limbs. Under the open sky next to a gnarled old stump washed down long ago, I set up our tent while Jude organised her kitchen. After that, we explored down by the river.

What an eye-opener! That yellow coating we'd seen from afar stank as if rancid butter. It coated everything; trunks, limbs, fallen trees, along with several discarded car tyres. Walking atop the heavily eroded bank that fell onto flats of crushed mining rock, we weren't surprised that nothing could grow as the air smelt acidic.

An uncomfortable night passed. Not that the moss wasn't comfy, but we feared being poisoned just touching the ground. So we made sure our hands stayed away from our mouths and cleaned ourselves thoroughly before slipping into bed.

Just after dawn, the maintenance train passed, and by the time we had eaten, dried the tent, and broken camp, the morning tourist run went past, leaving the line vacant until lunch.

Ten minutes walk from camp, we crossed the steel Quarter Mile Bridge and filmed the original one washed away in the '76 floods and lying in a muddle midstream. Shortly after that, a sign announced the next station, and we got alarmed when we heard workers and saw another locomotive. Stashing our sacks, we silently slipped closer to see what was up, feeling a bit like 007. Through understorey, we saw two large trucks carrying huge Huon pine logs – one more than two metres across – being loaded onto flat carriages. Snowy Morrison came to mind. He had told us about State Forest harvesting remnant logs from the Teepookana Plateau.

Snowy has been cutting Huon most of his life. He felled trees with his father and grandfather when a boy, and it was Snowy who told us the biggest and straightest Huon pines had grown on the plateau above what was called Teepookana, now known as Lower Station. In years gone by, Teepookana was where the ore was loaded onto ships for the journey abroad, and where the big Huon logs were rafted down to the mills at Strahan. Today, you can join a 4WD tour up to the top of the plateau, to a forestry lookout where you'll see what Forestry call a demonstration plantation. Different methods of growing Huon pine are being tried because they are the world's slowest-growing tree. They take 1000 years to reach a metre in diameter. When those on the plateau were harvested, they averaged 2000 years, and the oldest known was around 4000 years old. Plenty of trees on the Teepookana Plateau weren't good enough for the old piners. Bark inclusions, a bit bent, any fault at all, and they were left on the forest floor. Luckily Huon pines don't rot, a natural oil protects them. So, State Forest has hired contractors to dig 'em out, up to 50 truckloads per annum, supposedly to sustain the craft and boating industry. And as there's no road out, the trucks come and go on the railroad.

Well, after that train chugged out the station, we moseyed in, took one look up the steep forestry track, and dumped our sacks in the bush. We'd just have time to hike up to the Forestry lookout for a picnic lunch. Besides wanting to take in the view and see the demonstration plantation, our other motive was to check out that route as a possible way to the top of Mount Sorell. Before leaving Strahan, I had used Google Earth to search satellite images and had noticed forestry tracks to within a few miles of that mountain's slope. Of course, those few miles passed through Tassie's infamous 'horizontal scrub', exacting days of punishment perhaps. So we hoped to get a better idea from the lookout tower.

On the way up, two more trucks were coming down, carrying good looking logs and limbs, straw yellow inside, grey and smooth outside. Their drivers giving us a cheery wave, we calculated the loads worth a million dollars. At the sign welcoming us to the 'Huon Experience,' we studied the trial plantation layout before opting to first walk along the boardwalk.

What a lovely experience. There were several rainforest species on the way to the lookout and to read their names and details then see the rainforest trees up close was quite informative. We became more familiar with the uses and growth patterns of sassafras, blackwood, myrtle, and of course Tasmanian blue gum, which is a tough and durable timber, particularly suitable for bridges and wharves. Its pale straw to brown colour also makes it excellent flooring.

Raised on six poles, the lookout was well clear of the forest at the plateau's highest elevation of 275 metres above sea level. While the rustic sapling railing along the outside stairs was downright dangerous, especially for obese visitors, inside it was spacious with views all around through tinted Perspex. To a faraway sea and rising mountains ran a ruffled forest. Inside the hut, above our heads, an artist had drawn the landscape in silhouette with place names above their positions. And straightaway, we could see the route to Mount Sorell was fraught with difficulties. Thick, deep, green ravines hampered that route, and then Sorell's closest slopes were clothed in extremely dense vegetation.

"Hungry dear?" I enquired of Jude who just couldn't stop pointing her camera at the scenery. And when she didn't seem to hear, I took her sack and laid out our picnic of crackers and cheese. Alone, above the peace of Earth's forest on a clear day filled with blue sky, suddenly a noisy March fly broke our reverie, and it kept getting louder. Searching, craning our heads, a tiny pinprick quickly grew into a red helicopter that buzzed round 'n round until I wanted to swat it. Thrice around, it made a final approach then set down not far from us. A few minutes later, voices approached through the forest, and then we were joined by three mature aged visitors and their pilot Rodney, who we learnt was Snowy's cousin. Straight off, he captivated us with stories of his youth in forestry camps, occasionally pausing to show us how to pick out the drooping light green foliage of Huon pines amongst all the others, or pointing to the myrtle's dark green crown seen low near the understorey. He ended his informative talk by telling us how blackwood, a wattle, grows fast and tall to 35 m and is easily found by its olive green, lance-shaped leaves that are different from other forest species.

When they departed, Jude and I shared the tower's binoculars to follow their progress through the Huon pine demonstration plot, watching Rodney show his passengers the tiny scale-like leaves, spirally arranged on small limbs. Clearing our lunch, we soon followed and read that Huon pine reproduction usually occurs vegetatively; that is where a branch falls or touches the ground it forms roots and begins to shoot. Seedling regeneration does occur but is less common as reproduction only happens every 5–7 years. Therefore, Forestry is trying various cuttings, spacings, and plant mix to see which grows the swiftest.

Back down the hill, in hiding beside our packs, we brewed a tea while the afternoon train made its stop, and then after it departed, we saddled up to continue on down the tracks. Quite soon, bridge number 36 loomed ahead, recrossing the King by way of a large steel truss painted a god-awful red. Thinking of where we might camp, studying our map, not much flat ground lay ahead. But just across the river, we could see one. The question was how to reach it? On that far bank, the bridge truss sat in a notch cut through a vertical rock face.

After taking our usual photos and video of crossing the bridge, I raced ahead after detecting a faint line on that rock face. It proved to be an olden day foot track, overgrown and crumbling in places. But enough, I thought, for me with my pack. Of course, being directly above the river, one slip would prove disastrous. Obviously, in yesteryear, hundreds would have combed these hills, and some of their paths still exist. This one was a tippy-toe around the face then onto a moss-covered timber walkway missing half its planks. Gurgling below lay Virginia Creek, bordered by a lovely sandy beach. So I rushed back to help Jude negotiate the track.

What a perfect camp. We imagined it used by countless earlier workers, maybe even a favourite place for some to holiday as the creek poured pure mountain water into the putrid King River. And it held grand views over the entire steel bridge, its colour much nicer reflected off the black river, striking a sweet photogenic chord, especially when Thomas chugged home that night.

The rest of this saga is common compared to our journey of discovery. A comfortable night and then a trudge along more railroad flats for a further seven kilometres while witnessing an increasing amount of pollution. The heat of the day packed a punch by the time we regained the road at Lowana Station. Then a few kilometres ahead, beautiful Macquarie Harbour with the King River's mouth, a tragic example of man's lust and wilful disregard for our dear planet.

We can hardly say the folks back in 1900 didn't know any better. They knew precisely what they were doing, dumping toxic chemicals and waste down a pristine river. But, money ruled. Jobs were at stake. Jobs, jobs, jobs, so important everyone says. Some would argue, more important than Earth.

Politicians will debate and compromise, do anything to hold onto power while the future of our children and civilization crumbles, sunk by increasing waste and pollution. Now Jude and I are not superhuman, nor are we oracles, but from our travels, we feel Earth is heading deeper into trouble. And we think she's rebelling. Resources and space are getting tight. Wars and terrorism are on the rise and quite possibly will escalate to a scale that will put fear into every human heart - unless mankind finds another way to govern. It won't be easy; Put Earth First is what we say.

~ Chapter 14 ~

Assault on Mount Sorell

A WANDERING WAKE TOUCHES MANY SHORES, but rarely the same one twice. With so much beauty, adventure, and knowledge found in new destinations, why return without good reason? But, Jack and Jude have a peculiar quirk, and we love it, although it's both a blessing and a curse. You see this quirk drives us relentlessly, never letting up until we've achieved our objective. It's what got us up from the dinner table every night and sent us, not to the tellie, but outdoors whatever the weather, to bend cold steel and plane wood. That's how *Banyandah* got built, through sheer determination.

Last year in Macquarie Harbour, we met Trevor and Megs, owners of the charter yacht Stormbreaker. Trevor is a brilliant cartographer and loaned us three charts he'd drawn showing the harbour's many hideaways. They also noted numerous features in artistic ink. In nearly landlocked Farm Cove, where Sarah Island convicts had grown pumpkins and onions almost two centuries ago, his artwork shows a dashed line sweeping inland towards a series of concentric contours next to a note: Route to Mount Sorell – 15 hrs. Succinct, almost alluding to a stroll up the highest peak of Tasmania's south-western range that dominates every viewpoint along Macquarie's twenty-mile length.

The first time we passed through Hell's Gate, that infamous narrow entrance into Macquarie Harbour, a low afternoon sun was casting long shadows down from Mount Sorell's many peaks, turning its rocky ridges and verdant gullies into stripes like a Tasmanian Tiger crouching low on the surrounding buttongrass plains, as if freezing the last thylacine in time. Snow-capped in winter, swept by ferocious gales, from a distance, its lower slopes appeared as smooth as newly mown grass.

In Tasmania, buttongrass moors occupy more than one million hectares, approximately one-seventh of the island. It is low vegetation, dominated by sedges (grass-like plants) usually growing in poorly drained sites. It's the most common type of vegetation in the west and southwest of the State where annual rainfall exceeds 1000 mm. The common name, buttongrass, conjures up images of golf links made with tiny, round leaves matted together. But the name actually refers to its seed head, a dark chocolate bon-bon held teasingly aloft shoulder high on a slender shaft, gently bending, and so shiny it looks varnished. And instead of providing a smooth carpet to stroll, buttongrass grows in rounded clumps that over time become quite dense, forming tall stools that sometimes touch each other, but often do not. Elevated above the water table, at times they hide shallow-water channels.

Last year, Judith and I attempted to climb Mount Sorell. We left our vessel before dawn, landed at midsummer's first light, then forged through the razor grass guarding the moors. At first, we found the buttongrass merely a nuisance that required careful footing and lifting our boots knee high over, or onto, each tuft. We quickly discovered this soaked up our strength. Following Trevor's dashed line, and not realizing it was more an artist's indication than an actual route, we came to a bluff that exposed a deep chasm separating us from the main mountain slopes. Needing a warming cuppa to re-energise us, we then descended nearly five hundred feet into this dense verdant canyon, finding a wall of trees woven into a barricade by spaghetti vine so thick, the only way through was bodily throwing ourselves into it backwards. Our reward for conquering that, a mossy stream bubbling within a green maze, followed by a wall with vegetation so damn thick, on hands and knees we pulled ourselves through it, praying we'd not find one of Tasmania's deadly snakes coiled and ready to strike. That really sapped our strength, and so, on top of the next plateau, with the peaks still high above and the sun passed its zenith, we built a stone cairn to mark our achievement, then turned for home. Days later, Trevor revealed, that after three attempts, he'd not actually gained Sorell's summit, even though he once spent a night snowbound on its lower slopes.

Mount Sorell, at 1144 metres, is neither an Everest nor a Kilimanjaro. It's just a peak, several in fact of similar height. Its main difficulty is it has no points of access like its neighbours, and in general, remains relatively untouched compared to other West Coast mountains that have old mine workings and walking tracks. It was named for William Sorell, the third Lieutenant Governor of Tasmania, who in 1821 founded the Macquarie Harbour Penal Settlement on Sarah Island. At nearly 43° south, because of its dominance over Macquarie Harbour, it no doubt gave a sense of barrier to convicts with dreams of escape. Folklore claims leg irons and other items were found on its slopes by troops looking for escaped convicts. And Trevor had mentioned seeing a manmade rock wall somewhere on the flats connecting the ridges.

After completing our circumnavigation of Australia, when back in Ballina reviewing our Mount Sorell photos, the memories of those hardships had grown weak, and I felt a renewed longing to reach its peak. Viewed through the tinted lens of time, the other difficulties, those of reaching Tasmania through the Roaring Forties and Bass Strait, also seemed more rosy than dangerous. So I broached the possibility of going back to Judith.

"We might find Trevor's rock wall or maybe Matthew Brady's lost leg irons."

She's the original 'yes' girl and immediately began elaborating on the positives of my suggestion. And before either of us could draw another breath, we started planning the adventure.

This time we thought we'd establish a base camp on the plateau where we had turned back, thinking that one day of light would be plenty to hump tent and supplies to it. From there on the following day, we'd carry only daypacks when tackling the other half, reach the summit, and return to base. Spreading the attempt over three days would allow plenty of time to carry the extra kilos and time to search for historical remnants, or so we thought in the comfort of our lounge room.

From King Island, we sailed south directly for Hell's Gate, and once through those devilish narrows, our eyes were again drawn upon our goal, a beautiful but challenging vision. It came to pass that we then wandered around Macquarie Harbour, revisiting remembered sites, walking several tracks for fun and fitness, while waiting for a weather opportunity, which eventually arrived in the form of a very slow-moving, gigantic high-pressure cell.

As it approached, Trevor, who was just as keen for us to succeed, gave us a call. "Thought you'd be climbing Sorell," he said. "Been looking for you with my telescope."

"Tomorrow," I replied. "We'll make our assault on the peak Saturday." Then I chuckled. "Give you a call from the top."

Over the years, Judith and I have undertaken many treks, so we have our packing down to a science. She humps the kitchen and victuals; I carry the base camp, emergency gear, plus the video camera. We each bring our own down sleeping bag, change of clothes and extra warmth, and a pair of lightweight sandals to wear around camp. On this walk, we carried four – one-litre water containers divided between us. Our diet would consist of: Breakfast - cold cereal, with nuts, sultanas and dried apricots. Lunch - Cheese, tomato, (salami for me) on crackers. Dinner - A variety of packaged pasta meals. Snacks and treats - plenty of candy and muesli bars, soup and hot drinks; and of course, two litres of red wine to celebrate and dull the pain. All up, a load of about eighteen kilos for me, sixteen for Judith.

Just after arriving in Strahan on this visit, we met another lovely local couple, Max and Marie, who for many years have driven their forty-five-foot vessel around the harbour to "get away from it all." Max has ten years on me, and in his lifetime, he has walked nearly every square inch of the west coast. He's a true bushman who has been up Sorell several times, but oddly, he too has never actually reached the summit.

Our two boats left Strahan together, and then we shared several anchorages; the first in Kelly Basin where the failed North Mount Lyle Mining Company built a port amongst thick rainforest, only to be abandoned four years later. And while sharing a bit of boat hospitality, we talked with Max about that deadly difficult chasm, and he told us he always stayed low until under the first ridge, crossing the big creek on flat terrain. That made sense to us, and on our newly purchased topographical map, we planned a route accordingly. I made some marks then put those as waypoints into our handheld GPS.

Come the morning, it dawned crystal clear, just a bit of vapour rising off the upper slopes being burnt away by a bright lemon sun. The dinghy loaded, we locked up then set off for our departure beach a mile and half across Farm Cove. This time we searched the far eastern end of our landing beach, looking for an opening Max had mentioned. But, gosh, all that jungle seems similar. Plenty of vague paths were found, probably from wombats going through the scrub. But none went very far, and all ended in walls of thick scrub entwined with that dreadfully sharp razor grass. With heavy packs, we made the best choice we could, and this time found it easier to reach the buttongrass plains. In ten minutes, what had taken an hour last year, we were in the clear, and that seemed a good omen.

Then came the hard yakka. It seems everything worthwhile takes lots of hard work. Navigation was simple enough. We'd been here before and spied familiar sights. But, carrying that load hurt. I know Jude suffered greatly. But she stayed quiet and kept up. The main hardship was the uneven terrain and not knowing if your boot would find something solid or slip off a tuft and twist. So, every foot went down tentatively before shifting weight. By staying on the flatter ground, we also discovered that instead of one major creek, we had to cross several smaller ones, each overgrown with tea tree and bauera, which is nearly impenetrable scrub. Each stream took time. Firstly to find the narrowest passage, and then the effort of pushing a way through, wondering if snakes were lurking in the vegetation towering over our heads. After four hours of non-stop trucking, we came to that major creek, and I suggested lunch. We had not gained one inch of altitude, but we were now in line with the ridge going up to our proposed campsite.

Beginning the climb after eating, as is usual with full bellies after a stop, our packs seemed to have gained an extra ten kilos, and my legs started to complain with little cramps whenever I pushed extra hard. These, as the ascent became steeper, became a real problem.

It took an hour to win the first two hundred metres of altitude, grabbing at anything to pull ourselves up with each step. Then the second two hundred took half that again as I had to stop and massage my failing legs. We then traipsed across a flat neck to the last slope before our campsite. Seeing its increased steepness brought back the horror of our previous attempt when groping through shoulder height tea tree had torn our clothes and left red welts.

This time as I lead the way, I kept a watchful eye for white quartzite patches; slippery though they were, they gave respite from pushing through sharp tea tree, and relief for my legs.

At one point, I didn't think these old legs of mine would do it. With every step, they'd cramp, and I'd pummel each thigh with my fist, and then try to push up ever so gently. My main concern was a leg collapsing on a sharp rock when that heavy load might cause a fall and injury. As in many things we do, care is paramount. Strong minds had to stay focussed on the task. Until, by taking baby steps, we achieved a miracle. Breasting the last ridge, sweat wet and panting for breath, we had reached the campsite plateau and a most glorious view of gold glinting off the granite peaks signalled only an hour of daylight left.

Camp still had to be made and dinner cooked, but, first things first. I dumped the contents of my sack, found the cask of wine, and we toasted our huge success. That first slug flushed my cheeks and chilled my wet back, then my legs buckled and I slumped onto uneven ground. Jude, ever faithful, went to work massaging my paralysed limbs, and soon, through tears of pain, I once again straightened them. Putting an arm over her shoulder, she helped me hobble to some rocks where we sat and embraced while beholding a glorious sun setting over a picture-perfect harbour, and beyond to a thin finger of land and then to the Great Southern Ocean, a sheet of liquid gold floating away endlessly. The emptiness so vast, we dared not speak for some minutes. Our world perfectly at peace, a mountain songbird then graced our view of the harbour that had changed to one of a steel platter wrinkled by the *Lady Jane Franklin* leaving Sarah Island.

Even if we got no further, we had achieved a milestone important to us. To set targets, and then reach them reinforces confidence. More than that, it bonds a team together and glorifies the essence of life. Sorry to rave on, but Jude and I are getting on, so these small victories seem even more significant.

Of course, the reality was, I could hardly walk, and a flat place for the tent still had to be found, and Jude still had to whip up her culinary magic. So we kissed once, twice, and gave a laugh, then got on with our respective tasks.

After careful consideration, the place I chose for our tent needed some rearranging. Rocks littered the only bit of flattish ground, as did a couple of baby buttongrass tufts. But in half an hour, we had a home, and dinner was ready, which we ate ravenously under the increasing umbrella of starlight and the peaks of Sorell looking hauntingly down. Straight after cleaning up, we went to bed, only stopping long enough to clean our teeth. I slept like a dead man. No dreams, no thoughts, one moment I laid down, the next I perceived first light. Jude wasn't so fortunate. She had lumps under her, and while she normally curls around obstructions, in this case, she couldn't, and they aggravated her hip and groin, keeping her awake.

I arose to see a white soupy mist snaking about the dark forest along the Gordon River. Feeling the chill, I looked aloft. The five peaks of Mount Sorell, already sunlit, were inviting us to join them. But not just then, I could hardly walk.

From our rock kitchen, I could see *Banyandah* sitting quietly in her small bay, looking ultra-safe. So I hobbled about on rock hard muscles, knowing this was the day we had planned for and had sailed hundreds of miles to reach. The day we might achieve a dream.

Taking tea to Jude, I joined her in our little tent, drinking mine while she stretched and told me of her horror night. Not so pleasant as mine, but she was ready. In fact, more than willing. She was eager, determined, and looking forward to the great adventure of exploring one of Earth's rare locations.

I stretched, touched my toes, loosened hamstrings, but still painfully hobbled about taking longer to get ready than planned. A dawn start was what we had wanted. But, enjoying the moment so much, we didn't want to turn this adventure into just plain, hard work. Therefore, under increasingly warm sunlight, we sat warming our bones while marvelling at the majestic views.

Macquarie Harbour has several side pockets, all forested, and that morning each was filled with whipped cream mist. Gazing up at the peaks, we traced the route and let our minds wander, then finally got up to pack our daypacks. Medical kit inside mine, along with emergency beacon, GPS, warm clothes, map, and finally the video equipment slung over my shoulder. Jude carried the lunch, water, and her warm stuff. It was after nine when we set off up the first incline.

Straight above our camp, another bitch of a slope began. Loaded with plenty of buttongrass and short curly tea tree, it straightaway tested my legs and hampered our forward progress even though we carried light packs. Trevor had mentioned a 'road' traversing the white granite face we could see rising out the vegetation near the cleft between the first two peaks. During our previous visit, a waterfall had poured out that cleft. No water was visible this time, and that was worrisome because although we'd carried four litres up from the last stream, all had been finished at breakfast time.

That first slope drained an hour and a half of sweat out us, parched our lips, and dried our throats. We badly need a drink, so you can imagine our relief on hearing gurgling water as we approached the narrow cleft. Jude stayed back, perched on a rockslide, watching tiny mountain finches flit amongst the stunted trees while I slithered down through deeper vegetation until I stumbled upon a trickling stream. Straightaway I downed a full litre of cold sweet rainwater then filled all four to overflowing by topping them up using one of the caps. Climbing back, Jude sozzled a full litre non-stop then we packed a full one each, leaving the other two on a prominent rock, entering them as a waypoint on our GPS.

Gaining the ridgeline quite suddenly changed our expedition from total exertion to a relaxed wander through wonderland. Bleached, twisted tea tree remnants stood bent as graceful ballerinas, artistically bowed by westerly gales, white arms akimbo.

Passing behind the second peak, we crossed a mile wide saddle open in every direction. And each time I turned to check on Judith, a magnificent white quartzite dome that had been cleaved long ago by a glacier was seen in the distance. It was Frenchman's Cap, reminiscent of the Liberty caps worn during the French Revolution. Between it and us, the deep Clark River Valley fell away with Mount Darwin the highest point on its other boundary. Drier, it was crisscrossed with 4WD tracks from mining and made an interesting comparison to Sorell's unaltered wilderness.

By noon, we had fallen way behind schedule. The mountain peaks just kept appearing, and there were many stretches of white granite to negotiate where a slip or wrong footing could mean an emergency call for medics. That's against our creed of self-reliance. Meaning patience and watching every step was required. Maybe long ago I would curry up Judith, but now, we go safe. And if that means we go slow, well, I count my lucky stars to have a lady keen, willing, and able.

Trevor had been vague about which peak he had reached. Sorell has five in a row nearly the same height, but the last one north is taller by about five metres. That's the one with the tower and benchmark brought there aboard a Tasmanian Land Department's helicopter.

Cognisant that the sun's clock was ticking, after passing yet another gap between peaks, we were confronted by a sharp dip followed by a horrendous climb on tired legs to what I thought might only be Trevor's peak. If so, another drop and rise awaited us before our objective. It was nearly two hours after high noon, and that made it five hours on the trot, and hardly much more time than that till sundown, I began to fear we'd have to turn back after only reaching Trevor's peak. To have come so far, and fail…. Oh well. Probably best to just rearrange my thinking than spend a cold night on a Tasmanian mountain peak. Trudging ahead of my lady, I kept yodelling back that she'd best not stop for any more photos, when suddenly I came over a crest expecting a steep descent, and saw, not more than a few hundred metres ahead, a blanched white rocky peak, a few metres higher, and the vague silhouette of a steel tower showing through drifting mist.

"Hurry, c'mon, hurry," I hollered. "It's just ahead! We can make it!" And I sent an echoing yahoo skywards then rushed across the short rocky flat to scale the final summit. As soon as Jude poked above the

neighbouring peak, I started banging on the metal disc that was supposed to be on top of the tower, but which had been bowled over by some superstorm.

Of course, we did all the stuff we like to do, hugged, kissed and took photos in every imaginable pose, and then set up the video to act out explorers. Then the wonderful - I snapped one of us on our mobile phone and sent it to our kids with the text. "Hi from atop Mount Sorell."

Then out came Trevor's handheld VHF and we gave him a call. When he answered I couldn't help rubbing in salt, he's so good-natured. In reply, he swore he'd be following our foot tracks before the end of the year. And when I told him the Lands Department's beacon had been blown over, he replied, "Ah! So that's why we can't see it through my telescope anymore."

Our expedition established an important point. The professionals working on Macquarie Harbour rely on a VHF repeater located on the Cape Sorell lighthouse, and according to Trevor, it's nearly useless, hardly reaching halfway down the waterway. Mobil phone coverage is just as limited, so emergencies and even normal communications between Strahan and the many places in Macquarie Harbour are impossible without an expensive satellite phone. But, from a repeater on the summit of Mount Sorell, we proved all over coverage was possible.

A rusty biscuit tin was lodged at the base of the tower, and prising its corroded lid open revealed a plastic bag containing two sheets of paper, one discoloured by rust. Eight names in four parties in the eight years since 2003. Two had visited twice. One had returned with his son. The other noted, "First climbed in 1959." Proudly we added our names to the list.

Going home was simply more of the same. Beautiful. Inspiring. And we saw views missed when walking north. While the inland side plunges steeply into the Clerk River Valley, the ocean side races down spines of white granite, clad in buttongrass that spreads into brown plains fringed with forbidden forests.

Going downhill made quite a difference. Instead of searching the easiest route, I just let my weight push through the tangle of low branches, and as a result, we made super-fast time. In fact, we were back at base with still an hour of light, and guzzling the remaining red wine while watching the heavens turn to fire, our world becoming warm, fuzzy and happy.

After such an exhausting day, we slept late, and both of us awoke happy because I had smoothed out Judith's bed. Breaking camp, the beautiful expansive views of granite peaks around what appeared a steel coloured lake hampered our tasks until about ten when rucksacks were hoisted. The muscles complained, so we set off sedately down that murderous slope. Amazingly, it was easy with a bit of weight pushing us along. But we took care, especially after we'd both slipped onto our backside a few times.

Phase two began before we even hit the flats. Trevor had mentioned a manmade rock wall somewhere on the flats we descended, and both kept a lookout. Without tall trees, the view was unrestricted; anything upright and white wasn't hard to spot.

Made from flat rock neatly stacked like an English stone wall, it stood waist-high in a slight arc; whoever had constructed it, had not been a day-tripper. Far too much effort. First in locating the stone, and then meticulously stacking them interlocked. From behind it, Sarah Island was just visible, and convict history came into our thoughts. Intrigued, and hopeful of finding something long lost, we began searching the low scrub, hoping we'd kick up a rusty pair of leg irons or rotting shoe

leather. Our methodical search in ever-increasing circles lasted several tedious hours, turning over anything vaguely suspicious or unnatural.

Alas, finding something significant was not meant to be. But that didn't stop me from lying behind that wall and pretending to be escaped Gentleman Bushranger Brady planning my murderous attack on the penal colony.

On that rarely visited slope, who's to say Matthew Brady hadn't constructed this windbreak after escaping his duties in Farm Cove. Touching the stones one by one, I thought I heard hounds baying, and felt a chill of fear then sensed a defiant man persecuted until death seemed better than life imprisoned. Peering over the top stone, my breath rushed out upon seeing the island of ultra banishment and punishment, with *Banyandah*, my conduit to a rich, rewarding life in the foreground. Before tears could flow, Judith's warm breath was felt upon my ear, then her arms wrapped around me in a loving embrace.

~ Chapter 15 ~

One World to Another

HALFWAY ALONG TASMANIA'S WILD WEST COAST, the tidy town of Strahan lay on our doorstep, its single street reflecting the golden age of sailing ships loading copper ore at a rough timber jetty while giant Huon logs littered its black waters. *Banyandah* now lay upon those same waters, having come to witness the history of that long-ago era and to explore perhaps the last frontiers of wilderness. In the silence of dawn, all seems at peace - until looking skyward. Darkening wisps of mare's tails are being whisked off bare rock peaks, and at that moment we realise our true predicament.

Banyandah had journeyed halfway down the Australian Continent and across the notorious Bass Strait just so Judith and I could climb one peak. And now that we have conquered Mount Sorell, she is trapped on one of the world's most dangerous lee shores. To the west of those verdant green hills, the Great Southern Ocean is roaring with the unfettered might of ten thousand sea miles.

As summer turned to autumn, we had achieved much more than climb just one mountain. During our stay, several old-timers had greatly expanded our knowledge by telling us their experiences of timber getting, trailblazing and working the mines within this enclave of Nature. Also, we had walked forty kilometres along a historic railroad that once transported refined copper down from high mountains, along the infamous King River, a once pristine waterway now just a trickle due to acid mine tailings. Now our journey here has come to an end. A new destination beckons; South Australia, the driest state in the driest continent on Earth.

To take up this new challenge requires a 550 nautical mile sail northwest to South Australia's Kangaroo Island. That's a distance greater than Sydney to Brisbane, and it's not down a major highway, but across the open sea. Other small sailing vessels undertake such journeys in short hops, with the first, an overnight sail to King Island, then the second hop, overnight across Bass Strait to the mainland. After that, it can be managed in several day sails along the coast to our destination of American River on Kangaroo Island.

But Jude and I prefer to make these moves in one big jump. We like to reach open water, get our vessel set up, and then sail day and night around the clock. That leaves us ample free time to reflect and savour our last destination while pondering the next.

Aye, but doing this across the Roaring Forties requires particular care and good planning. Winds from southwest around to east would be the best. But those only occur when depressions pass under Tasmania, producing nasty storms, or when a high-pressure system passes north. A further complication, we had to time the outflow of the tide through the infamous Hell's Gate.

In the forty years since we began sailing, weather predicting has improved immensely. We can now access the Bureau of Meteorology's computer model over the internet. It provides wind vector predictions up to seven days ahead. That's what I was doing this morning in Strahan. Every day for more than two weeks, I have been checking the weather website and following the tides, searching for just the right conditions.

Never mind the wind clouds scudding overhead, they were only reminding us that here it can blow savagely anytime. This morning I was delighted to see the right combination of vectors appear on my screen. After the weekend, the wind will back from north through west to south and then continue around to the east over five or six days, sufficient for our journey to South Australia. We'll have light winds at first, and then these will strengthen as we close with our destination, theoretically providing the proverbial 'wet sail' taking us speedily to our destination. But studying the vectors also indicated we'd need an early start or be confronted with adverse winds before clearing Tasmania's north coast. So I informed Jude we'd be leaving early Monday morning.

It would have been grand if that day had brought a perfect dawn. But no such luck. Rain had fallen all Sunday night, and we got up under black clouds and cold drops of rain. Nevertheless, several friends came to see us off. First to arrive, Trevor's good lady Megs dashing between raindrops down the shiny wet wharf, her short fluffy hair framing her purposefully set red lips. And, as usual, her outfit perfectly colour-coordinated, jeans with a lime green blouse. Slinging her mauve knitted muff aside she knowingly ran a hand along our wet railing to displace the raindrops then slung her leg over before niftily ducking under our awning to escape the rain.

Jude was brewing a final round of coffee when Max and Marie sauntered down the jetty decked in rain slickers. Talkative as usual, well before reaching our boat, Max loudly wished us God's speed. Arm in arm with his lovely bride of more than fifty years, Marie beamed an impish smile that was further enhanced by sparks from her high voltage purple eyes. We all chatted and reminisced for more than a half-hour. Then hearing our ship's clock strike the hour, we shared

Jo and John from *SY Tiosjem*

one last cuddle. "Okay, let's go," I said reluctantly. "Sorry folks, it's time." And I started the engine. Its roar seeming to shake the quiet town.

"I'll shorten up the lines, Babe, while you take in the fenders," said I handing Megs' her bag over the railing.

"Bye, you two lovely people." Megs pouted playfully. "Be safe. And give us a call the moment you reach South Australia." Marie next to

Marie and Max ~ West Coasters

Megs, blew a kiss and Max grinning waved slowly. We were going to sadly miss these friends.

Untying our ship, Jude yelped. "Oh, my gosh! Going to miss you a lot. See ya." Then she took *Banyandah* off the jetty. And as she did, sunshine parted the dark clouds and bathed the town we'd come to love in brilliant sunshine.

Jude motored slowly past a collage of buildings while I stored mooring ropes and fenders in the cockpit locker.

"Hey, Jack," She nudged me.

Looking up, one building on the waterfront stood out from the rest. It was a ramshackle tin shed littered outside with stacks of dirty yellow logs and huge piles of bright yellow sawdust. Spread across its corrugated roof in huge black letters faded with age, 'Morrisons Sawmill,' the oldest working Huon pine sawmill in the world. And still family-owned after five generations. Snowy and Erin run it today, mostly to supply fine timbers to the craft industry, and to display the old ways for visiting tourists. Each afternoon when the *Eagle* catamaran returns from its Macquarie Harbour cruise, it lands its passengers alongside. That's when Snowy starts up the last working vertical saw in Tasmania and cuts timber to show them how his grandfather cut planks from Huon logs.

One World to Another

We were thrilled when from out the shadows of the open building came the four we had come to cherish, Snowy and Erin, and her sister June, and June's husband Gordon; those last two down from Queensland every summer to help with the mill. Standing in a pool of sunshine, they gave us a wave and cheery Bon Voyage. We'd been in their mill many times, talking timbers and the old ways, or just standing by the mill's wood fire on cold days. And they'd been over at our place for meals. Lovely times, listening to their stories, so we yahooed back at the top of our lungs and almost shed tears.

Once our friends merged into the background of buildings and forest, we turned forward to ponder our new adventure, and as we did, the last clouds evaporated from Mount Sorell's peaks. Magically bathed in glorious sunshine, each individual tree seemed to jump straight and tall out the mountains surrounding the harbour.

I won't pretend to know how Macquarie Harbour was formed. I can only say it's a unique place on Earth. Six times larger then Sydney Harbour, it takes *Banyandah* five hours to motor from one end to the other, and yet, no one lives along its shores. Two major rivers feed into it, and although their outpourings have been damned and diverted by white settlers, there are still hundreds of smaller creeks discharging huge volumes of mountain water. And like many waterways, it is tidal. But, Macquarie's rise and fall are hampered by an extremely narrow opening.

When first explored in 1815 by James Kelly, the man credited with its discovery, its opening was a maze of narrow channels coursing through sandbanks with a tiny rock island plumb in the middle. James Kelly and his group spent three days exploring its huge 285 square kilometres, and their descriptions of vast stands of trees had timber cutters entering the harbour within a year to cut down the magnificent

Huon pines. Nevertheless, early ships had little success navigating its torturous entrance, and many disasters occurred. So, between 1900 and 1902, the Macquarie Harbour Entrance Works constructed a training wall to form one deep channel between the rocky Entrance Island and the even more rocky southern shore. Since then, Nature has filled in the other channels leaving just the one narrow opening barely three houses wide. This is Hell's Gate. It's not named for the torrent that is always a threat, but by the convicts taken through its portal to a life in Hell on Sarah Island, the most feared penal colony in the world.

Once within the grip of Hell's Gate, we had no chance of turning back. Taken out by more current than our engine could challenge, it was then our journey began in earnest. The wind was not the favourable south of west we expected but from dead ahead. A bit peeved that our well-planned voyage was off to a poor start, we muttered oaths then tried sailing close to the wind. But our lady seemed destined to charge straight through the surf onto a nearby beach, making motoring the wisest choice.

Alongside us on the sailing ship *Tiosjem* were John and Jo, the couple first met in George Town. Leaving just after us, they were now bound for Geelong to complete their first voyage. So, in concert, we ploughed ahead into easy nor-westerly slop until darkness fell.

Saying Goodbye to *Hells Gate*

When an inky black sky was punctuated by a billion pricks of silver light, the light breeze shifted onshore, and Jude and I set full sail. Fortunately, *Tiosjem* continued motoring ahead on a different track, or we'd have fretted all night over the possibility of a collision. Great grandmother Jo had once asked if we still didn't get a wee bit apprehensive when going to sea and I honestly answered that we don't think that way anymore. *Banyandah* floats. She has in seas higher than many buildings. And she has for longer than many folks live. So, unless a disaster happens, which it might, she'll survive and so will we. With that fear removed, an ocean voyage is very special for many reasons. One is to experience the true wild side of Earth, where man's laws have little meaning.

The moment our engine's mechanical hammering ceased, Nature's sounds suddenly prevailed around us, and with them came the natural motion of Earth. Cool caresses ruffled our hair and lightly touched our cheeks, and the sea took us for a swaying, but soothing ride through the forever-ness of the heavens, and that filled us with great joy. Not for the first time have I watched our sails soar across the galaxies and wonder if other creatures felt this same great joy of life. Do sea eagles, when their wingtips lift on an updraft, smile inwardly with gratification? Does a gannet, its golden head gleaming as if dipped in saffron, feel joyful anticipation as it folds its bright white wings into a missile before piercing the sea to catch fish? And how does a grey kangaroo feel when lopping easily along in giant leaps across the red country with sweet spring growth filling its nostrils? At those magical times, do other creatures also enjoy life?

Our first night passed in tranquil ecstasy, first watching Sandy Cape's lighthouse blink ahead on a dark shore. And later, as it drew abeam and I had retired, Jude saw the full moon illuminate distant mountains.

"It was a spiritual vision, the moonbeam sparkling across the sea," she said next morning. And then narrated how she had weaved *Banyandah* through a fleet of fishing boats, revelling in the knowledge that she could go either right or left on a flat sea without laneways.

That morning, upon a perfect sapphire sea, the rising sun brightened *Banyandah's* taut white sails as she slipped smoothly northwards past the top end of the Tasmanian Island. By nine, all land had disappeared, replaced by a large flock of seabirds hunting nearby. Clouds then appeared where land had been, and the breeze eased to a quiet whisper, and yet we still managed an easy three knots towards our destination. When the moon rose that night, the breeze backed further to the south, forcing us to pole out the headsail at our midnight change of watch. And with the mainsail on our right, we waddled wing and wing downwind at little more than a fast walking pace.

Always the hunter-gatherer, each dawn after Jude slipped aft for her second sleep, I set out our trolling line then watched for the slightest twang. My eye often measuring its catenary to judge whether a small fish might be on. Twice I hauled in barracouta. Tasmanians call them Axe Handles; they're long, slender, silver fish with three dagger teeth. Stinky and slimy, and sometimes wormy, I set them free. But during sunset on day three, my line didn't rise gently from a Couta but snapped taut as a bowstring. Grasping hold, I felt the shaking head of a much bigger fish fighting for freedom, and from that moment, the battle was on. Hand over hand, I pulled as steadily as I could. No light tackle for us. This isn't a sport. It's food gathering. And if the fish is well hooked as this lovely ten-kilo Albacore Tuna was, well, it will soon be flopping madly about our cockpit. That's when I take a tight hold and pierce its brain with my knife, killing it instantly.

This time out of curiosity, I slit open its belly to see what it might have been eating and wasn't surprised to see something like a sardine slip out. And from the past, a distant memory stirred.

It felt just like yesterday. But the year was 1986 and the Four J's; Jack, Judith, Jason and Jerome, were on their run back to Australia after encircling Earth. We were five hundred miles out from the Galapagos Islands on a four-week voyage to Rapa Nui, what westerners call Easter Island. The seas were kind, the sky clear, and the wind fair when just before lunch our trolling line gave a twang and Jerome, the first to run aft, hauled in a ten kilogram Dorado with not as much fight as we would have expected from a fellow of this size. Why? Well, we found out moments later.

After the usual buzz of excitement while our fourteen-year-old dragged the beast alongside then pulled it out the sea in one powerful motion, in fact, not until it lay quite dead in the scuppers did I ask if he'd like to see what the beast had been eating. At times inspecting a fish's tummy can be quite an education. Inside the free-roaming fish like this

Dorado, we often would see a few remaining bones from digested fish, or maybe the remains of squid. I remember once seeing a seething mass of tiny shrimp in a tuna's stomach. As it turned out, this investigation proved an even bigger eye-opener.

"I wouldn't expect too much," Jerome said to me, our prize now on the aft locker with the blue of mid-ocean sliding past our work area.

Taking the sharp filleting knife from its sheath and handing it to my son, I replied. "Yeah, the poor baby looks like she hasn't eaten in a week."

"That's why she hit our lure." Jerome's cute boyish grin spread across his freckled face. "She was desperate!"

Dorado, Mahi Mahi, Dolphinfish; call it what you like, it's all the same handsome fish of great power. Rather thin and vertically flat, they are pelagic fish that individually and in packs roam the ocean as well as the seas around coral reefs. The bulls have a distinctive squarish forehead, while the females are a rounded shape. Both have tiny button eyes and a small mouth opening straight back for only a short distance that adds to the Dorado's mean puggish look. Inside their mouths, top and bottom are a row of small, very sharp teeth. The upper row is attached to a hard flat plate.

It's this plate that frustrates fisherman because often when the beast strikes the lure, the hook will jab that plate. Sometimes it will hold, sometimes it won't. We've lost more than a few, even had them up on deck when the hook let go. And that's meant one powerful fish thrashing about, smacking cabin and deck or anyone who tries to contain it. Usually, those ones win their freedom.

In addition to their fighting power and fantastic leaps, their appearance is made spectacular by a fin running full length down their back that erects like a sail. Often this sail matches the mood of the sea; a vibrant blue-green in the early morn and late afternoon; a lighter, sky blue around midday. Down from this fin, the Dorado slowly becomes a sea-green very alive with tiny dots of brilliant blue. About halfway down, splashes of gold highlight their pectoral fins and gill covers.

Watching this creature die demonstrated another astonishing fact. They change colours. From deep electric blue through almost all the blue-green combinations to a creamy yellow that eventually turns silver upon death.

Okay, Jerome has the knife, it's going in, and the flesh is being parted exposing the lighter pink colour of her intestinal cavity with her internal organs, long and bunched together, bound by a thin see-through membrane. There is no blood, no unsightly mess. It's all orderly, there's no overpowering smell. This is an intricate creature, a wonder to investigate.

"Dad, what are those dots of blue on the inside of her belly?" Jerome asked while he poked the knife at one of the many small blisters of swirly blue-green just under the fish's first layer of skin.

"I don't know son. Maybe sacks of concentrated colouration used to alter the fish's appearance." Then thinking of another sea creature that can change colour, I said, "You know, like those sacks of black we see in squid and octopus."

"Sure, I know the ones. Hey, remember when that squid flew out the water and hit Knobu?"

My son laughed and so did I remembering Knobu, the Japanese radio operator on the first Mellish Expedition. One fine morning he had been quietly taking the mid-ocean air, when out the blue, a squid flew over our railing. They do that sometimes in a panic to escape a moving boat. Next, Knobu is getting up with a big black splotch all over his immaculate white shirt. We all had a good laugh over that.

Still chuckling I said, "You know, your mom never got that stain completely out. But that's okay. Knobu took it home as a pop-art souvenir of his ocean crossing. But hey, why don't you give one of those blisters a poke and let's see what comes out."

Jerome, an eager investigator, never needed prompting twice, so before I could blink, he had stabbed several blisters and squeezed out a creamy swirl of intense green-blue.

"Wow, it's like glue," he exclaimed as he squished it between his fingers.

I dabbed my finger against his.

"Doesn't look like a worm, more like storage for the Dorado's blue colour. What do you think?"

"I don't know, but it sure stinks. Should I cut the belly open now?"

"Yeah, I'm also curious to see what culinary delights our lady's been eating."

Jerome pushed the bound bunch of organs free from the cavity then slid his hand up and around them, pushing aside the intestines then he grasped her stomach.

"Gosh, there's something pretty big in here."

I lent over and had a feel. It was slimy as fish innards are, but sliding my hand up and around the stomach, I felt something like a whole fish. Hmm, now my curiosity went into overdrive.

"Get on with it son, let's see what's she been up to."

Jerome used the knife to sever the stomach from the animal's throat, then exclaimed, "Hey, dad! That's a fish's tail."

Suddenly, I was not the only excited guy on *Banyandah's* aft deck. For sure, severing the fish's belly, a tail emerged. And sliding the elastic skin down, Jerome removed a whole fish about a foot long! It was intact - Yep, all there except for a gash in its stern area where Mrs Brute must have first chomped the little guy before swallowing it whole.

The poor little tyke, the stomach juices had already started their work, and he'd lost some of his colour. But even so, I knew it well, because it was a smaller version of the big lady Jerome had on the chopping board. Crikey! Might well have been one of her own.

Jerome was confused. As he pulled the little fellow out of the bigger fish's digestive machine, he cried, "She's got babies!"

Then he paused while confusion played havoc with his face.

"They don't give live birth, do they, dad?"

"Nope, they sure don't. She's eaten one of her own kind." And saying that, all the ill feelings I may have felt over killing such a beautiful creature left me. And I could only nod in agreement when Jerome said with some malice, "Cannibal fish!"

On our fourth morning, the forecast stronger winds started to roost, so I went to work rigging the hammock I'd purchased months earlier. While Jude can sleep standing on her head, I have trouble disengaging my mind when the boat is working hard, moving about, and making so many sounds. Normally on long passages, by about day three I'm so buggered I sleep through the night. But if it's been calm and then gets rough, the best I can hope for is a quiet rest.

So far, we'd had a good run across the much-feared Bass Strait, easy really. Crossed paths with a few ships on their rhumb lines to Wilson's

Promontory and then had a vacant ocean again. Later on that fourth night, mainland lights became visible, reassuring us that the outside world hadn't blown itself to smithereens while we'd been crossing from one world to another. A rainsquall the following sunrise increased the wind off our starboard quarter to more than we desired. And after reaching hull speed, it only made us rock and cavort down the waves, spoiling our peace, and making our jobs all the harder. But sailors take what comes. We enjoy the good times and make the not so nice a challenge.

Gosh, my antics trying to stop that hammock from swinging madly would have made you laugh. There I was, buggered, praying for sleep, and rocking wildly, while the devil burned his fiddle. I rigged shock cords with much exertion to slow its swing, but that only resulted in being jerked about. So, I carefully manoeuvred out of the hammock, praying not to be flipped, and tried lying against the hull. But our violent motion crushed my head into the pillow then levitated me into space, so I climbed back into the hammock. There I grumbled and cursed, while I heard the ship's clock strike every half hour of that dark, windy night. And all the time I hear Jude's hum and occasional giggle as *Banyandah* surfs the swell. Easing the pain, that day we doubled our speed, logging a very respectable 141 nautical miles in 24 hours.

With the first hint of dawn, I'm out of the hammock quite unsteady on my feet, and with the violent motion, slipped across the wet floor. Clinging desperately to the chart table, I struggled into wet sailing gear with icy downdrafts making me shiver. And in a comic act, in poor light, arms akimbo, I was first flung onto my back by one wave, then with the next, skidded headlong into a bulkhead. Immediately outside, spray wet my face, snatching the last warmth from my overly tired body. Suddenly wide-awake, I looked around alarmed that our ocean of deep blue had run away, replaced by one whipped white. With *Banyandah* carrying far too much sail, there's no time for coffee, and straightaway we went to work reefing the main, which requires me going forward.

I've done that a million times, and in far worse conditions, but leaving the relative safety of our cockpit is not a step taken lightly. One slip, an overbalance, could have me lost in those ocean waves with my ship speeding away. Imagine the panic Jude would feel trying to get rid of all sail before powering back across a white ocean. And if she managed to do that, then searching for something the size of a melon in its vastness. So, when stepping out the cockpit onto a heaving deck, if those images pop into my head, I block them out. Otherwise, fear will appear. And fear freezes the mind. It's a killer. Instead, I become single-minded, focused on my task with feet like a cat and hands like talons.

After several wettings while reducing our overly large main, we cranked in some headsail, shortening it to nearly its smallest. Then because the wind had shifted in the night, we switched both sails to their opposite sides, which required dropping one pole and rigging the other before pulling the headsail across to it. All rather hard work, especially now that we are seniors. *Banyandah* didn't exactly become a tame pony after controlling our bucking bronco. Instead, she became a wild stallion racing across the waves with us holding on tightly.

Wet from my work, my darling Jude briskly towelled me down while I dreamt of a strong brew of coffee. But before that, I had to dash aft and reset the windvane steering device. Then, just as I was ducking below, at last, Jude's squeal of anguish spun me around. Out the corner of my eye, I saw a vision of red flying away, like a sheet of newspaper flying away on a gust of wind. Realising what had happened hit fast.

"Oh! Shit! We've just lost the vane blade," was shouted in unison. And in that same instant, Jude lunged for the wheel as an out of control *Banyandah* slew round into breaking waves.

"What the?" I stammered, staring behind at the red dot quickly disappearing in an ocean of white. We'd had that vane blade since the earliest days. It still had our Four J's logo painted on it in blue. Emotionally stirred, tears welled, and we could have cried. The places it had taken us, the storms it had withstood. It had been a silent crewmember working day and night. From the wheel, Jude voiced her disappointment. "That was the last link with the kids." Then she muttered without conviction, "We should go back."

But the seas were running far too high to think of doing that, so I fished out the spare blade from the lazarette. Clamping it into position and standing back, its plain ply face brought home the fact that we'd just lost a long time friend.

From the vastness of the open ocean, distant land was coming into focus. Checking our GPS showed us approaching the narrow passage named by the intrepid explorer Matthew Flinders over 200 years earlier.

On the 27th of March 1802, he sailed between what is today the Yorke Peninsula and Kangaroo Island after having explored a long strait he'd named to honour his ship. Upon reaching the open sea again, he wrote.

> This part of Investigator's Strait is not more, in the narrowest part, than seven miles across. It forms a private entrance, as it were, to the two gulfs; and I named it Backstairs Passage.

And when abeam of our present position Matthew Flinders had noted.

> A white rock was reported from aloft to be seen ahead. It proved to be a ship standing towards us; and we cleared for action, in case of being attacked. The stranger was a heavy-looking ship, without any top-gallant masts up; and our colours being hoisted, she showed a French ensign, and afterwards an English Jack forward as we did a white flag. At half-past five, the land being then five miles distant to the north-eastward, I hove to; and learned, as the stranger passed to leeward with a free wind, that it was the French national ship Le Géographe under the command of Captain Nicolas Baudin.

At that time, the French were snooping around on a supposed scientific expedition, which the English feared was a guise to claim land for France. Baudin had passed south under Kangaroo Island, naming many headlands. That's why today we have Cape Bedout, Cape de Couedic, and Cape Gantheaume along Kangaroo's south coast. At the same time, Flinders had sailed along its north coast, naming Castle Hill, Marsden Point, and Antechamber Bay.

If you love history as we do, a book well worth reading is, "My Love Must Wait," by Ernestine Hill. It's the adventurous, rather tragic life story of Matthew Flinders.

Like the *Investigator*, *Banyandah* cleared for action, but not from fear of French attack, rather in respect for the steepest seas encountered on our journey. Jason and Amanda on the English catamaran *Pegasus*, who we met along the New South Wales coast, had written that off Cape Jaffa, our present position, they were forced to put the fourth reef in their mainsail for only the second time in their journey around the world. Obviously, this was a windy place.

When properly rigged, *Banyandah* loves heavy seas and strong winds. Her long keel and full forefoot keep her tracking straight on any wavefront. And though her rigging may hum, and spray wets her decks, she roars ahead.

Ahead, a bland, featureless, brown mass devoid of forests looms. A far greater contrast to the Tasmanian Island we could not imagine. Also ahead, amongst whitewater, three small rocky islands popped up equidistant to both shores. Flinders had named them The Pages. Then surprising us, a huge container ship suddenly appeared from astern and raced us for the gap. Jumping between lookout and nav station, quickly on our left, the Point Willoughby white light structure appeared brightly against beige limestone cliffs. And soon after, we were zooming past Antechamber Bay lying behind that cape. With great relief, that put us in calmer water, the fierce wind now rushing off the summer brown grass of Kangaroo Island.

This is always one of the best treats. Winds off the land carrying new aromas to enhance what our eyes perceive, and where details are limited, our imaginations fill in. Soon the buildings and small harbour of Penneshaw came into view, but it wasn't until they had passed that we saw the mainland ferry approaching. All too quickly, our journey reached its climax. Rounding Kangaroo Head, also named by Captain Flinders, we entered Eastern Cove with our sails still blessed with the wind now flowing across the barren island.

Kangaroo Island is Australia's third-largest island after Tasmania and Melville. It is located 112 kilometres (70 mi) southwest of Adelaide at the entrance of Gulf St Vincent. At its closest point to the mainland, it is 13 kilometres (8 mi) offshore from Cape Jervis, which is the southern tip of the Fleurieu Peninsula. The island is 150 km (93 mi) long and 57 km (35 mi) at its widest point with a coastline stretching more than 500 km around an island of rolling hills, the highest 307 m (1010 ft).

Our destination of American River could be seen across Eastern Cove during the hour we sailed across its calm water, and we noticed a beehive of boating activity near the river's entrance. And that seemed strange until we realised we'd made landfall on Easter Saturday. There was quite a throng from Adelaide holidaying on the island.

American River, with 120 permanent residents, was first settled by a group of American sealers, who had camped there in 1803, the year after Flinders charted the area. They had arrived on the brig *Union* and built a schooner from local timber that they named *Independence*. We had read this on our passage; so when seeing only dry twisted scrub, Jude and I reckoned they must have harvested every last tree.

Where Wild Winds Blow

After five days of only the ocean surrounded by unrestricted vistas and just our own company, in a matter of minutes, we were dodging speeding tinnies filled with landlubbers enjoying their brief respite. Handing the sails at the first pile marking the channel, we stopped long enough to watch with smiles on our faces the flood of humanity enjoying their few moments in Nature. Yes, we are blessed. We have a craft that can take us to the far ends of Earth, where we can live amongst Earth's many other creatures. Aye, but it can also be uncomfortable, tiring, arduous, even quite scary at times. For us, the rewards far outweigh the discomforts that we know will be soon forgotten, while the memories of our time in the wild remains cherished forever.

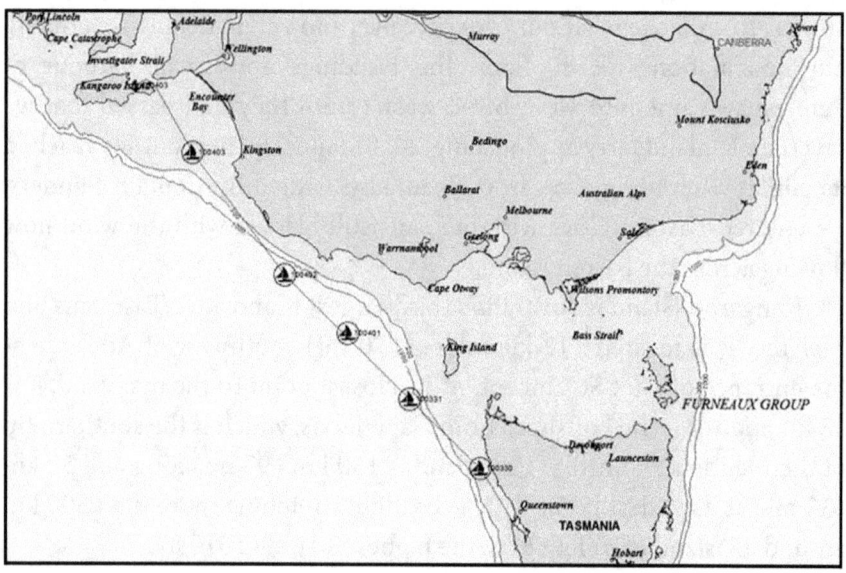

~ Chapter 16 ~

Tears in Paradise

FROM KANGAROO ISLAND, WE SAILED DIRECTLY to Adelaide to celebrate Jude's 65th birthday in style. And straightaway we were lucky in meeting the good folk at the Garden Island Yacht Club, who took us under their care, offering us a very secure berth not far from Adelaide's largest gas-fired power station.

Following Jude's birthday in quick succession, *Banyandah* sailed for Port Lincoln in the Spencer Gulf, a voyage of a hundred miles, where Timmy and Anna, two unique young people we met when circumnavigating Australia, joined *Banyandah* for a leisurely sail around the fabulous Sir Joseph Banks Group of islands. We had a fun few weeks observing the diverse flora and fauna in that island nature reserve then sailed back to the GIYC in Adelaide, packed up *Banyandah*, and flew home to our family for a winter of catching up.

Flip-flop; in the course of one plane ride, we had changed hats once again and became Nanni and Poppi to our small army of exuberant little folk. But once order had been restored and things settled down in our house overlooking the Richmond River, Jude and I started wondering what to do next. We'd achieve our original goals of witnessing Wybalenna and conquering the mountain, and now thoughts of what next kept entering our heads.

Our first book, Two's a Crew, covering *Banyandah's* circumnavigation of Australia, had not attracted an agent nor a publisher in the depressing climate found in book publishing today. Being first-time authors in a narrow genre had lessened our chances, as had the global financial crisis. But we have faced much bigger hurdles than this and took a step back from our disappointment. The book, we felt, had inspirational merit important to today's world. So we decided to dip into our limited savings and publish it ourselves. Ay-yi-yi! That opened a big can of worms.

Sitting here now, we can say that it also opened the door into a whole new kingdom. One filled with new challenges to be sure, but one also containing immense satisfaction after we had finally taken the challenge through to fruition.

Most writers understand that writing a book is comparable to producing a saleable product and marketing it. Straightaway, so many things had to be learnt. Starting with the basics, like what size book to create. To make that decision, costs had to be obtained, and layout and print fonts had to be selected. And because ours is a true-life adventure, there was the question of inserting colour photos versus the additional cost.

Creating Two's a Crew took up our winter in 2010. By the time we returned to *Banyandah* in November that year, we had produced and distributed several copies, which recouped some costs. However, the massive number of hours required, we donated gratis.

Marketing our new child proved the biggest headache. Normally this task is handled by the publisher through their well-oiled channels, but as new publishers, we had few contacts and knew very little. We had a product, and our next goal in life became finding ways to reach our audience. It was during a brainstorming session after watching a news clip of Jessica Watson at one of her book-signing events that we hit upon the idea of organising free showings of the film we produced of the voyage, at which we'd offer our book for sale.

While all that was underway, we were in communications with a much-loved cousin and her daughter. They had recently moved from Paris to the faraway island of Madagascar, after accepting a teaching position there. Enclosed with her first letter was a photo of a large villa surrounded by lush tropical vegetation and an invitation to come to stay with her.

Madagascar! What an evocative name.

Tears in Paradise

Suddenly, added to the burden of marketing our first book was the additional idea of sailing to a far distant land. Our minds were whirlpools. Oceanic winds and currents, routes, timing and even security in that underdeveloped country were tumbling round and round in my poor head. Talk about long days and restless nights!

Many years earlier, we had been to Madagascar, sailing there with our sons when we were called the Four J's. And it was the site of our most frightening mishap ever. And so, maybe you can imagine my tossing and turning in bed, this volatile mix rumbling inside my head when suddenly I jumped up wanting to reread a piece I wrote directly after that terrifying event.

In my dressing gown, I searched our bookcase lined with journals dating back to 1973, until I found the one with Madagascar written in large print across its cover. Jude, bless her, can sleep through a bomb blast, so my clumsy efforts at maintaining silence didn't wake her as I settled at my writing desk. Written in 1984, this story perfectly illustrates our lives when sailing around the world with our children.

Tears in Paradise is what I called the story back then, but I renamed the episode, giving it a more intriguing title when I wrote the book covering our voyage around the world. By reading this book, *Around the World in Ever Increasing Circles*, you will gain an understanding of where we came from.

The following is an excerpt from the chapter, The Dead Don't Cry.

Where Wild Winds Blow

From diary notes at Madagascar and letters written at the Dar es Salaam Yacht Club Completed Ventotene Island, Italy

The Dead Don't Cry
High Noon Port Louis

The closest planet to the sun could not be hotter than Jude standing in that airless room, staring at a bead of sweat sliding round and round a tight black curl, following it until a droplet formed. Falling onto a black neck, it joined others further staining the man's white collar.

A new droplet starting its journey sent Jude's fingers up through her own blonde strands and finding them wet, she mechanically lifted them from her neck, releasing a trickle of sweat, and that started alarm bells ringing.

Finding it difficult to focus, she followed its run down her arm until discovering wetness darkening the envelope containing her children's schoolwork released a sigh, followed by a deep groan. Shaking her head, she wondered whether stamps would stick to such a soggy envelope.

"Avez-vous parlé?"

The odd sound vaguely penetrates Jude's haze and looking up as if touched by a zephyr whispering across a flat ocean, two piercing mocha brown eyes demand her attention. Her brain still drowning in cement, instead of responding, she knits her brows.

"I asked if you spoke," said the gentleman who had turned in the queue. His clipped cultured voice had produced an exotic sound, and curiosity went to work like dynamite, and she explodes. "Where do you come from?"

From out a pink cavern rimmed in snow white, the young man laughed, maybe a bit too loudly. Recovering his composure, he announces, "I am Malagasy. From the island of Madagascar. Have you been there?"

Madagascar! Jude loved the sound and tried to roll it off her tongue as easily as the stranger, and repeated, "Madagascar." The sound igniting visions of green mountains and primitive people.

Her first try half-whispered, she said louder, "Madagascar." This time the sound flowed with the rolling of lips and darting tongue.

A puzzled, slow shake of her head at last brought the man his answer. "Err, no, I've never been there." And her smile extended the full width of her face. "But I live on a boat and could go there."

Somewhat unbalanced by her response, the black man steadied his weight as his eyes re-appraised the lady in a sarong that clung to her curves. Vainly he tried to visualise what she had meant, but not getting any images, he asked for a clue. "Boat?" he prompted.

"It's a yacht, actually. I'm with my husband and two children on a ketch lying in the main port."

Grappling with the aberrant image, he asked again, "Children? On a boat?"

"Yes, my sons; one's twelve, the other's thirteen. We're leaving Mauritius in a few days, sailing for Mombasa. What about you?"

Her question echoed around the cramped Port Louis Post Office, causing a few heads to turn while the black stranger continued to have difficulty conjuring up a vision of a family afloat. Silent moments passed until no longer able to resist the excitement beaming out the woman's eyes, he began.

"Please, you must pardon me. My name is Felicieu. Normally I am a student in Paris, but tomorrow I fly to Diego Suarez to visit my mother."

More exotic sounds from the young man's lips tightened her belly with anticipation. Never having met anyone from Madagascar inflamed her thirst to know more, and wanting her children and husband to meet this man, she blurted out, "Would you like to see my boat?"

Seven hundred nautical miles separates Madagascar from the island of Mauritius, which was uninhabited when first discovered by Arab traders in 975 AD. It was also home for thousands of fat birds which could not fly and tortoises which could not run. Mauritius remained little changed until 1638 when the Netherlands East India Company set up a settlement of twenty-five colonists who exploited the island's ebony and ambergris. In the following few years, a hundred slaves were imported from Madagascar and convicts were sent from Batavia. From

North Sea ports came free colonists, hardened men, settlers of desperation rather than brave idealists. Lawless years passed until one bright day in September 1715, Guillaume d'Arsel raised the French flag on a bluff overlooking what is today Port Louis, taking possession of Mauritius for King Louis XV, and naming the island, Ile-de-France.

Much has changed since that day, and upon leaving the Port Louis Post Office, Judith and the tall Malagasy were engulfed by a sea of people, a virtual tidal wave of humanity; some black, chestnut, others dusky or pale, in a mix of turbans, sackcloth, and straw hats. A third is Creole, mixed blood, mostly poorly attired.

The two had rushed around a corner and escaped through an archway, the only opening in a wrought-iron fence topped by sharp spears meant to keep the riff-raff out of the port area which now lay before them in something like a giant boot. Down the ankle led to open sea, and on both sides, cranes squealed, and ships groaned shifting bags of sugar into their bellies. On their right, along the foot stood a continuous line of corrugated iron sheds bearing cast metal nameplates attached to flaking paint. Alongside the dock in front of these were several small cargo ships from various nations, and perhaps a dozen dhows of weathered timbers, a few ornately painted in gay colours.

This harbour had given safe haven to Abel Tasman and James Cook, and here Matthew Flinders met a terrible fate. The port has also seen a steady stream of black misery. Where broken-hearted men, taught by voodoo that demons lay across the sea, had been shipped to hell around the world in slave irons.

Ahead on the quay, next to two brown masts, a crowd of dusky dockworkers burst out laughing as they jostled each other for a better view of the craft alongside.

"Come," Jude commanded, taking Felicieu's hand before pushing into the crowd, letting her white face be her passport. From the quayside, a tidy forty footer lay upon quiet turquoise water, her cream decks smooth and unbroken except for two small hatches and a central wheelhouse. On one side lay a blood-red gumdrop shaped dinghy, and upon the other, two bronzed demons raced for a rope dangling from the masthead. The taller, a little faster, leapt and claimed possession. But the other tackled him, and both went flying as if two pearls on a string out over rippled water. At the pinnacle of their arc, they dropped in unison, creating a beautiful white splash which brought a delighted roar from the crowd.

"My kids," admitted Jude, feeling an odd mixture of pride and embarrassment as she tugged her visitor towards the wharf's metal ladder.

After reaching the deck, she shouted, "Jason! Jerome! Dry off and meet Felicieu." Then stomping her foot twice, she called, "Hey, Jack! Meet someone from Madagascar!"

A few seconds later, leading him through the narrow companionway, a curious wonder spread over Felicieu.

"Magnifique!" he exclaimed. "I'm surprised. Like a house, only everything is smaller. I think it's lovely."

Behind him, the doorway filled with a dripping wet Jason sporting a mischievous smile.

"Yeah, but it's not the same." Reaching down, Jason said, "I'll bet you've seen nothing like this." And he gave the two-burner stove a push which set it swinging. Before Jas could answer Felicieu's questioning look, Jude explained, "That's so I can cook at sea. When the boat tilts, the stove remains level. Otherwise, we'd have lopsided bread."

A mop of snow-white hair scrambled past Jason and alongside the tall stranger. Looking up, taking his hand, Jerome asked in an eager voice, "Would you like to see where I sleep?"

"Where WE sleep." Jason pushed forward to chide his younger brother.

Felicieu chuckled warmly at the pair. "I shared a room with my two older brothers, and sometimes, I didn't like it either." His wistful voice hinted at lost pillow fights. "But please, let me see your bedroom."

Leading him forward, Jerome corrected him. "It's not a bedroom. On boats, they're called cabins."

Slamming lockers open, two young teenagers captivated their tall, aristocratic visitor with knick-knacks collected from around the world; intricate seashells, a Buddha carved from ivory, stamps, coins, postcards. When they ran out of goodies, Jude opened a seat locker and extracted several soft-covered books, and handed them to Felicieu. "These are books I use to teach *Banyandah School*. Each contains twelve lessons," she explained. "We mail the tests back to Australia for marking."

An educated man from a remote island, Felicieu appreciated the importance of comprehensive schooling. While leafing through the material, he explained that many on Madagascar wanted to learn, but there were too few teachers and little resources. Glancing up, admiration had softened his aloof nature when he announced that this meeting had inspired him to investigate introducing a similar system to his island.

Jude's small-town upbringing made her appear disarmingly charming when she asked Felicieu, "Tell us more about your island."

Rubbing his chin in thought, the expectant eagerness filling the boys' eyes touched him.

"The Malagasy people are a mixture of Africans and Asians who started arriving two thousand years ago," he began. "The first were Malay-Polynesian migrants who crossed the Indian Ocean in open boats from South East Asia. Later, Arab, Indian, and Portuguese traders arrived, and they brought slaves from eastern Africa. With them came European pirates and French colonists who mixed with the population to create the eighteen official tribes that inhabit Madagascar today."

Playful eyes engaged the boys when Felicieu whispered, "Do you know that not long ago, from bases along Madagascar's coast, over one-thousand pirates plundered ships rounding the Cape of Good Hope?"

Jerome rushed away to fetch the atlas and tossed it open on the saloon's small table. Both boys turned pages until a map appeared showing Madagascar long and thin next to the vast African continent. Felicieu pointed near the top.

"My family lives here in Diego Suarez. With a population of forty thousand, it is the north's administrative centre."

A thoughtful smile formed on his lips while he paused as if deciding whether to continue. Then he announced, "My mother is the elected government representative." His smile straightened. "But she's a member of the opposition party. And that's a big problem with today's Marxist government."

On the map, Jude put her finger on Diego Suarez, sitting as if by fate, very close to our route to Africa. After mentioning this to Felicieu, his reply gave life to a vague notion she'd carried since first meeting the dark stranger.

"I fly to Madagascar tomorrow. Why don't you stop there on your way to Kenya? You would be my guests."

Saying this, he put a hand on my arm, "I could show you some fascinating sights." He continued whetting our excitement by describing a Land Rover trek over mountains to isolated villages, and into national parks, home to lemurs and exotic birds.

His eyes flashed more brightly. *"Four J's*! Come and visit! My relatives would welcome you with a grand feast."

Was it fate meeting Felicieu? Should we stop at Madagascar under military rule; its borders closed as they had been for years. Mentioning this to Felicieu, he replied his family was influential and could help gain legal entry.

A great adventure beckoned, but should we chance it? Tapping my wife's finger, she turned with fire in her eyes. So I nodded, "Yes. We'll stop there if we can."

Available at
https://jackandjude.com/books/

~ Chapter 17 ~

Hard at Work in Adelaide

IT'S THE SPRING OF 2010, and after a mild winter at home, we have dragged ourselves away from our lovely flock of grandchildren and quiet river views to return to a boat filled with clutter needing attention. Every sail, rope, and piece of hardware we'd packed away six months ago has had to be hoisted from below and re-fitted. At the same time, all the paraphernalia brought from home has to find a storage spot. This kept us busy the first week, and then *Banyandah* was hauled out the water for a scrub and recoat! And on our minds, while we worked, was the idea imagined in Ballina that struck gold when the Royal South Australian Yacht Squadron enthusiastically accepted our offer to show our DVD at a book signing evening.

Adelaide is the driest capital in the driest country on Earth, and to welcome us back the temperature soared from low teens overnight into the forties next day. A jumper one day, scorched lips the next. But we kept working. We had to. The cradle was booked for another craft, so our time on dry land was

limited.

Just a few more days and our two-week working bee will be finished, and *Banyandah* re-floated. We're looking forward to life on the level again. In the cradle our lady slopes downhill. Everything's inclined towards the front, and every night Jude rolls on top of me!

On Friday, we'll have our first film night and book launch at the Royal South Australian Yacht Squadron. Should be great fun. I've been busy polishing the films, trying to squeeze a two-year adventure into eighty minutes. The audience should get their money's worth because admission is free! But we also think they'll be buggered by evening's end having sailed 9000 miles around Australia in one evening. Our fingers are crossed, hoping the book launch goes well because we've received our second shipment of books. The first lot sold out.

It's true isn't it that the busiest times are the least remembered. That sums up the following week. All we remember of our book launch is a room packed with friendly people and a better than expected oration by yours truly who actually choked up spilling a few tears when I spoke of my brave and beautiful wife. When question time came, to get it rolling, I mentioned a few facts about *Banyandah*. How she holds 700 litres of fresh water and 400 of fuel. And then a hand went up.

"Why did you build in ferrocement?" The Vice Commodore asked.

My mind shot back to Sydney, we were just kids about to have our first child, we'd been at the end of the road on Mount Kosciusko when Judith told me the news she was pregnant.

"We didn't actually set out to build a boat," I told the group and watched several turn to their neighbour and comment. "Back in 1970, Jude and I were young and travelling the world when she became pregnant with our first child, and I told her we wouldn't let the child change our life. She was as much a nomad as I."

That brought smiles and snickers from everyone, and I blushed and took a step backwards, almost shedding a tear with the impact that moment in our lives.

"We were just tourists at the time, had only been here a couple of months and travelling on little money that was about run out. So we went down to immigration and told them our story. This bloke said to us, 'So you want to stay in Australia,' and when we nodded, he took a rubber stamp and made us permanent residents - just like that."

Finding that hard to believe in Australia today, the room stirred with ruffled comments, and half of them gave a slight shake of their heads.

"Well, our first idea was to fit out a bus and take the kid around Australia, so we found a flat in Sydney and got jobs. But everywhere I went looking at buses, I'd find someone building a ferrocement boat right nearby. And when I talked to them, they didn't seem any brighter than me. So I began thinking, why not!

"When getting home one day, Jude was stretching on the lounge floor, belly full of child. As I said, we were just two kids in rented digs, just starting work, a child on the way and not a bean between us. So I blurted out something like, 'Hey, forget the bus. Why don't we build a boat and sail around the world with the bub?'"

Now, when I'd said that to all those faces, I must admit a tear did run down my cheek. My throat had gone dry, and I would have made a complete fool of myself if Steve, the organiser, hadn't yelled out, "My wife would have thrown me out." And the crowd burst out in laughter, and I shimmy-shammied around in one spot, took a sip of wine then smiled like I'd just had sex.

"Ah, Steve," I quipped. "But I've got the lady who always says yes." And the room roared.

For an hour after the show, the red wine poured while a couple of boxes of *Two's a Crew* were signed and went out the door.

We had a day to recuperate before relaunching *Banyandah* at 5 a.m. the following day, an early start to meet the high tide required to re-float her. Some wonderful GIYC members arrived early to work the gear and launch us. Since then, Jude has been flying up and down supermarket aisles filling shopping trolleys with six months of provisions. While I've been up and down the mast like a giant yo-yo, fitting our new running backstays. Why can't these things fit the first time!

We took a midweek break to stay with friends living in the hills on the south side of the city. Brisk forest air and the sounds of birds chortling were a very welcome change from the heat and buzz of mosquitoes that fills the air around the Garden Island Marina.

On the ride home, we picked up our life raft that had just been surveyed. It was the first time we'd seen it outside its hard case, and it looked brand new even though it is nearly ten years old. It's been our rule to see these life-saving devices inflated, to familiarize ourselves with

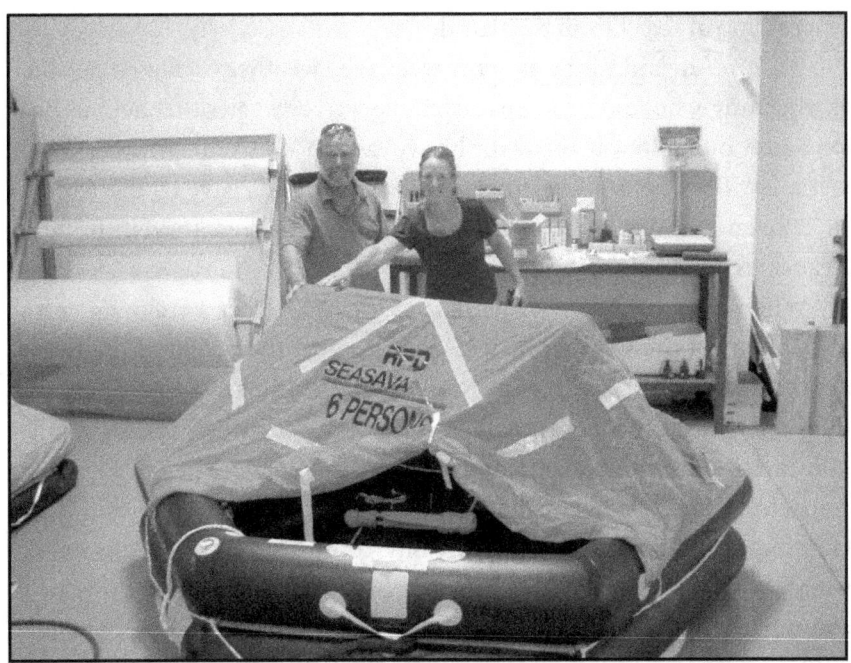

how to board it, and where the essential equipment will be found. Hopefully, it'll never be needed, but if it is, you can bet it'll be a highly stressed moment and quite possibly a dark night with high winds and big seas. We know it's wise to have some idea of what to expect.

Do you wonder why the need for six months provisions and the resurveying our life raft? Where in the world were we going? To answer that, we need to go back to the morning I got out of bed to reread our most frightening mishap ever. The morning star was just sinking into the river when Jude got up and found me in tears, and probably thought I'd had a breakdown. But not me, I'm just an old cry-baby.

After I read the account to her, she agreed we had unfinished business. Cuddled in each other's arms watching the new day begin we developed a plan to sail west, putting on free film nights until we were back along Australia's West Coast. At that juncture, we'd either continue across the Indian Ocean to our relatives in Madagascar or sail north around Australia in the opposite direction to our circumnavigation, clockwise to unwind. I somehow convinced Jude that that was a cool marketing idea, although she was far more excited with the prospect of exploring the sometimes-savage Great Australian Bight, said to have the longest line of sea cliffs in the world.

Back in Adelaide, for too many weeks the weather oscillated between excruciatingly hot days and unseasonable westerly gales that held us back long after our ship was ready for her voyage to Western Australia. Then, just a few days before Christmas, the weather gods gave us the window we'd been wanting. The season changed. Easterlies arrived, bringing clear skies and balmy weather.

When departing the Garden Island Yacht Club in a seagoing vessel, not only must the weather be watched, so must the height of the tide to negotiate the thirty-odd pairs of beacons leading to open sea. For *Banyandah*, that meant a predawn start at the top of the year's highest tide and risking with one little mistake, becoming long-term residents.

Before we sailed, we first express heartfelt thanks to the GIYC Committee for making all our dreams come true during *Banyandah's* winter layover. We highly recommend the GIYC to any yacht thinking of coming to Adelaide. This small club doesn't set out to make a profit from folks addicted to the sea. Their motto of 'make it happen, make it fun, make it cost-effective' exemplifies the true spirit of the cruising yachtie. And they set the bar where all clubs should aim - Two bucks for an excellent glass of red wine!

Being fresh off the slipway, our first sails were exhilarating. Our smooth bottom slipped through the sea like a wet baby on a plastic changing sheet. The slightest breeze got *Banyandah* going at hull speed, and with the increased summer hours, we made some impressive daylight runs.

We reached Kangaroo Island in two fast sails. The second, crossing the boisterous Investigator Strait wide open to the Southern Ocean, two days before Christmas. We saw no other boats - just empty sea, everyone must have been out Christmas shopping.

Her Majesty's Ship *Investigator* was the first ship to complete a voyage around Australia. Commanded by Matthew Flinders, she carried a crew of 78 plus a team of six scientists, their servants and Trim the cat. Built in 1795 to transport coal down the English coast, she was purchased by the Admiralty and refitted because she was well suited to exploration, she could carry large cargos and had a shallow draft that allowed her to sail close to shore.

Captain Flinders discovered Kangaroo Island at daybreak Sunday the 21st March 1802:

> Although the continuation of the main coast was not to be distinguished beyond the cape (Cape Spencer), yet there was land in sight at the distance of seven or eight leagues, from about south to S. 18½° W. Whether this land were an island or a part of the continent, and the wide opening to the eastward a strait or a new inlet, was uncertain.

For the *Investigator*, it then blew a fresh gale from the south-west. With much sea running, they hauled south under close-reefed topsails to gain the lee of this unknown land that was rather high and cliffy. At six in the evening, they came to anchor in 9 fathoms, sandy bottom, within a mile of the shore. Neither smoke nor other marks of inhabitants had been perceived although they had passed many miles of this strange land's coast. By then, too late to go on shore, every 'glass' in the ship was pointed there to see what could be discovered. Several black, rock-like lumps were thought to have been seen in motion by some of the young gentlemen, which caused their imaginations to be much admired.

Next morning, Monday the 22nd, on going toward the shore, several dark-brown kangaroos were seen feeding upon a grass-plate by the side of a wood, and the party's landing gave them no disturbance. Flinders had with him a double-barrelled gun fitted with a bayonet, and his companions had muskets. It would be difficult to guess how many kangaroos were seen, but Flinders killed ten, and the rest of the party made the number to thirty-one. Taken on board during the day; the least of them weighed 69 pounds and the largest 125 pounds.

After this butchery, Flinders, carrying his surveying instruments, scrambled with difficulty over fallen trees and through brushwood to reach the higher land. There was little doubt that this extensive piece of land was separated from the continent because the extraordinary tameness of the kangaroos and the presence of seals upon the shore concurred with the absence of all traces of man. Flinders named their landing place Kangaroo Head.

At the far northwest end of Kangaroo Island, close to where Flinders had first perceived land at seven or eight leagues, hidden behind steep cliffs is a magical cove that had once been a yachtsman's heaven. Aqua clear water runs up a pure-white sand beach surrounded by bizarre sandstone cliffs perforated by spooky caves. Inland, grassy slopes lead to stumpy green forests.

Carefully feeling our way in through its narrow rocky opening, we were delighted to see the mooring that Steve had offered to us with not a soul in sight.

"Trust me, it'll hold a destroyer," he had told us on the night we'd showed our film at the Royal South Australia Yacht Squadron. And from the size of the mooring rope and huge stud link chain, we knew Steve had not exaggerated.

Snug Cove at one time had been a sheep station but was now owned by Steve's friend. After stowing our sails and putting up our awning, we started fishing just under the boat. This was nothing short of fantastic, just like Steve had promised. Plainly visible a few feet below our keel, several varieties of edible fish were sauntering along the white bottom. Quickly at work, in no time we were eating scrumptious fresh fish, our first since returning to *Banyandah*.

Next day, the owner arrived in his motor launch, bringing his grandchildren, two daughters and their husbands. Our solitude was broken, so we rowed ashore to join the festivities, and found a place everyone dreams of owning. Acres of undulating land hidden from the maddening crowd with immense vistas across Investigator Strait, the best fishing, balmiest climate, and yet with a capital city just an hour's flight or day's drive away.

From Snug Cove we were bound for Port Lincoln where we hoped to organise a free film night. We had previously contacted the local newspaper who would publish a column about the time of our expected arrival, with info on our background and the need for a venue. Two hours after its publication, which happened to be the morning we anchored off town beach, we'd hardly caught our breath when our phone rang, and the Axel Stenross Maritime Museum enthusiastically offered us their theatre.

"Sure, the public is welcome free. We are only too happy to help," said the cheery voice of Rob, the museum's director. "Our theatre can accommodate one hundred, and if need be, we can add extra seats."

Axel Stenross, born in Finland around the turn of the century dreamed of a life on the high seas. As a young man, he achieved his dream and sailed the world, and of all the places he saw, he loved Port Lincoln so much he went ashore in 1927 and set up a business. He and partner Frank Laakso built ships for sixty years. Alex was still making boats right up until his death at the age of 84. Ever since then, enthusiasts of his wonderful life have kept his memory and his workshop alive.

When Jude and I called in, straightaway we were taken back in time by the equipment and tools almost as they were when the business was running. The Axel Stenross Museum is one of South Australia's most distinctive. It is a historic house, but not the grand home of a rich landowner. Axel lived humbly in his corrugated iron complex, some of the walls we saw were made from old tea chests. Boats and boat memorabilia were everywhere on display, and our slow saunter around bestowed upon us an appreciation of Axel's hard life using skills that are lost to today's generation.

What also impressed us was the theatre that boasted comfortable seating and a modern overhead projection that normally shows a short film introducing Axel's life to museum-goers.

After arrangements were made for our show in a week, they offered us the use of a mooring so we could spend New Years' with Timmy and Anna, our vagabond friends first met in Carnarvon. They lived just up the road a few hundred clicks and were expecting their first child in a few months. Strange how life ebbs and flows. These two had joined *Banyandah* earlier that year, and together we had explored the wondrous Sir Joseph Banks Group of islands lying just north of the port. In our two-week adventure, one topic discussed was family. We told them quite sincerely, "The best thing that ever happened to us." A few short weeks later, Anna became pregnant.

Catching up with them on their small property near Elliston and gently rubbing our hands over Anna's tummy was the first joy of many, as we also witnessed how people can live very comfortably when closely in tune with Earth, and doing it without the fuss and possessions that seem to trap many other young people starting out.

Hard Work at Adelaide

In a simple mud-brick dwelling surrounded by a modest bit of land that was by no means fantastically fertile until their energies transformed it into a lush garden with a chook and duck run and an orchard that produces literally a ton of fruit that these two either dry or bottle for later use. To pay their way, they rely on frugal living and bursts of employment teaching schoolchildren orienteering and water sports. For sure, their life is not for everyone. Too much hard work and too few comforts, not to mention that today few kids have the necessary skills.

Jude and I have had a similar journey through life. We have attempted and then developed a range of skills that still serve us well as we get older. Built a boat, navigated the world, leant carpentry and mechanical repair, we even created our own house. Doing it just takes an extraordinary amount of hard work, a fair bit of patience, and a positive outlook. In addition to maintaining good health, that's really all it takes because so many help those that help themselves.

Our free film night received support by the local newspaper, and on the night, we think the museum directors got a shock with the crowd that turned up. Young and old, including a couple nearly ninety, a few with their grandkids, all supported us handsomely, and everyone enjoyed seeing the wonderful adventure of circumnavigating Australia. The questions that followed clearly indicated that I was learning to be a competent speaker. Helped greatly by retelling stories from when we were sailing with the boys and known as the Four J's.

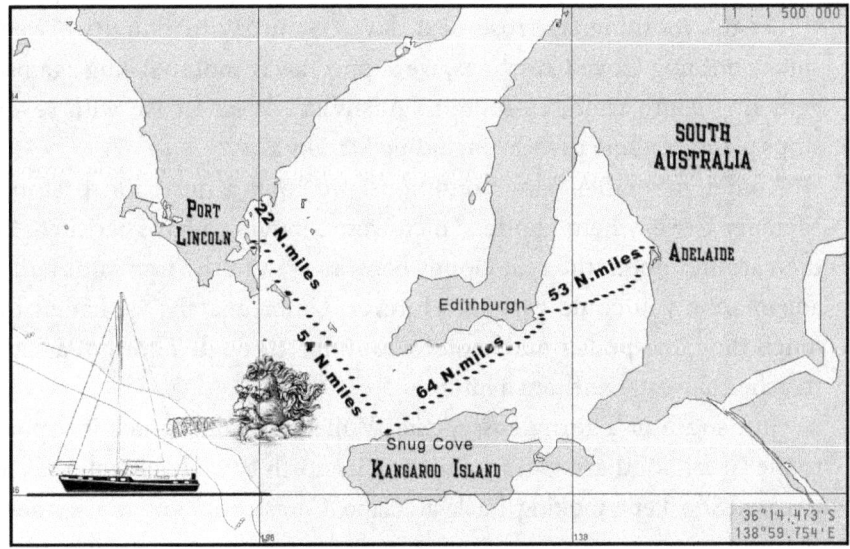

~ Chapter 18 ~

Streaking Along to Streaky Bay

A GOOD PERFORMER KNOWS TO EXIT WITH RAVE REVIEWS, so late the day after our show we unhitched the borrowed mooring and sailed into the sunset so to speak. We only went a few miles, to a quiet beach off the Lincoln National Park, which contains the Memory Cove Wilderness Protection Area. In 1802, a month before Flinders discovered Kangaroo Island, there had been a tragic event. While fetching water, their cutter was lost with eight men on board. Flinders was deeply affected by this disaster and named the headland near the sinking Cape Catastrophe, and the straits he named Thorny Passage.

As the morning star rose next day, a Saturday marking two weeks since our Snug Cove Christmas, we slipped away motor-sailing against a gathering south wind, en-route to Australia's West Coast, with several stops planned along the way including Streaky Bay.

Under miserable rainy conditions, we took a quiet lunch stop in Memory Cove, where Flinders' men were thought to have perished. But then around noon, the rain clouds blew away, and the waters turned an aquamarine you could gaze into forever. Unfortunately, we hadn't that much time and pulled our hook to continue through Thorny Passage's treacherous water without a hitch.

Just south of Thorny Passage lies Williams Island, which is exposed to the Great Southern Ocean. Entering its north bay, I could tell Jude felt uneasy. She kept looking back at Cape Catastrophe, at the immense white explosions of ocean swell bursting high up those cliffs. This was the beginning of a dangerous ocean, and a tightening in my belly, the first of many, warned me to take extra care on the journey ahead.

Once anchored, darkness rushed down from the heavens while Euros, the god of the east wind howled just next to our heads as we hunkered down for a rocky rollie night at Williams Island. With first light, we sailed, hoping for a fast daylight passage west. We needed four of them to reach Streaky Bay.

An important part of managing a sailing ship is voyage planning. First and foremost, we are wind sailors, so it's paramount to observe and understand wind systems. In the tropics, a pressure cell moves slowly, and a sailor may be blessed with steady winds for months. But down here in the higher latitudes, things change fast, and sometimes get furious. Our many sea miles have taught us to plan every day. To identify the dangers and currents, decide the best route and have a fallback plan. Out at sea, a small sailing ship can hunker down and wait. But next to huge combers, an error could prove fatal.

Ahead were forecast four days of strong winds straight from Antarctica. Cold, blustery winds upon which to reach Streaky, the next all-weather port. Then those winds would shift into our face, making the dry cliffs along Australia's Great Bight a dangerous lee shore.

Leaving Williams proved a perfect departure day; we even caught a fish, our first since Snug Cove. A stinky barracouta that we chucked back. That hardly helped ease the pain from our lack of sleep. You see, we had dragged anchor at Williams, forcing us to haul out our newly modified Admiralty anchor, hoping it would cope with the weed on this coast. Feeling unsettled after setting it, we left the GPS running all night so we could check if we dragged again in those blasts off the cliffs.

Instead of having a Sunday morning lie-in, followed by a lovely cooked breakfast, that day *Banyandah* ran down sixty miles with white caps chasing her. Dodging reefs and rocky outcrops, she whizzed past Perforated Island, the site of numerous White Pointer shark attacks. Then after rounding Whidbey Point on the mainland late in the day, she raced up the blunt end of Coffin Bay dodging more breaking rocky outcrops.

We'd towed two lures all day, landing two more stinky barracoutas. They too, had been chucked. We were very disappointed considering the remoteness. Mind, at these speeds only smelly barracouta or fast tuna could catch our lures. So, when something big hit our lure as we flew along in the lee of Coffins, with windblasts driving our decks into the sea and sheets of spray wetting us, I was right onto him. At those speeds, it was hard yakka hauling in our dinner, when suddenly off to our right a pair of red balls whizzed past. Crikey! Cray pots! Looking up, more were coming, a whole minefield.

Struggling with the fish, I yelled to Jude, "Turn a little right." She was steering the last miles through those windblasts. And just as she altered course, more red floats whizzed past, one really close to our trolling line. And immediately, an almighty jerk nearly took my arms out their sockets. Then snap! Only our braid remained. Lure, wire trace, and 50 metres of 100 kg monofilament, gone with our fish.

At the end of our run, we pulled into a sandy cove called Sir Isaacs with the same wind screaming through our rigging. Suffering from lack of sleep and a big day, the GPS was left running a second night, so we could keep checking that the rocks behind us weren't getting closer.

Another big day was coming. Flinders Island lay sixty miles further to the northwest. Not sure what we'll find there, the pilot warns of a rock bottom and other obstructions. But we can be sure it'll still be madly blowing like this. If we can't find a secure anchorage there, might sail overnight for Streaky Bay for a well-deserved break.

Isn't the internet a wonderful tool? While sheltering in that shark bite out a sandy coast called Sir Isaacs, we perused the internet and found a beaut anchorage behind an island just north of Elliston where Timmy and Anna live. There's no way we'd attempt Elliston's wicked entry in winds as big as these, so it's a good thing we had that time with them over New Year.

Several times during the night, I found Jude peeking out the window checking our position, and I got up once after a big blast rocked us to verify that the GPS icon was blinking in the same spot.

Strong winds make for little sleep, that's simply a fact of life for sailors. The flip side came with Monday morning's golden sunrise, easy winds that gave us hours of fun sailing, which only got faster and faster as the hours after lunch ticked past. By four, we were hanging on tight, *Banyandah* charging down the wavefronts, her rigging singing to the melody of crashing whitewater.

Over winter, we had ordered new hardware to rig a set of running backstays that I installed at Garden Island. With mighty Euros blowing up our backside, for the first time, I ran around setting up these new mast supports that would enable us to safely carry our staysail in strong winds.

Sails harness Nature's forces that are sometimes gentle, other times vicious, destructive. Transferring this energy to our ships are our masts and rigging. In olden times, masts were heavy solid posts, and their rigging were ropes that stretched and wore. Today, using the essence of physics, we use light spars supported by immensely strong cables with little or no stretch.

A modern sailboat's mast is designed to withstand compressive forces, and it's the rigging that gives a mast lateral strength. On *Banyandah*, rigging wires attach four ways at the first spreaders to provide a solid base, with four more at the masthead resisting the pull on the forestay. That's the norm for sloop-rigged sailboats with one headsail and one mainsail. But because we also carry a second sail forward, called a staysail, which attaches three-quarters up the mast, the pull from that sail must also be supported; otherwise, the mast could buckle at that point. We have two permanent rigging wires attached there that take the side strain, and we have two more restraining the forward pull of the staysail, but they don't lead far enough back to give adequate purchase in strong winds.

Why? Well, rigging wires mustn't foul the sails. Modern sailcloth is so hard the stitching sits proud on its surface, and any sail touching rigging wire will chafe the stitching. Those wires from the second spreaders are commonly the ones that rub the mainsail when it's set a long way out, like when running. So their angle is kept just enough for normal forces. Therefore, on yachts with a second headsail, it is quite common to rig what is called running backstays to restrain the mast in heavy weather. Running means the rigging is set up and not permanent. So a running backstay is one that is permanently attached at the top, but its bottom end has something like a snap shackle and multi-fall block and tackle to tension it.

Managing a sailboat in heavy weather is obviously nothing like driving a car in a storm. The forces are immense and must be harnessed by manpower without getting hurt or busting gear. So imagine two aging veterans holding tightly to a craft rocking about in a near gale that's blowing the sea into mighty marching soldiers, the noise nearly deafening. With our roller furling headsail in moderately tight and the smaller staysail poled out to windward, our new running backstays holding the mast steady, *Banyandah* left a creamy wake while our much-loved windvane hummed a cheerful tune keeping us tracking straight down the wavefronts.

Today's navigation is so much simpler compared to yesteryear. Instead of plotting course lines then charting bearings from headlands or lighthouses, to determine a safe route today we peruse a digital chart that's displayed on our GPS. Then by pressing a single button, we can lay a course line, and the machine will display mileage and ETA. Easy! Easy to make mistakes as well. Prudence requires a close examination of that course line, especially here, where rocks jut up from great depths, and big Southern Ocean swells would soon dash our ship into very small pieces.

That day's turning point proved a disaster waiting for the unwary. On our digital chart, which didn't show land heights, we presumed it was a tall island, but in fact, it proved to be a flat pancake rock. If we hadn't kept our eyes keenly on where the strong wind was driving us, it would have taken only minutes to be surfing powerful waves to certain destruction. But, we survived, and turned the corner, gybing all sail to run into Waldegrave's lee and a heavenly anchorage.

Pup seals and sea lions raced *Banyandah* towards sculptured saffron cliffs until a pure white sand bottom shining up through aquamarine gave our Admiralty a good bite. It's a wonderful feeling when we can see sand on the bottom as it almost always heralds a good sleep. That ended our workday, and once again, Jude and I kicked back elated and exhausted at the same time.

Streaking Along to Streaky Bay

In a wide bay with nothing but open sea behind us, we shut down the GPS, and then as the sun spread fiery gold across a clear horizon, we closed our eyes and slept like the dead. Must have slept in because my first sight was canary-yellow tickling the black underbellies of morning clouds.

What a lovely spot behind Waldegrave Island. We dawdled instead of setting sail in the soft early light. Had coffee in bed and listened to the radio. And what a treat to eat brekkie at a level table. The wind was just finding strength when we raised our mainsail to meet it. In fine practised form, on greased rails, if you like, *Banyandah* was set up running towards a small bay called Sceale, 54 miles ahead.

Coming away from Waldegrave, the now soft pink light graced us with a breeze that softly filled our reduced sail plan, and this created such a relaxed mood that while the pale limestone cliffs slipped away, we sat watching far ahead white breakers pop up from a flat emerald sea that highlighted the sunken rocks off Cape Radstock.

Everything was so perfect we could have gazed at the horizon for days, but such an easy motion after a sound sleep started us on our worklists. Jude, bless her, made fresh bread, its aroma driving me crazy as I rigged a new safety line from our life-ring to its emergency light. There is another line connecting the life-ring to our danbuoy, that's the pole that floats upright with an orange flag at the top. Just as I finished making a new lure to replace the silver one lost to those pesky cray pots, fresh salad and a few of Anna's eggs hard-boiled complemented Jude's freshly made bread. YUM.

That Tuesday morning crept along real slowly, but who was in a hurry. We knew the afternoon would roar, so we savoured the slow miles ticking past while being amused by pods of dolphins leaping out the low swells. Poor fellows, *Banyandah* was too slow for their fun, and they were soon bored waiting for her to run.

Down here in the Australian Bight, with the desert not that far away, the mighty midday sun heats the land, and this sucks the cooler air off the sea. This effect produces powerful afternoon sea breezes that often reach gale force. By 3 p.m. our home on the water started moving at a greater pace, and our peace was shattered. Distant pale cliffs came up quick and whizzed past while our log recorded 7s and 8s; a perfect speed to fool a fat muscly tuna with my new silver lure made from the bladder of an empty wine cask. With a bang, our bungee cord stretched to its limit. Hauling the brute alongside, Jude gaffed him. Then we both heaved, bringing on board a perfect size bluefin tuna.

Clearing the rocks off Cape Blanche, we hardened sails and took bullets from the cliff tops that drove *Banyandah* onto her beam-ends and wet us. With the wind on her side, its true ferocity could be gauged. And tired from several long days, these last miles frazzled my patience.

"This too shall pass," kept rolling around my head as I strode forward to bring down the staysail. Its tension released, it immediately began flogging like a tormented demon, and taking a slap in the face with the metal ring in its clew angered me more. Then when the sail knocked my knitted red beanie over the side, I exploded, cursing Zeus and all his cohorts. Thankfully, our newly altered Admiralty took an instant bite into a sand patch that jerked the bows around to face the township of Sceale Bay. We'd read 40 people reside there. Founded in 1888, a jetty once graced its shoreline. Built in 1910 to export wheat, and knocked down in 1972 for lack of maintenance. Today, only a few holiday houses mark a stronghold of unimpressive Nature.

The anchor down released me for more pleasurable chores, and I immediately cracked open a couple of cold beers to celebrate the fact that only a short hop separated us from our destination. One more day, a short one at that, and the weather set to ease.

Four windy days on the trot had sapped our energy, and it was a good thing the last morning dawned carrying a kind gentle breeze with a drop or two of rain helping to ease our pain. Day sailing is so much harder than crossing oceans. Sounds weird I know, but getting underway each day, settling into the rhythm, and then closing down the boat, worrying about the anchorage, sort of drains your energies little by little. Whereas, crossing a sea you set up the boat then settled back for the ride, day and night.

That last morning, *Banyandah*, fortunately, seemed to know her way around Speed Point, evading the rocks a mile off that cape, thank goodness, because Jude and I were pooped. All we could do was sit quietly watching the parched land slip past. True to form, around noon the breeze did pick up, but by that time we were ready for a bit of excitement.

The countryside stretching ahead to the limestone cliffs of the Bight were rolling flats of wheat country. Dry and without trees, as we rounded Cape Bauer, we were impressed with the pretty patterns created by harvested fields of wheat. But then, taking the breeze on our beam got us going really fast and suddenly everything was busy. Close inshore the water got kind of skinny with weed and sand patches whizzing past just under our keel. We held our breaths. It's a bit disconcerting the sudden changing of colours. But the chart showed a steady bottom, so we steadfastly stuck to our course and let the adrenaline rush. What a blast, standing atop the bow rail searching a clear path ahead while hot wind rushed through my salt and pepper locks, my lady beaming a big wide smile, and me shouting left, right, whatever the case. There's beauty all around, danger too, powerful forces helping to pound the blood through our veins.

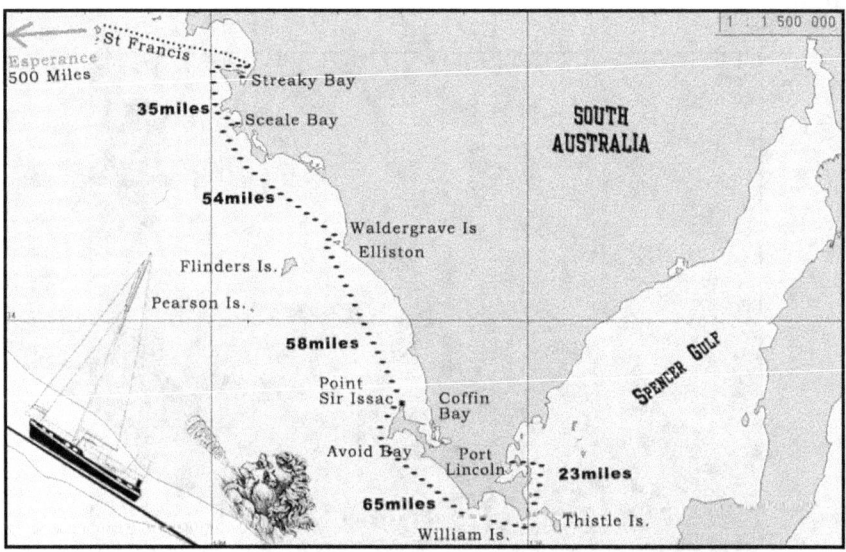

Soon the entrance into Streaky Bay came into sight. Past a yellow sand spit leading to Point Gibson, radio towers popped up, followed by wheat silos then buildings. First discovered by the Dutchman Peter Nuyts in 1627, that's a hundred and fifty years before Captain Cook. Flinders came next in 1802. He wrote in his log, "The water was much discoloured in Streaks... and I called it Streaky Bay."

It is now thought these streaks were the reflection of sand and seaweed or caused by the release of oils of certain species of seaweed.

Interestingly, Flinders thought the streaks were caused by the outpouring of a river. His mistaken belief prompted Australian explorer John Eyre to speculate that a great river flowed across half the Australian continent from the Great Dividing Range to enter the sea near Streaky Bay. After Flinders' visit, this nearly landlocked bay lay empty until John Eyre went looking for that river in 1839. Not finding one, he continued exploring the land to Albany, Western Australia.

Today, Streaky is a sleepy hideaway for just a thousand people. In the summer, Grey Nomads probably outnumber the residents. Also, we have heard there are never more than a couple of cray boats and two or three shark fisherman on this magnificent expanse of protected water.

Our arrival that Wednesday took the number of craft to two, and after a few circles to find the best spot, we dropped our anchor off the town's long timber jetty, which brought cheers from several tourists and locals.

Our journey complete, 235 nautical miles (400 km) from Port Lincoln in four hard days of sailing, had used 10 litres of diesel. Most of that when leaving Port Lincoln to get us into the stream of wind. The rest of our journey had been compliments of Mother Nature!

Ahead, a 550 nautical mile crossing of the Great Australian Bight to Western Australia. But first, we'll have a few meals out and some cold ones at the local, not forgetting a few blissful nights of undisturbed sleep.

~ Chapter 19 ~

A Journey Much Feared

JOSHUA SLOCUM, THE FIRST PERSON to circumnavigate the world single-handed, chose to avoid it. Jessica Watson experienced some of the worst seas of her entire round-the-world journey there. Yes, the voyage across the Great Australian Bight has many perils. Without a single safe haven for 550 miles, the prevailing winds send stricken vessels towards a hostile shore of limestone cliffs. To a coast that doesn't hold much hope for life - unless you're a lizard, snake, or rough n' tough kangaroo. Beyond those cliffs, a desert begins that sweeps nearly all the way across the great continent. And in the other direction, there isn't any land until Antarctica. This body of water passing under Australia is unique. It's the only ocean that completely encircles Earth. Swept by storms that build so much latent energy, its surface jumps in peaks even after days of calm weather. And when the wind comes, the Bight quickly becomes a monster. No wonder few yachtsmen attempt this voyage. But we did, two retirees aboard a homemade sailboat undertaking their third crossing.

Streaky Bay in cool early light seemed heavenly. From our boat resting quietly upon the bay's still waters, the few buildings appeared suspended in time; the coast road was vacant, the long timber jetty abandoned. Through a gap between two low buildings, the way out of town promised unknown adventures. It too was silent. From the aft cabin, a low moan reached me and turning, Jude looked a kitten curled up in only a single sheet. She breathed another low moan and stretched.

"Make you a cuppa," I said. Then with a wink, "Nothing going on up here, think I'll join you in bed."

Those first hours after making a difficult passage, when your destination has been achieved and there's no further call to action, fills a soul with heavenly laziness. They are moments of affection and admiration for your partner who has shared those hardships and helped achieve the goal. Only a select few can know this feeling. To have faced dangers on our own, to have worked synchronously as if an exquisite pair of gears harnessing Nature's immense power has fused our souls into one.

Rowing ashore sometime later, I was concentrating too much on my lady's divine torso lifting and stroking the oars instead of paying closer attention to filming the historic jetty coming closer. Glinting diamonds shone above her sweetly curved bare shoulders as she manoeuvred under the big timber beams, to a platform with stairs next to an enclosed swimming area. Seeing the mesh fencing got me thinking they do have a serious shark situation here.

There's something about long jetties leading towards outback towns, their parallel lines trained our eyes onto historical buildings in soft federation colours, and that had our imaginations working overtime. Old buggies could almost be seen on a dusty track. Instead, we walked up to the town's esplanade. A pub across the road, veranda strategically placed held a panoramic view over the bay with *Banyandah* peacefully awaiting her next assignment. As if sharing the same thought, our eyes met long enough for a knowing smile to part our lips.

"Good place for lunch," my lady giggled.

"Yeah. Or a coldie tonight." Then giving her arm a soft caress, I said, "But first let's find the tourist bureau and see what this town has to offer."

Up the main drag, we spotted a small supermarket, a fish and chipery, hardware store, and pharmacy. Good, I thought, I need some sunscreen, or my lips are going to perish in this sun.

Streaky, we found out, is endowed with several historical building, and the visitor's bureau had thoughtfully made up a walking trip down memory lane to over 33 plaques, temples, churches, cottages, monuments and cenotaphs. The majority situated within the CBD, and steeped in mystery and intrigue according to the brochure.

That began a memorable day. Oozing from the harsh dry countryside was a relaxing contrast of interesting houses and buildings. Rounding every corner, we expected John Eyre to be there with his packhorses. Not seeing him but stumbling instead upon two concrete workers sweating in the dry heat, we stopped for a short natter. They were pleased to down tools long enough to tell us not to miss the National Trust Museum next to the playschool they were fixing.

"The main building is closed." The big one said in a slight stutter. "Got lotsa bird's eggs and shells, and indigenous stuff belonging to old Daisy Bates." Then the younger one cut in. "But the sheds out back have heaps of early agricultural machinery, blacksmith tools and printing equipment dating from 1912. And an old cottage like they used to live in."

"Think they'd mind if we took a look," I said after I read a plaque indicating the old building had been Streaky Bay's first school.

"No-o," the big fella stammered again. "No-one gonna bother you."

So we walked down the lane to an open lean-to chockablock with quaint fire engines, thrashers, tractors, and next to it in the far back corner a finely restored example of a 'Pug 'n Pine' cottage that, with a slight push of the door, revealed furniture and clothing used by early settlers from 1886.

Back home that night, I was at my workstation searching the internet for information on the way ahead. We knew the Dutch had discovered the area three centuries earlier, and that Flinders and Eyre had followed. But what about the first pioneers. That day, we'd seen first hand the harshness of the land and realized there were heroic stories yet to be discovered. One website intrigued me the most. A photo showed two derelict houses on a barren saltbush hill. Stark in the extreme, but what attracted my attention, they were located on St. Francis Island.

"Hey, Jude," I called forward. "There are some old dwellings on that island fifty miles out. You know, the one I said was on our way to WA."

Reading on, I discovered that the Dutch Captain of the Gulden Zeepaert had discovered the island in 1627, naming it after his patron saint. But I wanted to know who had lived on such a remote island, when, and why. So, while Jude cooked up a fresh veggie stir-fry delight, I kept digging deeper into the mystery.

Four days later, church bells were calling the faithful to prayer as we set sail before a strong easterly that was painting the bay steel grey streaked white. Strong winds had returned, and therefore our journey began under double-reefed mainsail and reduced headsail. Swiftly we passed the Point Gibson sand spit, and leaving behind the bay's protection, laid a course for the last land before the Great Australian Bight.

In 1606, more than one and a half centuries before Captain Cook had discovered Australia's East Coast, the first European landing in Australia was a Dutchman named Willem Janszoon, captain of the *Duyfken*, who came ashore on Australia's North Coast. But the continent's south coast remained a mystery for another twenty years, until June 1627, when Captain Francois Thyssen aboard the *Gulden Zeepaert* (Golden Seahorse), with Peter Nuyts, Councillor of the Dutch East Indies, became the first Europeans to see Australia's southern seaboard. Why they came to be so far east is a mystery. Probably bad weather had blown them off-course or a navigational error. Nevertheless, they charted the southern coast from Cape Leeuwin, all the way to present-day Fowlers Bay, where they named two islands, St Francis and St Pieter. No one really knows what happened after that. Some believe they retraced their route and sailed on to Java. Others believe, with prevailing west winds, they kept sailing east in the hope of seeing the coastline turn north. Later on, Matthew Flinders named the region Nuyts Archipelago to honour the Councillor.

Our first anchorage in the Nuyts Archipelago, St Francis Island, fifty-five miles out to sea from Streaky Bay, is the second-largest in a group comprising twelve islets and rocks. According to the online encyclopaedia, its mix of grassland, saltbush, and low shrub supports a huge population of sooty petrels estimated at 273,000 pairs. They're commonly called muttonbirds because of their oily meat. The island has a long history of agricultural use, as well as guano mining, and its highest point, 81 m above the sea, carries an automated lighthouse and radio beacon. In years past, two homesteads had been built upon these two square kilometres of limestone that covers a granite base.

A Journey Much Feared

As we cleared the northeast tip to enter Petrel Bay, named by Matthew Flinders because of the large numbers of muttonbirds he observed, the ruins were starkly visible on the treeless slopes. Before us, rose an easy gradient of low scrub fronted by a line of white sand splodged randomly with needle-sharp limestone rock, leaving the bay solely to our ship, apart from a slight swell. We had caught a ten-kilo bluefin tuna on the crossing, and I was cleaning him by the golden rays of the setting sun streaking up through the gathering night clouds. As I did, the sky darkened further with muttonbirds returning to the island. In family groups, they soared in wide circles right above us, squawking their news until the noise was deafening.

All work stopped. Jude came up and joined me, our heads skyward as we witnessed one of Nature's mysteries and miracles. As if an unseen conductor had raised his baton, their noise ceased as each of them zeroed in on their particular nook, their hole in the ground amongst so many. How they knew which hole baffled us; especially as these migratory birds travel thousands of miles each year and return to exactly the same tiny opening. And humans think we're so clever. Humph, can't find anything without a fancy onboard GPS telling us where to turn.

This area is biologically unique due to the influence of the Leeuwin Current that flows down Australia's West Coast and then eastwards across the Great Australian Bight, and it brings features more typical of western than southeastern Australia. In and around the archipelago, the subtropical Leeuwin Current meets and mixes with the colder waters of the Flinders Current creating a biodiversity hotspot attracting many fish species.

Next morning after launching *Little Red*, we landed through slight surf then walked to the island's highest point to view the navigation light and radio tower, having to be very careful when negotiating around the muttonbird burrows that numbered many thousands.

Across the low scrub blew a strong east wind carrying the pungent smell of guano. And in plain sight was death. Decaying bodies of brown birds and bleached bones dotted the grey and green of sharp saltbush. While across the island, two odd shapes broke this empty vista.

"I love this," Jude squealed pointing her cameras at just about everything, framing shots with an azure blue sea backdrop. She had discovered a bush with purple berries, and a prehistoric shell with whorls decorated with tiny raised stars. And of course, the lighthouse with its modern array of solar cells.

"Must have been very lonely living here," I mused thinking of the newspaper article I'd read concerning the death of Mrs Arnold just before Christmas 1914. Apparently a suicide.

"See that edge," I said, pointing past the derelict houses. "Tracks were found and followed to a cliff where the tracks were lost."

Jude stared, slowly shaking her head. "I couldn't live here."

"Well, I read Mrs Arnold had, for more than twenty years. Grew market vegetables and raised sheep. Evidently, the soil is very rich, the result of the bones and droppings from millions of muttonbirds. The newspaper said it would grow anything, including watermelons and tomatoes, so long as there was a reasonable rainfall of about 12 to 14 inches."

Next day, after a morning working bee getting our ship a bit more ready for her voyage, we strolled along the shoreline until under the ruins. The day before, having nearly collapsed several muttonbird burrows, we felt it best to minimize our travel inland. According to the National Library website, the dwellings were built before 1900 and have been abandoned for more than forty years, since the time these islands were declared a conservation park.

A Journey Much Feared

They proved fascinating. Built from lumps of limestone chiselled out the shore rock, the walls were then lime-mud filled. Unfortunately, all except one iron roof had collapsed. Easy to understand with fierce winter storms unrestricted across barren terrain.

"Come on, I'm going in." And I struggled carefully under a fallen roof that lay on a low rock wall, into a room with a timber floor. Finding the only timber wall defaced with graffiti, I touched a clean spot of whitewash next to an opening, my gaze settling on the blue horizon. And for a moment, where *Banyandah* sat quietly, I imagined the island's ketch *Sunbeam* that had been built in WA from Jarrah. A smile spread across my lips when I remembered what her builder had written in her specs. "In order that she may not be delayed, she will, when becalmed, utilize for propulsion a 10 hp engine."

Even with our modern hulls and precise navigation, few of today's yachts would venture into these waters with anything less than five times that power.

While my mind tried to conjure up an image of Mrs Arnold preparing her last meal, I remembered she had been forty-two, and not well, and probably missing her two children, son Francis, aged 18, and daughter Clara, just 13. The investigating officer had thought she had suffered sunstroke, but why had she ventured so close to that edge?

Jude and I began play-acting living on such an isolated island. She was Mrs Arnold collecting eggs from the chook run while I carried water in from the tanks. But it was all too depressing. The unlimited blue vista hardly made up for the lack of trees, the hot wind, and zillion muttonbird burrows in which to break a leg. Moreover, with no medical facilities or radio contact; our situation afloat suddenly seemed like Nirvana.

We walked home along the beach depressed in thought until seeing a family of dolphins working the shallows back and forth, obviously herding a school of fish closer together. Occasionally a frisky one surprised us by racing pell-mell around his brothers and then jumped clear out the sea as if leaping through an imaginary hoop. Cheering us up immensely, we thought who needs Sea-World.

The following morning, an hour's motor-sail brought us to Masillon, the next island south; to an anchorage recommended by a fisherman who had said these two spots were his favourites. Masillon is a strange island, much smaller than St Francis. During Baudin's expedition of 1802, it was named after the Bishop of Clermont, Jean Baptiste Massillon.

Rising abruptly out the blue sea, it sports a white collar of crustaceans marking the start of pockmarked, golden yellow calcarenite. On its flat top, healthy shrub and saltbush reportedly house another forty thousand muttonbirds.

The anchorage we almost missed. It was nothing more than a narrow chasm ending in an eroded cliff that had been undermined by sea action. Three caves added a bit of mystery.

"That doesn't look safe," Jude said at first sight. She must have been thinking of the strong winds and powerful sea running just beyond the opening.

"Let's have a look," I suggested. "It's either in there, or we're going back. We still have the dinghy to pack before our crossing."

Jude looked over her shoulder at St Francis, so I pressed her button. "Go on, take us in. Just stay away from the surge along those walls."

Inside the narrow gorge-like-bay was a fantasy. The sounder recorded huge depths going in until the last bit when the bottom rushed up quickly to 35 feet, hurrah! Here we could swing on the anchor

A Journey Much Feared

without hitting the cliffs, perfect to risk an overnight stay. The surface of the water, now completely out the breeze, was glassy calm with just a bit of tolerable surge. And after searching around, I lowered our anchor into a sand patch amongst scattered clumps of weed.

The easy surge where it ran against craggy orange limestone, rose and fell like a bubble of water coming to boil. So excited we didn't wait, but straightaway relaunched the dinghy to get even closer. Jude rowed, while I filmed *Banyandah* against limestone caves. Then I had us swap around. I wanted to thrill Jude by rowing into one of the caverns with the surge then back row to get out before we grounded. The first time we were lucky. Jude hung to *Little Red's* gunwales concern on her face as the unpredictable surge sucked us towards a rocky death. The next time I had to work like a demon when a sudden downdraft propelled us against our wills towards the open sea. Deciding caution was wiser than bravado, I took her home to absorb the scenery from the safety of our ship.

After a glorious sleep and rising into cool splendour, we got stuck into our last task, packing our dinghy with emergency supplies. Secured under the thwarts were ten litres of drinking water, several flares, a knife, and watertight drum containing medicines and essentials. The evening before, Jude had put together our 'grab bag,' a stout, bright-yellow sail bag with a long lanyard attached to a buoy. Into this, she had put additional essentials such as dried food, medicines, fishing gear, more flares, and sealed packets of water. To that lot, well waterproofed, she added some flotation. That 'grab bag' stores within easy reach inside a cockpit locker, ready in case of a disaster. These are our normal precautions for crossing any large expanse of water, as well as having an in-date six-person life raft that self deploys. We've sailed too many miles not to have the greatest respect for the sea, plus we heartily support the old sailor's code of looking after oneself.

Being prepared made us feel relaxed and confident. And so, on the foredeck after lashing the dinghy down, we snuck in a wee bit of a cuddle. And while in each other's arms we heard three honks, one after the other, from a pair of white-bellied sea eagles soaring on thermals above the clifftop. Their landing with a good view over us seemed to signal that it was time to go. With two fellow devotees of wind watching us, we hoisted our Admiralty anchor, stowed it under the saloon floor then hoisted the mainsail, putting in one reef. The video recorded one last good look around, and finding all ship-shape, it zeroed in on the eagles. Giving them a farewell wave, I directed Jude to take our floating home out to the open sea.

Giving her some throttle, Jude wrote in the log.

0935 A well-oiled departure. Genoa unfurled to starboard, swell more than expected ~ 2 metres from SW.

After settling *Banyandah* on her course, I had nothing to do but sit and gaze at the distant horizon while Jude finished her last task of marking new columns on a few more pages of our logbook.

At 11 a.m. she wrote, The *last island abeam, sea routine established. Jack reading, 'Whaling around Australia' by Colwell. Speed 5.3 knots.*

There was nothing more to report until 5 p.m. when she added, *Mobile phone connection! 72 NM from Ceduna. Talked with Ally (daughter-in-law) and Lottie (one of Jude's best friends).*

It was a dream start to what can be a journey much feared. Laid back, at 6 p.m. Jude recorded one of my favourite comments. *Sailing down the sun, orange ahead – silver astern, full moon rising. On a beam reach.*

We had a peaceful first night, so important when trying to become one with the ship's motion, which helps avoid injuries. Miraculously, we both found sleep while our baby tracked easily across the sea under brilliant moonlight.

A Journey Much Feared

Unfortunately, a cold front was approaching. We knew it was coming. On a passage lasting nearly a week down here in The Bight, you'd be lucky to avoid one. But the calm before the storm arrived much sooner than we had hoped. Maybe I scared away the wind when my ugly mug arose from bed just after sunrise and forgot to give my wife her three kisses. First, it backed to the NE, then the NW, and then it vanished, leaving us wallowing in a troubled sea. Jude went below to catch up on her sleep, so I started the engine and ran it slow to steady the ship. We chugged along for several hours, the sea quieted, and it was after Jude had gotten up and we were eating lunch that we noticed a long easy southerly swell starting to roll by. Hmm, swell with no wind means something is coming. A bit of breeze soon arrived and we were sailing again. But then that party-pooper wind left us once again dead in the water and rolling. The 3 p.m. log entry tells the story. *Sooty petrels and albatrosses sitting on calm water.*

Knowing the front was coming, we had left Masillon because a larger one was forecast in four days, at which time we hoped to be anchored somewhere in Western Australia. The forecast for this first front was upwards of thirty-knot southwest wind. That's a headwind. And to prepare for this, we had travelled left of our course line, thinking that when the front struck, we'd tack across the wind and be able to ease the sails while heading back towards our course line. That was the plan.

Fronts can be hundreds of kilometres in width. The air behind one is much cooler than the air in front, often by 15° C. The cooler, denser air wedges under the less-dense warm air, lifting it and often creating clouds along that wedge. This is because as the warm air rises, it cools and condenses; commonly bringing a band of precipitation that can be very strong, maybe with thunderstorms, hailstorms, even tornadoes.

Around four, I was below having a poppy-nap when after light misty drizzle came icy blasts. As the boat groaned and laid-over, I'm suddenly bowled out my quiet repose. Rushing topsides in only a thermal shirt, suddenly I'm shivering and turn for a jumper, but see there's no time. A greenish-black roll cloud is about to attack.

"Quick Babe! Let's reef the main." I shout.

In freezing rain, we put in a double reef then rolled in the headsail until just a single dot showed. Even short rigged, once we'd tacked, we still couldn't hold our desired course. Instead, *Banyandah* started getting pushed towards land. The seas built quickly, and by darkness, our decks were awash.

Fronts are not like trade winds that blow steadily from one direction. They attack in blasts that blow waves into sheets of wetness and fine mist. One moment all is fine. The next, a series of bigger blasts buries our ship, and we have to tightly grip something or go flying. During their onslaught, every movement must be timed to the sea. With at least one hand on the ship, otherwise, injuries happen.

Of course, the motion took away any chance of sleep. Jude lay in her berth listening to the ship's clock strike every hour until midnight. Then after the change of watch, I lay next to the hull tensing whenever rigging hummed and shrieked. And not just that, the gurgling and sluicing of seawater across our decks had me thinking of the sails stretched so tautly that I lay planning an emergency strategy, over and over until the portholes started to lighten.

But this was never going to be the ultimate storm, just a plain vanilla cold front that is a regular event in higher latitudes. And even though it was uncomfortable and worrisome, by the time the grey morning lightened, the wind had backed to the south and was easing.

By noon our third day at sea, a comfortable wind of 12 to 18 knots had backed around to the SE letting us sail on our course with a single reef and 70% of the jib.

Some of Jude's log entries for that third day's journey were:

1300 Caught a tuna. Shearwaters enjoying a feast on bits thrown in. Not one drop of seawater on their feathers after diving for scraps. Beautiful, robust chocolate brown birds.

2100 Moon up – Sweet Ride – slowing down.

2400 Day's run 116 NM made good. 127 NM sailed.

Day four began with a three-quarter moon peeking through 90% cloud and 2 m SW swell, *Banyandah* rolling along nicely in just 10 knots of ESE breeze.

0600 Sun up. A bit more blue sky. Supposed to be 15/20 SE today. Need it to reach an anchorage tomorrow and beat the next front.

On day five, when the sun should have come up, instead grey cottonwool filled the sky and took away every vestige of wind, leaving us bobbing around on a left-behind-sea. Again, to help ease the motion, I started motoring, letting Jude catch-up her sleep.

Steering from under the dodger hiding from a light drizzle, I'm humming Dylan's 'Shelter from the Storm,' when off to the right bearing north by northwest, vague mountains peeked through the opaque mist. As a child watching adventure movies at the pics, I always wanted to cry out, "Land ho!" The reality is, children only see the adventure of crossing oceans, but not the euphoria of surviving days on an empty platter doing battle with Nature's forces. My first few times were scary, but now they're intoxicating. More than that, it's empowering to know that alone, without the police, army, or SES, we can survive and achieve our goals.

We motored until 1 p.m. then sailed for an hour when the breeze freshened, but it left us again about the time Bellinger Island rose ahead.

No matter how many crossing we make, the first sight of new land still amazes us. From dry South Australian limestone with scrubby growth, arm in arm on our foredeck Jude and I watched beige granite tors rise from the sea. Thickly covered in gold and green succulents, the shore moved with black patches that became families of sea lions.

We had arrived at a very remote part of Australia, the nearest town some hundreds of kilometres away. That always raises our awareness of danger. And so, after stowing our sails, slowly under power, we approached the island, me at the front holding onto a stay, Jude following my instructions. Both of us had already studied the digital chart, memorized the dangers, and left it available onscreen back aft.

Bellinger is a low unremarkable island close off the south coast of Western Australia. It is one of the first islands in the Archipelago of the Recherché, an amazing group of 105 uninhabited islands stretching 125 NM (230 km) west from Israelite Bay to Esperance.

As we approached, a yellow-hulled cray boat suddenly took shape out of the gorgeous yellow-green succulents. He was parked rather away from the shore, which had me wondering whether dangers lay closer in, so Jude eased *Banyandah* within hailing distance.

"How you going," slipped out easily after a week on our own.

"Yeah, good," came the reply from a scruffy fellow in his late forties. Towards the back of his open deck area, his offsider was not more than a nipper wearing a big cheesy grin.

"Just made the crossing from South Australia," I said, and watched them exchange glances. "I'm wondering if it's okay to park closer to shore."

Both did a quick look over their shoulders, and then the older one put his barefoot up on the gunwale.

"Sure. We just park out here 'cause we'll be going early in the morn," he said with a few nods of his head. "What're ya doing for tea tonight?"

I looked at Jude, who scrunched her shoulders. So I looked back and put both hands up. He smiled and waved us in closer while telling his deckie something we couldn't hear.

Well, blow me down with a feather, the deckie saunters over carrying a big red crayfish. Crikey! Now, all we had to figure out was how to get a hold of the beast. There being a slight ripple running, our two boats might collide. But Jude manoeuvred our 13 tonnes up to within reach of our boat hook that held a plastic bucket on its end. And the skipper dropped in our treat.

"Welcome to Western Australia," he said, so I gave him a wink.

Once our anchor got a bite of the weedy bottom, a good bottle of red found its way out the locker. Then I sat back to celebrate with my lady. Exhaustion battled the drink. One breath I was ready to take my honey below for a cuddle, the next, my eyes slipped shut, and it seemed too much trouble to open 'em.

While eyeing my wife, she did her bookwork, then shut down all the electronic gismos before reading out the stats.

"We did well," she said with that cute little twinkle I love so much. "Four hundred and ninety miles (906 km) made good in four days and seven hours... Um, that's an average of 4.8 knots or 115 NM each day. Max speed was 7.8 knots! Not bad at all."

Two's a Crew had conquered the voyage much feared, so I raised my glass to my lady and whispered, "I love you." After that, our crayfish dinner had to wait.

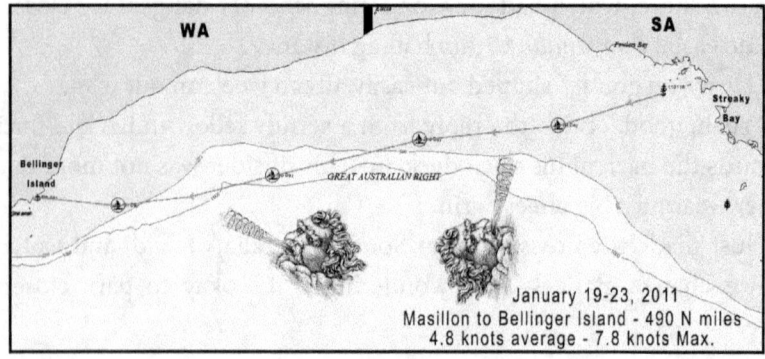

January 19-23, 2011
Masillon to Bellinger Island - 490 N miles
4.8 knots average - 7.8 knots Max.

~ Chapter 20 ~

Chasing a Wild Goose

ONCE IN THE ARCHIPELAGO OF THE RECHERCHÉ, the safety of the open sea was replaced by dangers all around. In 1814, Flinders succinctly stated in his log, "this extensive mass of dangers..." when describing the 125 nautical miles that contain 1200 obstacles to shipping. Perusing the chart after a great sleep and waking to find our spot at Bellinger being attacked by an increasing east wind, we discovered there weren't many safe anchorages near us. Lickety-split, with just a coffee in hand, we were underway, our sails taking *Banyandah* through seas obstructed by rocks marked, 'position approximate' or 'evidence doubtful.' By the limited soundings shown, this area had not been well surveyed.

Twenty-five miles ahead, rising out these little-explored waters stood Middle Island, the largest in the archipelago at 11 square kilometres. In 1792, d'Entrecasteaux went searching for the missing French explorer La Pérouse who had disappeared without a trace after leaving Botany Bay in 1788. D'Entrecasteaux skirted the edge of this dangerous area and named the island in the centre of the archipelago - no surprises for guessing - Ile du milieu, Middle Island. According to our guidebook, the island contained a pink lake, Lake Hillier. This archipelago had also been the favourite haunt of Australia's only documented pirate, Afro-American Black Jack Anderson, who first worked the area as a sealer. He became a pirate almost reluctantly, or so the story goes, but soon became proficient and embraced his new career. He wreaked havoc along the south coast for about a decade before his crew decided enough was enough and murdered him. Our information says his treasure has never been found.

Fortunately, our voyage to Middle Island passed without event. And by late afternoon, we had successfully slipped past the sunken rocks off Cape Pasley, 'position approximate,' and by hardening our sails, had skirted the breaking reefs off Miles Island then sailed close round the North East Point of Middle Island, snapping photos of the beautifully polished granite awash with white surf.

One of the great joys of the south coast is its magical turquoise waters and brilliant white sands that now held us gobsmacked as *Banyandah* entered Goose Island Bay. The seas calmed, the SE wind that had gained strength during the day now only blew high above our heads, leaving us drifting silently towards the lovely anchorage nearest the pink lake. Eucalypt clad hills and tea-tree rose behind it. Sheltered from NE through S to W, *Banyandah* anchored in a sand patch 5 m deep, fairly close to a steep beach with a small surge.

Eager to explore, *Little Red* was chucked in, and within fifteen minutes, we were snapping photos of the most amazing pink lake and finding it very salty. Looking around, especially aloft to the bare granite peak, Jude chuckled. "We could stay here for weeks."

A few mornings later, I was aft reading a most interesting account by Captain Flinders in his, "A voyage to Terra Australis."

FRIDAY 15 JANUARY 1802
The botanists landed in the morning upon Middle Island; for I had determined to stop a day or two, as well for their accommodation as to improve my chart of the archipelago. I went to the northern island, which is one mile long and near half a mile in breadth, and found it to be covered with tufts of wiry grass intermixed with a few shrubs. Some of the little, blue penguins, like those of Bass Strait, harboured under the bushes; and amongst the grass and upon the shores were a number of the bernacle geese (Cape Barren Geese), of which we killed nine, mostly with sticks; and sixteen more were procured in the course of the day.
After taking bearings from the uppermost of the small elevations of GOOSE ISLAND, as it was now named, I ascended the high north-western hill of Middle Island (Flinders Peak), which afforded a more extensive view. The furthest visible part of the main land was a projecting cape, with a broad-topped hill upon it bearing N. 58° E., six or seven leagues. This projection not having been seen by d'Entrecasteaux, was named after the late admiral Sir Thomas Pasley, under whom I had the honour of entering the naval service. The shore betwixt Cape Pasley and Cape Arid is low and sandy, and falls back in a large bight, nearly similar to what is formed on the west side

of Cape Arid. Behind that cape was a high bank of sand, which stretched from one bight nearly to the other, and had the appearance of having been the seashore not very long since.

We find it fascinating to read what was written hundreds of years earlier about remote locations that are little changed today, and then be at those places, standing in our cockpit, seeing the same view and imagining ourselves on board, in this case, *The Investigator* exploring this unknown southern land. With his words before me in the silent cabin, I remembered what I had read earlier about Flinders' second visit to this island a year after his first when they knew the ship had rotten timbers and was leaking badly. In May 1803, Flinders was returning to Port Jackson from Timor, his crew ailing from the long months of restricted diet and deprivation, and taking their toll were the diseases contracted in Timor. Flinders himself was severely incapacitated, but he remembered this haven from the previous year and stopped again at Middle Island for fresh food and supplies of salt. As always, fresh water was required, as was lamp oil from seal blubber.

But his dreams were not realised. There was no salt, which they thought was due to recent heavy rain. Neither were there many geese. Only 12 were shot, not enough to give strength to the large number of invalids on board.

Imaginative as ever, in my mind scenes danced and I saw in flickering lamplight, the boatswain's mate wet a delirious man's brow as he lay mumbling, "Mary, Mary, I love you."

Then with a sigh, the man's head slipped sideways into silence. From between darkened decks, a tall, sickly figure struggled forward resplendent in gold braid.

"How's the boatswain?" he wheezed. The mate simply shook his head.

In the dim light before dawn, Charles Douglas, of His Majesty's Ship *Investigator* was sewn into a piece of old sail and loaded into a longboat then hauled to shore. In the year of 1803, before an assembly of his shipmates, Captain Flinders read the eulogy.

"Charles Douglas was an honest man who served God and his country. He will not be forgotten."

"Hey Jude," I called from my writing desk. "The Investigator's boatswain is buried on Goose Island."

She joined me in the cockpit, and together we looked across the bay.

"Any idea where?" she asked.

Overnight, cool air from Antarctica had driven the heat haze away, and now the sandhills surrounding Cape Arid stood crisp and white against a perfect sea and sky. On our left, rising sharply against a tiffany sky, Flinders Peak dribbled old blood that was now streaked with sunshine. Between the two was Goose Island, a deep emerald rising from a sheet of sapphire.

"Where?" I laughed. "All the guidebook says, when discovered in 1999 his grave was inscribed Charles Douglas HMS Investigator May 18, 1803."

Instinctively our eyes searched that half-mile-long island as I added, "It doesn't say where. But my guess is it'll be close to a landing and probably face the rising sun – that's where I'd like to be laid to rest."

Like a schoolgirl seeking a treat, Jude asked. "Shall we go and look?"

"Sure! What a thrill it will be to connect with something from *The Investigator*. But, let's shift *Banyandah* first."

Just past the low limestone cliffs on Goose Island, a finger of white sand sparkled beneath bold Caribbean blue, and where the sand met the sea, a picturesque limestone archway rose. Jude, watching me work the oars, became radiant as a distant memory began dancing in her eyes.

"Reminds me of Ventotene," she trilled, which brought a cherished memory of making love on just such a beach, hidden inside just such a cave while the sea lapped our feet.

"I'll row now," she declared. "Those spooky caves with limestone teeth will look great on video."

So we switched places, and while she pulled the oars, I watched her breasts rise, and firm, and ideas of returning to that cave started spinning around my head.

Past the craggy headland, a perfect white beach ran a hundred metres before it reached the channel between the two islands, where assisted by a low surge we grounded then quickly dragged *Little Red* up the hard sand. Immediately I documented our landing by panning from the beach through the archway to *Banyandah* tugging at her anchor.

"He won't be buried here," I declared, looking to Jude brushing wet sand from her toes, her boots and socks standing ready. "The grave wasn't discovered for nearly 200 years, so it won't be next to the only decent landing site."

D'Entrecasteaux, we know, first recorded these islands in 1792 and later explorers mostly avoided the area because it's littered with so many obstacles to shipping. It's far-flung from mankind, without any roads nearby as there is no need. The ground is sand or rock with no resources of note. It's a place for Earth's other creatures, and they abound in variety. Each year, flocks of seabirds come here to reproduce. They live underground in burrows dug by their beak and webbed feet, and each year they return to the exact same hole. Flinders wrote of the sky being turned black for hours by their passing millions. However, today, though man doesn't hunt these creatures anymore, their numbers are greatly reduced. Why? Because we take their food. We harvest huge schools of pilchards at a time – to feed our cats. And we capture baby tuna from the sea then fatten them in nets. How we expect them to procreate is beyond Jude and me. It's got the tuna baffled too! Many species of tuna are now listed as highly endangered. It might help if humanity remembered that every form of Earth life is connected. What our growing population takes makes other species suffer.

Picking our way carefully, we zigzagged past thick tea-tree and sharp scrub towards a rock shelf rising up the weather side. Avoiding muttonbird burrows that hollowed the ground like Swiss cheese, between them on the bare earth, we saw the tiny shuffling footprints of the little blue penguins that also live on the island. Surprising us next, we found large areas of round spoor and prayed it came from small marsupials. But soon we were disappointed to catch sight of a small rabbit bobbing away.

"Pretty one, that," Jude exclaimed facetiously.

I'm sure she was thinking of her childhood pet because although this one had lovely black fur tinged in rusty gold, we both knew it was a disaster. Memories of totally denuded islands flashed through our thoughts.

"Wonder how they got here," I mused, shaking my head.

Rabbits are hugely destructive. First, they destroy the moist refugia around rocky outcrops, which causes the decline of medium-sized mammals. Then, as their numbers increase, they devour all plant life. Like humans nibbling away, first along the edges of wilderness, little bites at a time until there's none left.

Along that rock shelf, we travelled the weather side, watching glorious blue sea bursting white on polished granite while traversing higher in the direction of an eagle's nest. Then as we gained the ridge, that nest became an immense rock cairn atop the island's summit. Jude added our stone, having to hike herself up to reach its top.

Flinders Peak on Middle Island from Goose Island

From that vantage, the small island spread in a delight of complementing colours surrounded by a blueberry sea. Ripe avocado had been brushed along the leeward side facing the anchorage, but it had died in places leaving brown patches intermingled with splotches of flat rock that made it look as if the island had been injured, and these were scabs.

"I see what you meant," Jude said as she finished scanning the island. "Charles would more likely be interned on that ridge there, or that one," she said, pointing to two separate fingers running parallel towards our ship.

"That makes sense. *The Investigator* would have parked just a bit further out from us." Then I suggested, "If you like, let's first explore that cave. See? Up in that rock mass at the far end, then we'll search for Charles on the way back."

Exploring a far distant island turned us retirees into children by energising our spirits. The air carried more vigour; our eyes noticed more detail, our minds asked questions, and we soon forgot our aches and pains.

The cave proved no more than an overhang popular with sea birds. Fishbones littered the earth among a white carpet of excrement and shattered seashells. But around it and spreading up a shallow valley were gorgeous succulents the colour of fire at dawn. Polyps, billions of them. While filming this grandeur, Jude, wearing her backpack like the hunchback of Notre Dame, frightened a massive wedge-tail eagle into flight and the parade of colours and action through my lens made me gasp.

When only three fingers separated the sun from the sea, it told us to hurry, or we'd be spending the night surrounded by noisy penguins. Heading home through the low slopes of brush, every step brought new hope of stumbling across Charles. Over and over, I imagined how I'd react to finding a direct link to *The Investigator*, while in my head ran the constant chant of, "I've found it!"

What would I see first? A headstone? Probably not. More likely a neat pile of stones. The island had had two hundred years of growth. Those nearby trees were not here then. And Charles could be at rest under them or be under any of the thicker growth.

Finding the boatswain became hot, sticky work, hopeful, then disappointing. A metal stake set my heart racing. It led to another by some trees, and the words of discovery were ready to fly from my lips. But all I found were half-buried plastic bins, being used for some sort of scientific experiment similar to those we'd seen on other islands. Catching rats, I suppose.

Exhausted, sweaty, thinking of a shower and a cold beer, totally spent from our day's excitement surrounded by Nature's beauty, we began talking of rowing home. Finding Charles may not have been meant to be. Rest in peace Charles Douglas.

Now I must add a humorous footnote to this adventure because when we emerged from our communications vacuum at Middle Island, after arriving at Cape Le Grand, 25 km before Esperance, and able to connect to the worldwide net, we did a search for Charles Douglas.

He wasn't easy to find. But we finally found that he had died of dysentery on board *The Investigator* as they approached Middle Island, and Flinders had named the island nearest them in his honour. When leaving Middle Island, we had sailed past Douglas Island wondering if it had been named to honour the boatswain. But his final resting place? Aaah! Our guidebook had it wrong! It was May 1803, the winter seas were big, and Flinders' crew were sick and weak. Even the captain couldn't land on Goose Island, so Charles was interned behind the third bay on Middle Island! And you'll be amused to read that we had parked right by him the day after searching Goose. And had walked within cooee of his grave during our jaunt up Flinders Peak on Australia Day. Oh well, it had been a marvellous wild goose chase!

~ Chapter 21 ~

Feeling True Blue

GROWING UP IN LOS ANGELES IN THE 50s, the most anticipated of all holidays, except perhaps Christmas, was the 4th of July, celebrating the day in 1776 when the American colony declared independence from the Kingdom of Great Britain. Commonly associated with parades, carnivals, picnics, baseball games, political speeches, and fireworks, and coming just a few weeks after school broke up for summer, usually no one left on their holidays until after the 4th was celebrated. My family always organised a huge gala picnic with lots of family and friends. We almost always gathered in Griffith Park near the Observatory, spread blankets on the lawn, played heaps of baseball, consumed huge piles of BBQ chicken, potato salad, jello, and my favourite, a chocolate layer cake my mom made that sent me straight to heaven. It was always hot, and we kids could drink all the soda pop we wanted. Oh, my belly nearly always ached, ready to burst by the time we went home or to a relative's house to set off fireworks.

Every year, for weeks before the 4th, on vacant corner lots vans splashed with bursting stars sold a huge range of pyrotechnics. I can still see row upon row of Venus Volcano's stacked on the counter and imagined them erupting and shooting sparks. As well, spinning Piñatas shooting sliver streams round and round faster and faster till they went whoosh. And my favourite, Piccolo Pete's, a small tubular whistling firework that exploded as a finale. Dad was always our conductor, making us kids stand well back, and maybe occasionally handing one of the older ones the glowing punk used to light the fuses. The fireworks represent the battle for Independence, although we kids only really knew the excitement and noise.

But here in Australia, our history is quite different. Separate states developed from separate colonies, and each guarded its own sovereignty. Therefore, there really isn't any date Australia became independent as such. Australia's road to independence is more a journey of many steps. Having our own constitution in 1901 was the beginning of nationhood. Still, we weren't fully independent in 1931 when Britain passed the Statute of Westminster that established legislative equality between the dominions of the British Empire and the United Kingdom. A simple test is a fact that Australian Troops returned from WWII on British Passports. You certainly can't claim to be an independent country without having your own passports. The actual date Australia became an Independent Nation was 3rd March 1986 when all legal jurisdiction over Australia by the British Nation ceased.

With all these various dates, the most important has become 26 January, the date commemorating the arrival of the First Fleet at Sydney Cove in 1788. As you can imagine, it is not well-loved by Aboriginal Australians.

The tradition of celebrating 26 January began early in the nineteenth century with Sydney's almanac referring to First Landing Day or Foundation Day. Some immigrants who had prospered, especially those who had been convicts, began marking the colony's beginnings with an anniversary dinner, - "an emancipist festival" to celebrate their love of the land that had given them a new start.

Back then, Australia, as a nation was still forming. Van Diemens Land, occupied in 1803, became a separate colony in 1825. Three years later Britain claimed the western third of the continent to forestall French occupation, and settlers, not convicts, began arriving at Swan River in 1829. The settlement of South Australia followed in 1836. These colonies celebrated their own beginnings, rather than the Sydney celebration of prosperity. Therefore, the attitudes towards celebrating 26 January were mixed. South Australia's Advertiser took pains to point out that New South Wales, though 'senior', was not the parent colony of all the others.

Feeling True Blue

On 26 January 1988, when celebrating the bicentenary of the first fleet landing, Sydney Harbour was again the centre of attention. This time, the extraordinary spectacle attracted some two million people watching the arrival of Tall Ships from around the world and the First Fleet re-enactment. In preparation, in 1981, a forum put forward the theme, 'ONE NATION — ONE FUTURE', and speakers looked for ways Australians could find unity in diversity. As the composition of Australia's population had changed dramatically after the end of World War II, with fewer British people wanting to migrate and increasing numbers of immigrants coming from Europe and other parts of the world, for a country that had taken pride in being British and white, the change was remarkable. Between 1970 and 1990, the percentage of immigrants coming to Australia that were born in the British Isles dropped from 47.3% to 19.4%. At the same time, Aborigines were pressing ahead in their campaign for citizens' rights.

Being a laid-back society, Australians had not used the name, Australia Day, to mark that date until 1935, and it was not declared a national holiday until 1994. But, each year since then, pride in being an Australian has grown as our awareness of the wider world has grown, so that today, Australia Day is widely celebrated in a similar vein as the 4th of July.

Clearly, Flinders Peak beckoned us. After all, this was Australia Day, and the peak was shining delightfully in the sunlight. Bold granite faces of ochres and greys just begging to be explored like it had when Flinders and his men climbed to the top to gain a better view of this great archipelago. And what better thing to do on Australia Day than to climb Flinders Peak named for the very man who had first called this great continent Australia.

Just that morning we had shifted *Banyandah* into the bay closest to a starting point for our climb and had carefully positioned our anchor to be as close to the shore as we dared, to be out the easterly swell still crossing the bay.

During the previous night, when parked off Goose Island, we'd had northerly winds as forecast. Unprotected from that direction, it had caused a rolling sea until mid-morning. Nothing dangerous really, merely uncomfortable until late morning, when the wind changed to the east, and we moved here.

Preparing a daypack with water, first aid, and a little food, we launched *Little Red* then left *Banyandah* to fend for herself. We began our walk along the sandy shore to look for an easy way through the tangle of scrub. But being a cunning pair of old bushies, I straightaway lead Jude into the thick stuff, and we headed straight for the rising rock slope. Crikey, it was then that we were probably no more than a few steps from Boatswain Douglas, but we didn't know that. An hour's climb through moderately thick bush found the top. And while it could be tackled by anyone fit, on our return, we found a few white posts marking an easier route.

An open smooth granite dome provided spectacular vistas at every point of the compass. Sparkling blue lay dotted with a myriad of tiny islands in front of the Australian coastline brushed with white sand that nearly blinded us. Being a million miles from the rest of the world, it was easy to become Matthew Flinders, spyglass in hand, scanning the magical islands, and drawing a map with carefully noted bearings and distances.

Below us, *Banyandah* danced quietly on the little arrows of swell, while up another two fingers, Lake Hillier shone as if a crimson plum split in half on a bed of leaves.

"Look there," I said, pointing across a light blue sky stippled with pearly wisps of mare's tails. Following my gaze to the far side of the island, unseen until then, Jude reacted by uttering a surprised gasp.

"Oh gee, that's a deep crack. Bet that's the pirate's den."

"Yeah. Quite a hideout, hey?"

Big in stature, violent in character, Black Jack Anderson had been a whaler on the *Vigilant* from Massachusetts when it arrived in King George Sound in 1826, at the settlement now called Albany. King George Sound was only a trading post then, with a general store acting as purveyor, liquor outlet, and community centre rolled into one.

The *Vigilant's* battered crew found themselves drinking at the store with another ship's crew that night. A fight broke out, and one sailor was killed, the volatile Black Jack blamed, though there is no concrete proof it was him.

Perhaps his next actions were more of an indictment – he stole a small whale chaser and fled with several other crewmen, heading for the dangerous Recherché Archipelago.

The group drifted through the islands living off seals, before making their base at Middle Island where there was soil, vegetation and, most importantly, fresh water. Sealing and raiding passing supply ships, they lived there for 10 years and did very well for themselves. Sealskins were sold for six shillings a skin on the spot. There was also a romance with a captivating, as opposed to a captive, Dorothy Newell, his English mistress. Dorothy, her brother Jimmy, her sister Mary, and Mary's husband, Matthew Gill were among nine people shipwrecked at Thistle Cove near Cape Le Grand. Afterwards, they sailed a lifeboat to Middle Island, presumably for food and shelter. Black Jack Anderson met his fate in that same manner of his life, in a fight, a bullet hole blown in his head. The legend states his chest of treasure was never discovered.

Overhead, our world changed. The cirrus clouds thickened into cirrocumulus, and on the water, a sea fret started to form. We discovered our mobile phone had found a connection, and with great excitement, Judith called her children, hearing their voices and telling them we were safe. In our lifestyle, contacts with family can be far between. The last they had heard, two weeks earlier, *Banyandah* was sailing away from the previous island before the Great Australian Bight. While Jude danced with joy around the rock cairn on Flinders Peak, hearing her grandchildren one at a time tell their adventures, I listened to their conversation and watched our world turn on the magic. Where azure sea had flowed to the far arc of Earth, it became spooky mist with just the tips of islands poking through, giving the impression of mermaids floating on their backs with just the delicious curves of their bodies and beautiful breasts poking through.

Despite first appearances, the Recherché Archipelago has suffered from the impact of man in the last 200 years. Sealers, whalers, fishermen, and hunters have taken their toll. Though water has always been hard to find, the seeming abundance of Nature has diminished on these islands. Two hundred years ago, it was believed that the supply from Nature would never run out. Today current estimates are that there are no more than 1000 of the South Western Cape Barren Geese alive today, making them one of the rarest geese in the world. Tuna are listed as threatened, and with the advent of rabbits, there will soon be little vegetation. Then all the little critters will perish. Are Jude and I just old fuddy-duddies wanting Earth to remain intact, wanting Nature to prosper as humanity has? Or is it Earth's fate to have her majesty and beautiful wild kingdom erased forever.

~ Chapter 22 ~

Pirates at Esperance

A FEW WEEKS LATER, *BANYANDAH* ARRIVED IN ESPERANCE and with the help of the local newspaper and generosity of the Esperance Bay Yacht Club, we staged one of our free film nights.

Taking over the main dining room on the night, Jude and I were pleasantly surprised by an amazing Sunday night turnout of about a hundred. In row upon row, people covered the entire age spectrum. One of the first to arrive were two old dears, each hobbling along with the help of walking sticks, they took pride of place in the first row of chairs. A few minutes later, an elderly gentleman arrived, mentioning when we greeted him that he was 86, and rarely went out at night anymore. As the crowd grew, several families came in, including a few with young children. And by the time we started, the room was full of eager faces, who all turned to listen to the club's commodore introduce us.

I took the floor and spoke briefly about our ship, how she came to be named *Banyandah* and gave a few facts of our sailing life. Then I said, "Sit back and enjoy your journey around Australia by sail." And I punched the play button on the handheld remote.

We always hold a question and answer period after its showing, giving the audience a chance to learn more, and if they're enthusiastic, I spin a story or two.

Pirates? Had we ever been attacked by pirates, the wrinkled lady who had to be at least eighty asked, and the room that had held many side conversations suddenly fell silent.

Standing before our hundred guests, I ran my eyes over the crowd thinking of the time the Vietnamese had shelled us in the South China Sea. The old guy up front would remember those troubled years, but the young lad next to him wouldn't understand that that had been more a military decision.

A vision of big Black Jack Anderson popped into my head, and I remembered how his on and off life of crime had been forced upon him by circumstances, and that train of thought took me straight to Africa. A knowing smile briefly touched my lips then I looked to the wizened lady at the front. Her eyes looking like runny eggs bore straight into mine with great interest.

"I remember an encounter taking place far away near the Horn of Africa, near the pirate hot spot of Socotra, just off the shores of Somalia."

Everyone there knew about the pirates of Somalia, and several sucked in their breath, while others turned to comment to their neighbour.

"This pirate encounter took place when our sons were just entering puberty." And I pointed to the lad near the front and said, "About your age."

The lad looked both ways with embarrassment, and I asked if he might be about twelve. He nodded and so I said to the audience, "Our sons were just twelve and thirteen when we decided to sail for Africa and go on safari. Once there, we hired a Suzuki 4WD, one of those tiny ones that we crammed full with camping stuff. And then we went driving about East Africa's game parks. Jason and Jerome saw more wildlife in that month than they had in all their lives.

"From Africa, *Banyandah* sailed the thousand miles out to the Seychelles Islands for a tropical holiday, and while there, we decided not to sail home as planned. Instead, continue on to Egypt and Europe as the boys were studying ancient histories, thinking what better way to learn than to witness and touch. That meant travelling the infamous Red Sea."

For a moment, memories of an earlier delivery voyage up that wind-blasted sunken valley reminded me of how hard a journey sailing up the

Red Sea is, and how dangerous. It also brought back visions of the doldrums and the many miles of windless ocean.

"I remember pulling our boat up to the fuelling dock on our last day in Port Victoria, capital of Seychelles, and having this swarthy, arrogant so and so demand a hundred dollars just to tie up.

"'But I'm going to buy fuel and oil,' I protested.

"When he smirked then shook his head, three gold teeth twinkled in the sunlight. 'A hundred U.S. dollars,' he repeated.

"Raising a family afloat is quite a bit harder than on land. Work opportunities are few and far apart. Therefore watching our cash flow was paramount. Besides, I always hated being taken for a ride, so I ranted and raved trying to persuade the man, but in the end, he only looked away with disdain. And that broke my dam.

"'You're an asshole!' I shouted, and then chucked my lines free before motoring off towards the vacant north horizon."

In my head, I could see Jude's concern at the time and could hear my sons verbally agreeing with me.

"None of that mattered after we'd raised our sails, flying away at great speed while feeling smug that we hadn't given that pirate any of our hard earned cash."

Just then, a vision a flat pancake sea invaded my head – windless and silent.

"When we hit the belt of doldrums that circle the Earth near the equator, we lost all wind, and without fuel or oil, we began to drift just like olden day sailors. In our previous travels, we had already crossed this windless belt between the two trade wind systems several times and knew it might take days. And so when our home on the water became quite still, school proceeded daily and we waited. Jas and Jerome got stuck into that year's first term with teacher Jude cracking the whip and sharing the educational fun."

Jude then piped in. "It was great, I got to learn all that I missed."

"And she did a wonderful job. I wish I had her patience. So we drifted, and anytime a skerrick of breeze happened our way, we worked the sails."

The room had gone deathly silent like that ocean. Drinks remained untouched on the bar, and at the back, the sandy hair commodore gave me a nod.

"For nearly a week we crept northwards, mostly taken that way by currents. Then one morning I'll never forget, a wind squall attacked." I said this looking into two hundred eyes but saw only the wild ones of my youngest son when he slammed open the aft cabin doors.

"Jude and I were still in bed when this monster wind slapped us down, catapulting our mainsail across the ship.

"Our son's frightened eyes had snapped us wide-awake, but his first words made us dash topsides. 'Dad, the rigging's just broke. The mast is about to fall down!'"

The silence in the room silence erupted in gasps, and oh my gods as each pair of eyes seemed to ask, what'd you do?

"We were five hundred miles off the coast of Africa, a thousand yet to Aden and five hundred miles back through the doldrums to Seychelles. We were in quite a pickle. Life had not only taught us survival, it had also taught us resourcefulness. The rest of that day I spent aloft rigging ropes, while down on deck our two sons secured them to steady our mast."

I must have looked pleased with myself remembering the spaghetti of lines because one old salt at the bar called out, "That must have slowed you to a walk." And the audience laughed relieving the tension.

Bobbing my head, I agreed. "We didn't break any speed records after that, like a cripple hobbling along a cliff edge. But I'd better get on about my pirates because they're still coming."

"Did they catch you when you were crippled," a lady called from the back. And a few around her said, "Bastards."

"No, no, we actually sailed right into their lair. Going so slow, our bottom became really thick with gooseneck barnacles. They loved the warm sea slowly drifting past and were loving each other too, making a thick carpet of babies on our hull. *Banyandah* went slower and slower."

A vision popped into my head of their many thousands fornicating, with their feather-like organs touching all the others around them and I remembered how shocked and helpless I'd felt after diving in for a look under our boat.

"We needed somewhere to dry out and scrape off, or we'd starve to skeletons before reaching help. Searching our charts, ahead lay a few islands off the Horn of Africa called Socotra. But our pilot book warned of them being historically used by pirates. Aye, but we were desperate, and I was so naïve, I believed as I still do, that no one would harm children. After all, kids bond all the world's people.

"We used our last fuel to make a beeline for the last island in the group, Abd al Kuri. It lay a mere fifty miles off the Somalia coast. And when it popped up, we got a huge surprise."

Chairs scraped as some of my listeners sat more upright while I paused to bring back the vision, and with it came the fear we had felt.

"The eeriest sight, it was like an asteroid with jagged pinnacles sticking straight up like millions of daggers. Not a blade of grass. Nor a green leaf. No vegetation. Just grey rock, as if shouting a warning to stay away.

"I had our double-barrel shotgun loaded and ready as we rounded the far western tip, Jude nervously pacing up and down, looking all around. And the boys, young as they were, were holding back their excitement, calling out things like 'spooky' and 'aargh' when they playacted a sword fight.

"Well, the bay was empty. Just a quiet black sand beach. And immensely relieved, we dropped anchor and got busy. All of us put on facemasks and jumped in with scrapers. And in a few hours, we'd mowed off nearly all the barnacles down a few feet. The ones nearer the bottom of our six-foot deep keel would take another attack.

"Towelling off and shovelling food into our mouths, I think we all froze when engine noise was detected. All our eyes followed it down to the point, and we collected together by the aft rail as three low timber vessels came into view and turned our way.

"We were alone. One man, his lady, and two kids a million miles from authority. Easy to hide four bodies out there, simply feed the sharks.

"These three boats made a beeline straight for us and without a 'may we' or even a 'hello' the first one came alongside and four scruffy, tattered blokes started mounting our railing."

"What'd you do?" The old dear squealed, and I hoped she was not about to have a seizure while my mind's eye was reliving the moment every sailor, every family man fears most.

"I started pushing them back, yelling 'No! No, stay on your boat.' And Jude did the same, and so did the kids. But they kept trying to board, and every time one got a leg over, we'd push it back and yell, 'No.'

"It was scary, but you know, I think the fear was kept in check. Until the other two boats tied alongside the first, and then there were twelve blokes.

"Oh, gosh, they were so poor. The tatters they wore barely hung from their shoulders. But, no AK47's. No rocket grenades. And more to the point, no knives flashed between their teeth. And in time, we got them to stop trying to board us."

I scratched my beard, rubbed my face, looked to Jude, and she seemed to say, "Were we lucky or what?"

"They were all jabbering in their own lingo, gesticulating, and such. Then one grabbed my arm and motioned for me to come aboard his craft.

"You can imagine my thoughts. Get me out the way, and my family would be easy pickings. But though his teeth were broken and discoloured, his eyes were pleading with me. So I motioned if they let go of my boat, I'd tie them aft, and come on board. Jason ran for a long line, and I turned to Judith, 'Get the kids below and take the gun.'

"Their craft had no wheelhouse, only tarps stretched across a curved deck, and they lead me aft to a sunken cockpit then beckoned me down a short set of steps. Below, I can't recall a more pungent smell of ammonia, but as I stepped off the last rung and onto their cargo covered in burlap, it gave a little. You know, firm but squashy.

"Leading me around the ladder, I saw a small diesel engine, and the fella pointed to some piping and playacted lighting a welding torch.

"You've got to understand, a minute earlier, I'd been Errol Flynn battling to save my loved ones, so none of this made much sense. Until, in a jumble of strange words, another fisherman cum pirate jumped forward and cranked the engine. As soon as it burst into life, a big jet of water came squirting out that pipe where it joined the engine.

"Aha! I remember saying when I clapped the skipper's shoulder. Ugh, it was greasy and stank. Then I shook my head as I pointed to my boat and replayed the act of lighting a torch. And I was wondering whether that would be the moment they would slit my throat, kill my family, and steal my boat.

"They were collected together on top of their cargo, and I remember wondering if I should make a break and escape. But I really wanted to help. And that's when I remembered some high-temperature epoxy I had stashed away.

"Oi, I called motioning them over. Then using hand signs, I tried explaining my idea and pointing to my boat, indicated they should stay put.

"Of course Jude wanted to know what had happened, and while rummaging under our bed, I explained that they were shark fishermen with a broken engine pipe and that I was going to attempt fixing it with our epoxy."

I love telling stories of our early life. I get a buzz reliving the experience, and by the intense chatter going on, these folk were enjoying it too. So I started wrapping it up by telling them that the fishermen removed the manifold, and then from my bag of magic, I fixed it. Next day, after it had cured, I had the satisfaction of seeing the engine run without it leaking. The tattered grimy owner embraced me and kissed both my cheeks while his crew clapped me on the back. Boy! Did I feel great.

We spent nearly a week with them in that bay. Being an almost full moon, the tides were growing bigger, so the next day they drove their boats up on that black sand beach, propped them and cleaned their bottoms as the tide fell. We did the same with *Banyandah*. Side by side the new with the old world, we worked on our crafts, exchanging many hours of looking at the other and trying to communicate.

When I took out my half-empty tin of anti-fouling paint, they started a fire and chucked in lots of coral, burning it down to form lime. While at the same time, they boiled up a few sharks to mix with the lime to make a white paste. This they said, kept their ships barnacle free.

Every morning after their schooling, our sons would row to their camp with bread Jude had just made, and then the boys would watch the men use their sharp knives flensing the jaws out the sharks. As the pile grew taller than our sons, they hunted out a supreme collection of jaws and teeth.

After the Esperance group had given us a loud round of applause, I silenced them with a cute bow followed by raising my hand. I then spoke from my heart about these troubled times and the distrust rampant around the world.

Where Wild Winds Blow

No matter where in the world we have travelled, we've found people are much the same. They want a future for their children, and a bit of space to pursue their own lives. And thinking of those poor fishermen who are now the most active pirates in the world, most folks condemn them as brutal beasts without really knowing the facts.

Starting about the time we were there in 1985, years of drought brought increased hardship to their country, and in 1991, the government collapsed in that poor African Nation. Two parties stepped into the vacuum and fought for supremacy. While they did, certain large corporation's took advantage of this. European ships started appearing off the coast of Somalia, dumping thousands of barrels of toxic waste into the ocean. The coastal population began to get sick. At first, they suffered strange rashes, nausea and malformed babies and many other symptoms. But lacking proper medical attention, most of this was overlooked. Then, after the 2005 tsunami, hundreds of the dumped and leaking barrels washed up on their shores. People began to suffer from radiation sickness, and more than 300 died.

Thousands of Somalis once made their living as fishermen. But Somalia has been without a central government for nearly two decades, so there's no active body able to effectively protect the country's coastline, and the once-abundant supply of fish it held. And due to the willingness of foreigners to exploit fisheries off Somalia's coast, many of these fishermen, probably including the twelve we knew, are finding their nets empty. And without the ability to bring home even a sufficient amount of fish to eat, many of these fishermen justifiably grew desperate. Initially, many of the now-termed "pirates" were vigilante patrols, steering their boats to foreign fishing vessels found illegally snagging their seafood or dumping toxic waste in Somali waters, and they demanded they pay a tax. After this proved ineffective, something closer to organized piracy developed.

~ Chapter 23 ~

Wild Stopover at Investigator

ALL THE TIME IN ESPERANCE WE HAD BEEN HOPING we'd be able to stop at those twin exposed rocks in the Great Southern Ocean called the Investigator Islands. Originally called Rocky Isles when first spied by Matthew Flinders in 1802, then later renamed to honour Flinders' ship, they are no more than two gigantic granite boulders rising out a tempestuous sea. This rarely visited outpost for Nature invited our investigation, and we planned to anchor there overnight if conditions allowed. Lying fifty-five miles west of Esperance and fifteen miles from the mainland, when first seen ten miles ahead, Judith and I were in seventh heaven. A full main and headsail poled out were both filled by an easy caressing breeze, our first since leaving Adelaide eight weeks earlier. Occasionally gazing at the approaching humps gaining colour and taking shape, I was aft cleaning a recently caught two-meal tuna. At the same time, Jude nattered in my ear about hoping the swell wouldn't affect the bay trapped between the islands.

The Investigator Islands are the furthest west in the Recherché Archipelago; in an area poorly surveyed, so ships avoid them and few if any small vessels stop. Therefore, using the chart as an indicator only, we sailed into a bay surrounded by rising granite massifs, skirting the shallow patch off its head before proceeding with great caution expecting the bottom to rise abruptly. Looking about, there were no sandy beaches, just steep bare rock all around, so it wasn't surprising that we had to sink our anchor down into great depth thinking it was most probably rock.

Once settled, on our next look about, sea lions littered the polished rocks slopes. Too late to row around, we didn't mind, in half an hour, the sun would be melting gold behind black rocks, and there was plenty to see from the comfort of our floating home. A group of what looked to be NZ fur seals were cavorting about in the rocky gap between the two islands, dark shapes starkly contrasted against the white breaking Southern Ocean swells foaming up and over from the far side of the gap. Through binoculars, their dripping wet coats reflected the orange glow of the setting sun, through which seabirds were already flying home.

The whole world around us was wild, stark, menacing, and cold. While downstairs was warm and cosy, above decks lay Earth's beauty. The setting sun set afire the carpet of orange vegetation, a backdrop to dark creatures lugging slug-like bodies up the slopes, or their heads posturing aloof. Forked tailed terns, bright against scudding cloud, darted about, their eyes striped black – inquisitive or hanging perilously aloft on fragile wings right above our ship – on their way home to roost and maybe looking for the last fish of the day. Life was in abundance – or was it?

For an outpost of Nature, our experience said there should be more. Memories of dark clouds that became masses of seabirds were replaced here by visions of a dotted presence. And sea lions for as far as the eye could see, substituted with peppercorns scattered here and there. Who took away God's creatures? Or did mankind take their food?

The Australian Sea Lion is an endangered marine mammal found only in Australian waters. Today it's estimated only 10,000 remain in the wild.

Australian Sea Lions are threatened because their populations were decimated by hunting in the 1800s and their population has never recovered, and now there are concerning signs of decline again. Entanglement in fishing equipment, particularly shark gill nets, is a major concern. According to the Environment Department, the reported annual kill rate is at least 1.3% of the population, the third-highest for any pinniped (seals, sea lions, walruses) in the world.

Overnight we were gently rocked to sleep, then awakened and kept alert by intensified gusts of wind through the gap between the islands.

Drifting back into slumber, we were awoken this time by the yelps of seal pups demanding a feed.

Over our radio, the forecast came for light winds to increase after noon. Sunny patches had already begun peeking through morning cloud, so we quickly launched *Little Red* and rowed around for a look. Anticipating a landing, shore-going gear was packed, but two attempts had to be aborted. Much of the twin islands emerge from the sea in large surf polished ramps covered in treacherous black slime. Once, I got both feet out the dinghy standing on a slippery slope but didn't dare let go else I would have slid into the briny. Jude back rowed furiously to keep from being sucked away, and I had no choice, but to step back in smartly. Immediately after, a swell swept the dinghy away. Lucky me, dry inside.

But we did get ashore. I had spotted a nick behind a large rock within the gap between the two islands and chanced rowing us over submerged boulders on top of a surge. As luck would have it, we came nicely into a perfect harbour no bigger than *Little Red*. Over its transom, we scrambled onto a dry, flat rock about a foot above the water, and then hauled *Little Red* up after us.

First look around got our bearings, noting what was close at hand. Two bulls not far away were giving each other a hard time, their land-lumbering bodies looking as if they could easily cause real damage.

Watching them bully one another, Jude nodded when I said, "Keep a keen eye out for them. Not good to be caught by surprise."

And as we began our sortie, taking our first steps with some trepidation, she checked behind every rock before we walked past.

Three or four sea lions, one with several scars, were curious and we thought territorial enough to charge, so we backed away to give them their space. And when we came upon one mum taking time off to bathe in an elevated pool, we surprised her pup unintentionally. Poor thing kept screaming a frightful yelp from a ledge some way from her. Both looked very healthy, and we hoped they'd stay that way.

That is something that plays on our minds, this going ashore on isolated islands rarely stepped upon. Apart from sitting atop the island's summit to watch Bridled Terns soaring about, we touched little and did nothing that could interfere with the islands' integrity.

By sitting still, we soon found the terns landing beside us unperturbed, to shelter in the overhang. How great to see them just a few feet away or when on the wind, floating like gliders at eye-level in front of us. Down nearer sea level, a moderate flock of Crested-Terns with their distinctive scruffy black crest and pale yellow bill preferred to rest on the smooth granite. And in the far distance, a pair of sea eagles soared above the island on the upswept wind. As we watched, one swooped and caught a tern in flight. Flying away, its prey facing forward, a talon clutching each wing, really, it looked just like a bi-plane.

Below the islands' beige granite tops, in shelters protected from the worst weather grew a thick mat of succulents, their fleshy leaves like bunches of green grapes though some were orange to bright yellow. They were heavily interspersed with delicate purple flowers. These islands have little other vegetation.

Wild Stopover at Investigator

From our high viewpoint, we watched an old bull, perhaps an outcast, take up residence slightly downhill from where we sat, while across the bay a smaller female lumbered up that island's slope then along the ridge. When back aboard just before dusk we thought it was her scanning the far horizon from the top.

So lovely and unique, filled with the majesty of Nature, we'd spent the full day observing the other creatures live life, which confirmed yet again that they do pretty much the same as us. Care for their young, find food, and investigate life. What joy that brought. We are one, the wild ones and us. Each wanting the same, a future for our children, and the time to enjoy this magical creation we call Earth.

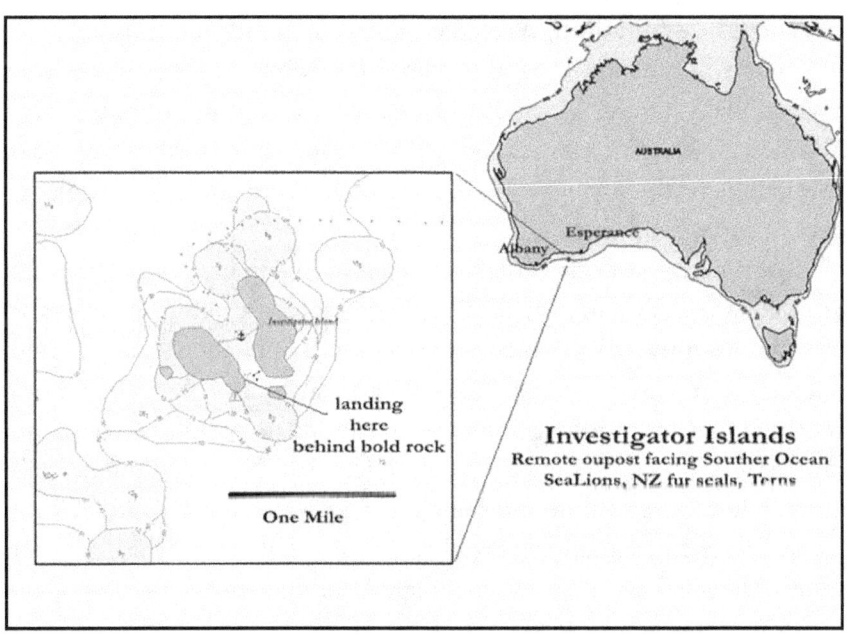

landing here behind bold rock

One Mile

Investigator Islands
Remote oupost facing Souther Ocean
SeaLions, NZ fur seals, Terns

~ Chapter 24 ~

Too Many Choices

WE LEFT INVESTIGATOR ISLAND OUR MINDS ILL AT EASE. After following our dream for so long, suffering hardships and savouring experiences new to us, we realised that reaching Albany would be the last point for an early return to loved ones. And suddenly we found our future in question and had to pause and consider all our options. Which way should we go? North, West, East, it became a difficult decision.

To go home north via the wondrous Kimberley was filled with navigational hurdles including fast currents and turbid water. Additionally, there are crocodiles all along the north that make swimming death-defying. And then after Darwin, we would probably have to battle headwinds.

Continuing west across the great span of Indian Ocean to Africa had been our main aim, to visit relatives in Madagascar before returning to Australia via tiny St Paul in the roaring forties. On many a black night, watching our sails arc across the heavens, we often dreamt of making another long ocean passage to explore exotic lands. But, in going that route, there would be no easy communications: No video phone calls, no mobile coverage, little internet. We'd be isolated even further from family and friends, and for more than a year. That would not have been so terrible years ago when a single-family before we acquired so many devilishly cute grandchildren.

Upon reaching Albany, a third choice came up. We could turn around and sail back east. Return to Tasmania, back to that beautiful island filled with unspoilt Nature. Jude and I, when cuddled in bed-sharing visions of our future, often discuss basing our floating home in the Apple Isle. We'd spend winters at home with our family, summers cruising Tasmania's many bays and rivers, and have the added closeness of New Zealand enticing us to sail across 'the ditch' for a summer cruise. Then there's the possibility of a journey north running with the trades to New Caledonia. What a treat to trade-wind sail once again!

Making this decision caused many sleepless nights in Albany, because once around Cape Leeuwin and into the predominantly southerly winds, it'd be much harder to turn back. Therefore, a decision in Albany seemed mandatory.

Since leaving Adelaide nine weeks earlier, 1500 miles had roared under our keel. That's more than halfway across the huge Australian continent and reminiscent of years ago when we used to clock up seven to ten thousand miles every year. Whether caused by global warming or cyclic change, this summer's weather had been rather ordinary, either very windy or wet or both. We'd had very few balmy days, where a swim in crystal clear waters would have been idyllic. Quite the contrary, in fact. Blustery winds had made our anchorages uncomfortable, forcing Jude and me to constantly ensure we were not dragging our anchor. Nevertheless, we'd had several great outings, climbed many beautiful granite massifs and wandered lovely heaths. But relaxing? Not exactly.

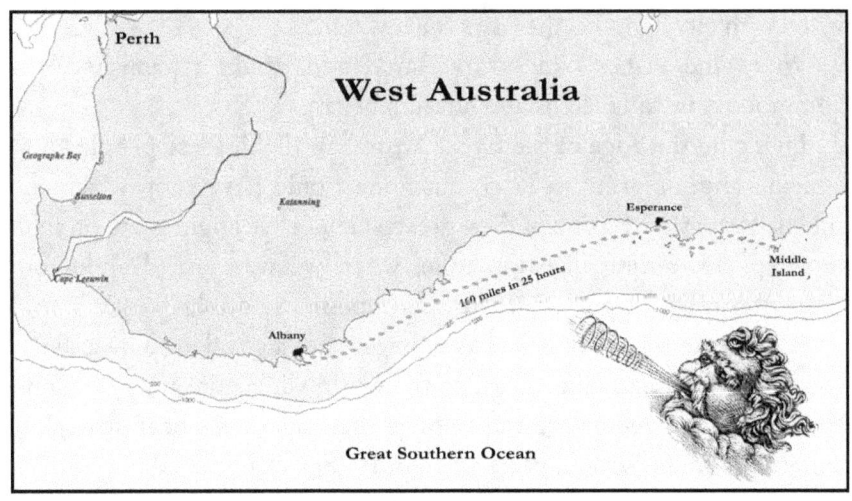

In Albany, we planned two shows, the first at the Princess Royal Sailing Club. We were getting quite a kick out of sharing our experiences with so many interested folks, and these two shows plus a couple of excursions into the southwest forests kept us entertained during our month-long visit.

The second European to visit this area was George Vancouver, who entered King George Sound in 1791. The first, Pieter Nuyts was there in 1627. During the two weeks Vancouver spent here, he named several islands and points and took possession of the area at Point Possession.

> This port, the first which we had discovered, I honoured with the name of King George the Third's Sound, and this day being the anniversary of Her Royal Highness Princess Charlotte Augusta Matilda's birth, the harbour behind Point Possession I called Princess Royal Harbour.

Albany is actually blessed with two landlocked harbours in addition to the open roadstead Vancouver had named after King George. The second is accessible only to small vessels through a narrow sandy channel, and Captain Vancouver called it Oyster Harbour because of the number of oysters he found. Not surprisingly, there are no wild oysters there today.

The main shipping facilities are located adjacent to the city in Princess Royal Harbour. On its southern shore, The Princess Royal Sailing Club, established 1909, serves meals in a large room with several picture windows looking across the majestic harbour to the city flowing up and over the hills. On our film night, the room was noisy with members and guests enjoying a meal while the setting sun's orange glow mixed with city lights on the bay's silver waters.

When the dishes had been cleared and drinks replenished, the Commodore introduced us and our film began.

Living on the edge of the Great Australian Bight, these people knew a fair bit about stormy weather, but none would have known Jack and Jude had experienced one of their greatest challenges right there on their doorstep. So, during question time, when we were asked about our greatest storm, Jude picked up the microphone and off she went.

"Well, you might not know," she began, her face taking a deep flush, "that during our early life we sailed the world while educating our sons. And earning our keep was always a huge challenge. We'd been struggling hand to mouth for several years when in 1978, Jack began talking with an

Australian on our amateur radio. To cut to the point, Harry, who was in Sydney, quickly became aware of our financial situation because we'd already told him we were on our way to Europe to find work. And out the blue, he offered to charter our yacht. He was organizing an Amateur Radio DXpedition and needed a boat to take his team of four, seven hundred miles out into the Coral Sea."

Jude then took a minute to explain a DXpedition, that the amateurs have awards for the number of countries they contact, and that the rarest 'countries' are just mid-ocean specks of land, and that the only way to contact them is when someone takes radio equipment out there. DX means long distant communications, and DXpedition is their word for one of these operations, which are usually funded by donations.

Jude's not the greatest orator, but she can get animated, and painted the picture pacing up and down, hands flying out. Stopping abruptly, she shot me a glance and then gave a girly grin extracting a little wink from me, which made her flush even more deeply. My eyes urged her to get on with it, so she suddenly snapped forward, and when she saw over a hundred faces watching her, she sucked in a deep breath.

"Well, aha, it seems we had taken on a mammoth task because we were then in Sri Lanka. But we needed the money badly, so turned around to meet Harry in Sydney in time to take his crew into the Coral Sea before the next cyclone season started. That gave us three months to sail six thousand miles of ocean.

"Sri Lanka to Fremantle took thirty-eight days and chopped nearly four thousand miles out the distance. And it was a great sail - until our landfall late in July when we ran into a humdinger of a westerly gale. Closing the WA coast not long after dark, we'd seen a plane taking off almost dead ahead. Then at midnight, from the hot tropics to a cold, windy night, we were off the winking light on Rottnest. Most of you will know Freo's coast is quite low, and without today's satellite navigation, only Jack's spot-on navigation found the light.

"Well, that gale grew so severe it was the first time, and only time, we laid ahull. To tell the truth, to have the boat pressed hard over by such a strong force, with whitewater crashing over us, well, I know I was frightened. You couldn't sleep shut up like a drum. And all night, all I could think about was the boat's drift towards shore. How far were we making and how fast? Without a GPS, how could we know?

"Next day, when weak light showed sickly green water streaked white, we were basically lost. Clouds of misty spume hid a horrendous lee shore. Having to do something, we unlashed the helm and bore away under bare poles."

Here she stopped and shook her head. "Pity those first Dutch sailors running unawares towards spume and combers on a dark night. At least we'd seen a light.

"Luck was on our side that morning. We were on the verge of panic when the yellow fairway buoy whooshed out the backside of a wave, and with a scrap of sail, we hightailed into what was then the fishing boat harbour. We rode right through the gap on a big breaker. It would have been exhilarating had I not been so damn scared and concentrating on Jacks' directions."

The audience hardly moved, looking expectantly at Jude as she paced up and down, her eyes blazing with excitement. Looking up as if hearing a wall of whitewater about to strike, she grimaced, her eyes steeled then she went on.

"Umm. Well. With the wind onshore, and us not quite in control, once in sheltered water, we dropped the pick straight off the bat and fortunately swung around to face the wind. The boys were still below in life jackets when Jack and I looked out to huge breakers coming right over the wall, and we thanked our lucky stars. The boys then quickly found a yellow satin pillowcase to use as a quarantine flag, replacing the one lost in Galle and pressed it into service up the mast on a halyard. And quick as a wink, a voice yelled out, 'You want Customs?' And Jack raised his arms in the affirmative.

"An hour later, Jason's shout got us on deck to watch a car pull up. Six strapping boys in light blue uniforms piled out, and one waved for us to come alongside the empty wharf.

"The sudden appearance of those big bristling officials talking in loud voices and jumping aboard had a sudden, unexpected effect on us. We'd been at sea so long Jack could hardly speak. The boys and I didn't have to. We'd snuck forward. Jason, on his bunk, tried to read a book. But all the while we could hear Jack dealing with official questions. 'Galle? Where's that?' And when they still didn't catch on, Jack's astonished reply, 'Galle! It's the southern port of what used to be called Ceylon. You know, next to India.' I remember hearing his frustrated voice and looking around the bulkhead to see him pointing off in Galle's general direction. I think right then we all felt invaded and craved solitude again."

Jude looked to the ceiling as if remembering that morning and then she smiled and shook her head. Fastening her gaze onto mine, we both grinned like idiots.

"It got a bit overwhelming when the six packed down below with the four of us. Jack began shuffling papers and answering questions, so I made a big pot of tea. Most had a cup. Not surprising considering how cold it was. Our de-briefing then warmed up. They laughed when I told them about the previous night's disastrous landfall dinner. Then Jason rushed in telling everyone about catching his first big fish. The minute he was through, Jerome startled everyone with his report that he'd fallen overboard.

"Comments flew with that. And the customs chap wearing a gold wedding ring asked if he'd been scared. I'll not forget the adorable look Jerome had given his dad when he said, 'I almost was.' You see, Jerome would have cried had his father not gotten him to take control of his fear."

A buzz ignited the room, and everyone looked straight at me, so I jumped to explain.

"It is life or death on a small boat at sea. Disasters happen instantly and what saves lives is clear thinking. Panic freezes the mind. The boys had a wonderful childhood, loads of fun, and many adventures. But they also had to learn about the danger and taking control." I was enjoying hearing Jude tell the story and turning, gave her a nod to continue.

"Umm. Well, when Customs mentioned we could lie alongside over by Cicerello's Fish Shop, it was welcome news because the heavy surge had already bumped us hard against the dock a few times.

"Once secure, we felt better. But you know while cleaning up, we heard our names on the radio, reported as recently arrived with the storm. And right after, we heard that a one hundred and fifty-foot Japanese longliner was in danger of sinking, having turned turtle in huge seas off Cape Leeuwin. Imagine our shock! I'd never given it much thought in Sri Lanka, but realized right then that we were in with the really big stuff and knew we'd better be prepared."

Jude threw her head back with a chuckle. "Next day I gave the boys ten dollars to spend on warm clothes at the OP shop saying, get prepared boys. And those two little lads, they were just a month off seven and eight, did a really great job of kitting themselves out."

My lovely partner then stepped back to take a breather and looking over the room I reckon she knew the news about the Japanese longliner had dampened their elation of our safely crossing the Indian Ocean. They knew Fremantle was just our halfway point.

I took the microphone and started telling how we had a week in Fremantle, where it stormed and rained every day. How Jude had the cockpit overflowing with sails under repair while I built storm-boards to block our companionways, cutting thick plywood blanks to seal half the height of the door opening. Our panel doors, two in each passageway, were by no means waterproof, and if we got doused, we'd take plenty of water through them. And if the cockpit filled, we'd take heaps. When completed, the permanently attached storm-boards sealed the doorways higher than the cockpit seats. A bit hard to get in and out, but eminently wiser.

"Since the radio had also announced our intention to sail on to Sydney, we had a steady stream of visitors; fishermen and port officials dropping by to discourage us from going. We often heard 'Don't attempt The Bight in winter.'

"At the time we were both mid-thirties and didn't feel we were extraordinarily brave, or stupid. Just that we knew our boat and felt the 'B' could take whatever came. And so, with blind perseverance, we continued our preparations.

"A week of gales had made me well known to the local meteorological office as I called every day. And when on our way for a meal with friends we'd met on the ship coming to Australia in 1969, I suggested a stop at the Met Office.

"It's still clear in my head, us being ushered into an open plan office cluttered with desks, two teletypes and a full-size drawing board, and only two people working there. This tall, lanky fellow introduced himself as the forecaster I'd been speaking with on the phone. And without hesitation after ruffling the hair of my youngest son, said something like, 'Glad you came today. I was wondering why no phone call from you. Are you ready...? A break in the weather is on its way.'

"And I thought, Ah good, tomorrow. Then felt the usual tightening in my belly.

"Well, he led our little group over to the large prognostic chart on the drawing board and ran his finger over the prominent features. A big high was coming, followed by a low-pressure cell tightly compressing the isobars against the backside of the high. Pointing to an area off the coast that had widely spaced lines in concentric circles, he mentioned that the high was moving rapidly towards us, but that he expected it to slow once it hit the coast. Then he said, 'If you go straight away you'll have time to get around Cape Leeuwin before this low moves in.' And here he bounced his pencil against an area considerably darker, filled with many more black lines and continued, 'After the Cape, even if this low becomes a gale, you'll have the wind at your back.'

"That's what I loved about this meteorologist; he understood the workings of a sailboat. But straight away? Surely, that meant tomorrow at first light. 'No Jack,' he said, 'within thirty-six hours that low may be here and if it is you'll be clobbered by another bad westerly before you have a chance to turn the corner. You should go now while the wind is calming.'"

I guess a good storyteller reacts to his audience. Many parents were hanging onto our every word, so I tried to mimic our sons' reaction.

"Now?" I cried in a child's whinging voice. "Both boys and Jude had said it in unison as if wired together. Oh my! To see those three pairs of very disheartened eyes, uh oh, I felt really bad. But I was the captain." And here I shook my head. "I make the decisions, sometimes with a heavy heart. And so I said to them. 'Okay, guys. You heard the man. Cheer up. This will be our last big voyage. That's a promise. After this, we'll be in Sydney and no more sailing. Okay?'"

Several parents got a chuckle from my child-like whinge, and in their laughter, I heard my sons moaning that they had wanted to go over to Warren and Vicki's to play with their children and my answer that we were not going there, but back out into the briny.

If there's one thing raising a family afloat gave us, it was control over our children. We set boundaries, then lavished them with love. And we had great fun sharing life together 24/7. Both sons prospered by knowing just how far they could go. No meant no, it didn't mean maybe, lets debate. And physical punishment was hardly ever necessary once boundaries were established. And once they were, it allowed them even greater freedom because we knew they were responsible, and this, in turn, allowed the family to take on much more dangerous pursuits knowing the child would follow our orders.

I had wanted to tell these sailors and armchair adventurers every detail of our silently heading back on the train to the port, and how, within the hour, we had the engine ticking over and were untying the 'B', while overhead, the sky was mauve and pink, and breathless. But our story had a long way to run, so I quickly said that we had an easy motor out the same crack, and as there was no one there to wish us a safe journey, to fulfil our needs how we had heaped plenty of calls of 'so long' onto a slightly baffled rock fisherman.

Then I quickly described our uneventful motor under a hushed sky atop a sea that lifted and fell in giant size ripples while our barometer continued to rise until it peaked at 1031 mb early the next day. Steadily, under increasingly glassy conditions, we clicked off the miles towards Australia's most southwesterly point. Everyone in that room knew that Cape Leeuwin has the distinction of being the world's third-worst cape. But at thirty minutes past noon on the cold sunny day, we went around, it was a millpond. Reaching it, we found that it was not an island as first appeared, but connected by a thin isthmus that looked as if it must go under in a big storm.

Rounding the cape, we altered course to the east, for The Bight. As we did, a faint nor' westerly sprang up on cue, and I issued a special thanks to our forecaster friend.

Heralding the wind, the barometer had begun to drop. And for the rest of that day and night, it continued to slide. As it did, so the wind increased. But we didn't mind, it was from astern, so wasn't a problem. In fact, it was the next thing to heaven. The 'B' was running down the miles far faster under sail than she ever could under power. And neither Jude nor I had to steer, a chore we hate when powering.

The morning after rounding the cape, we were scampering along, and I was teeter-tottering over a decision to enter Port Albany or keep right on trucking down the miles. It was the old rhythm thing again. Once we got going, we rather hated to break our routine. But when rounding the cape, a vee belt on the engine had snapped, and my replacement was not all it should have been. A new belt would solve the problem. So, about eleven, when the wind started to pick up to a solid twenty-five, gusting thirty, I decided to make it a race; Albany before nightfall.

The wind off the land left the sea fairly calm considering its force, and it blew over the stern quarter, two conditions for a perfect sail. As the day rolled on, the wind touched gale force, making it an increasingly great sail close to a shore of polished granite boulders in the loveliest soft yellow-tan. Under a bright winter sky, the sea was a cold blue while, close at hand, the breakers constantly exploded into the most brilliant of whites. And then with everything so sharp, a pod of black and white killer whales leapt out the waves right behind us. Six, eight, ten, hard to tell, so unexpected. Don't think any of us will ever forget them racing close alongside. The awe, and fear, of such powerful creatures.

By three, we had sped through a group of off-lying islands, zigzagging with wild exhilaration through the deep channels that split them, and were beating our way up a wide empty bay of smooth water.

At this point, as I had gone quiet thinking of those whales and rounding our first big cape, Jude took the microphone, and striding front and centre she declared, "Did you know *Banyandah* came here in 1978?"

That brought everyone's focus onto her with several shaking their heads.

"Just on dusk, we were alongside your old timber jetty surrounded by a rim of hills that brought much-appreciated peace and made your town look quite dreamy actually. Our boys were charged up, hoping to get ashore, industriously collecting their strewn Leggo as instructed. Then came the magic.

"We were still cleaning up when a man and lady rapped on our railing and said, 'bet you could use a hot shower.' A whirlwind immediately followed our meeting Ted and Jeannette, who whisked us off to their house overlooking the harbour, into hot showers and then fed us big steaks. They were building a Hartley South Seas, the same design as *Banyandah*. And asked all sorts of questions until long after the boys fell asleep in front of their TV. Next day Jeanette and I baked at her place while Jack was taken to buy the V-belt. Two days later, the first of August, we departed Albany. Dead of winter as you know."

As if a winter breeze chilled my spine, Jude's recollection of departing Albany suddenly had me seeing those winter seas. Taking the microphone, I started by rubbing my arms.

"Brrr! It was so cold. We were lucky a 1020 millibar high had drifted over Albany, bringing stable, clear weather. Geared up and ready, we went out and found our friend the northwest wind off Breaksea Island, and that started our marathon run to Harry in Sydney.

"The first three days of northerly weather were great sunny days that had Jude and I wondering why all the fuss over The Great Australian Bight. It seemed just like any other body of water. But then that north wind suddenly stopped. And within an hour, it had turned southwest. Okay. No problem. We put the sails on the other side and kept going. There followed another three days of super sailing. Only this time, more gloom, with drizzle and long periods of rain with the barometer on the rise again.

"A week out of Albany, about as far from help as one can get, the barometer peaked and started to plummet. I have told others, my eyes looking mad, about the time we made that winter crossing with me on the aft deck cudgelling the heavens trying to match Nature's fury as a menacing black front approached. Earlier, before the fury had even begun, a passing ship had been lost to sight in seas taller than most buildings. We'd been most impressed by the huge half-mile distance between the crests. The air so cold, we huddled below with a pressure lantern blazing out heat and light.

"Fast approaching from astern, rolls of greenish-black cloud spitting lightning would soon be flexing her powers. Already short rigged, our mainsail down, furled tight, we only ran with twin headsails aloft. But seeing the fury behind us, I ran forward, dropped and lashed one, leaving only the storm jib poled out.

"I wonder how many have been bowled off their feet by the sea?" and stopped speaking to give the audience time to muse the question. Some shook their heads others pursed their lips. "Well, you could see it coming. Great sheets of white spume ripped off the wave tops tumbling and rolling towards us, the ocean seething grey white. The wind, trying to flatten the swells. Its attack felt like being hit by a freight train. The rage we heard coming. *Banyandah* began lifting to a wave towering twice the height of her mast. And when the top third tumbled and turned white, froth flew from its crest. And in a deafening roar, just like a train, it chased *Banyandah* down till it washed right over us.

"Catapulted off my feet, my hands locked around a wire stay. Desperate to hang on, my legs out like a flag in a gale, the sea tried to take me down to meet Davy Jones."

"We all got quite a shock from that and suddenly felt quite alone in our isolated world.

"Instantly learning new respect for the power of the sea, we could see that storms are not just one wave, but many attacking relentlessly. They sink ships by ripping sails, disabling machinery, tiring the crew. It's far more powerful than you can ever imagine. And to her great credit, *Banyandah* proved herself a fantastic sea boat. She tracked straight down wavefronts, no hint of broaching, helped by being pulled along by a headsail only. And her stout rig held firm.

"A few years later, we got flipped upside-down in the middle of the North Pacific. Her masts fully buried, when we came back up, they were intact, but the sails were in tatters.

"But that's another story. This retiree is ready for bed. So if we've answered your questions, maybe should we wrap this up?"

Later on in bed and still excited from our presentation, Jude and I were unable to sleep and relieved our tension by comparing our Southern Ocean crossings. The first, tantamount to the scariest ride imaginable, we had survived, and through the tinted glass of time has become one of our greatest adventures. Our crossing from Albany to Tasmania two years before defied all expectations by being the most wondrous experience. Full of Nature's beauty, and surprisingly, heaps of wildlife. And this one just past, the shorter crossing of The Bight that brought us to Albany, well, as you've read, a most enjoyable experience.

In the short debate that followed, sleep thickened our thoughts and blurred the image of our seven grandchildren into a warm cuddly glow that decided us to turn *Banyandah* around and sail a fourth time across the Great Southern Ocean, back to Tasmania.

My last thought as I drifted off; well, we're really just big kids. Once inside the candy shop, our lines off the dock, a change of mind still might be made!

~ Chapter 25 ~

Bound for Tasmania

WHEN THE SEA ROARS LIKE A PACK OF HUNGRY LIONS and the wind howls as if a world of living dead, who amongst us are warriors?

Oh, my head still hurts as if it's going to shatter. Aye, from too much celebrating. You see, we made landfall yesterday. And my body still aches. Not from too much celebrating, but a thrashing by an angry sea.

Jude and I may have been bound for Tasmania from the West Australian coast; however, the weather gods had other ideas. Have a peek at this weather chart covering the waters between Australia and the South Pole, and you'll see a crisscross of swirling depressions that if anything, makes the weather down there unpredictable.

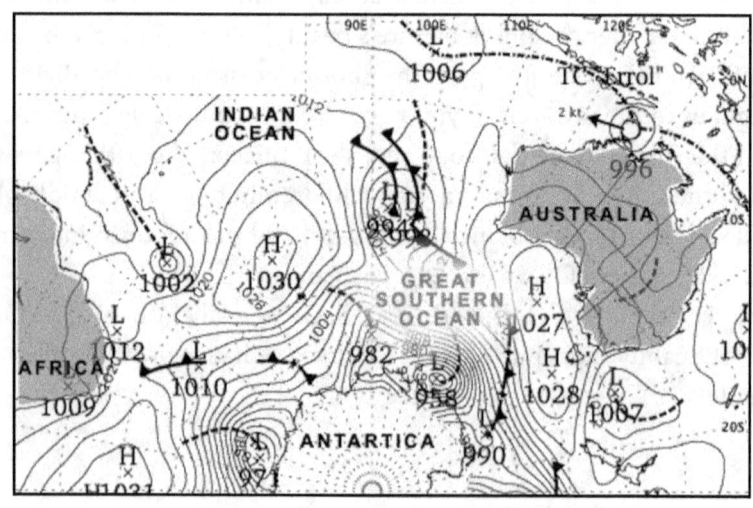

Bound for Tasmania

Two years ago, we completed this very same passage very successfully. When setting off this time, we were going to follow the same plan by first finding a way through the coastal headwinds to the westerly flow on the other side of the summer anticyclone. Although gales and storms rage down there, that earlier crossing to Tasmania had been as placid as sleeping kittens. Taking sixteen days and nights, we had purred along surrounded by Nature so pure Jude, and I felt we were the only people upon a pond stretching to heaven.

This time we waited in Albany for a perfect weather pattern, and we had to wait weeks, our resolve sorely tested. When at last a gigantic high-pressure cell established itself over The Bight, I assiduously copied five days of weather maps that showed we'd have nothing but north winds off the backside of that immense high-pressure cell. After that, well, we'd be at the mercy of King Neptune. What I didn't see was those winds would be vicious.

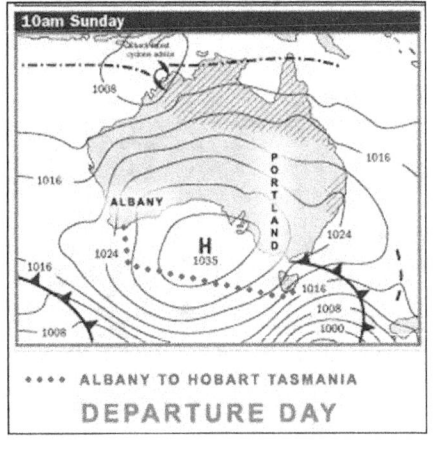

When departure day was set, last invites poured in from our Albany friends, and hectic though it was victualling our ship, we enjoyed some of the finest moments before the sea claimed us. And when departure day arrived, a Sunday morn with church bells ringing and motorboats speeding past, Jude and I packed emergency supplies into our dinghy then lashed it upside-down on our foredeck. After a last look round revealed everything locked in place, we started the diesel and began a journey into the unknown.

We left with little wind, and while motoring across King George Sound, our phone rang. Old Jack, a dear friend in poor health, was at the lookout. Turning the binoculars his way, we exchanged a wave. Sadly, that would be our last sight of a man met by chance, who had won our love and respect. Old Jack's heart of gold always shone through his sometimes cranky moments as he spun endless stories of a long-ago

Albany when he worked harbour boats. It's people like Old Jack that make our travels richly rewarding.

Almost every long-distance voyage begins with relief. The exacting preparations, hectic last goodbyes, and worry over what might lie ahead extract a tiresome toll. Therefore, by the time the real journey began, we were relieved to be lolling back somewhat exhausted, marvelling at the receding coastline. That coastline, bold with beige granite mountaintops, the world's whitest beaches and bluest waters was sighted as early as 1627 when the Dutch ship Gulden Zeepaardt sailed across the Great Australian Bight. Based on Nuyts' report of infertility, the Dutch showed no interest in settlement. But the map he drew inspired Jonathan Swift when he wrote *Gulliver's Travels*. Swift located the land of the Houyhnhnms just south of present-day Albany. With some kind of precognition, Swift had Gulliver landing on the coast, eating oysters and being chased by aborigines. Could he have known that 65 years later George Vancouver would enter one of the bays of King George Sound and name it Oyster Harbour? Or that a clan of aborigines lived on its shore?

Ominously for us, when the huge granite outcrop Vancouver had named Bald Head loomed just ahead, our path crossed two Police vessels bringing in the dead body of an 18-year-old lad swept from rocks by a king wave. Once past that point and into the king waves of the Great

Southern Ocean, the north wind found our sails, and there was no going back.

Engine secured, peace descended, but it was soon shattered by sloppy waves splashing our aft deck. Moving under the cockpit's protection, unbeknownst to us that would be our last walk around our decks for nearly a week. When a black moonless night filled the heavens with twinkling stars and land gone from sight, the wind began to moan.

We are cautious sailors. Why get out of a warm bed to battle too much sail when it's so much wiser to reduce sail area before losing daylight. So, our first night saw us flying under double reef mainsail and a tiny headsail.

In the following first light, the seas were extraordinarily steep and sloppy. Not sure why, maybe the north wind driving against the southerly swell produced not flanks of white soldiers marching against us, but erratic, individual suicide bombers. And the wind just didn't moan, it now began to howl. And with each screech, Jude stood grating her teeth pleading for it to go away.

For five days we flew at some of our greatest speeds while the sea crashed into *Banyandah's* side, sending cold green water over our ship, filling her cockpit, flooding her seats, forcing Jude and me to stay below behind the protection of our leeboards. Naturally, with water being so forcefully hurled at our poor baby, seawater found every tiny entry, and with what we tracked below on our sodden garb, *Banyandah* soon became waterlogged. Our best food in that time was pumpkin soup from a pan lashed to the stove, and cold cereal. The jarring simply sent more stuff flying.

Day five saw the high-pressure cell chased away by a developing low. I was grabbing weather maps off our amateur radio each day through some fancy software that converts faxes into images. And at first, the developing low didn't look severe. But that changed. Guess that's why they are called 'developing.'

Not all bad weather precedes a front. As with this one, it was much worse after it passed, on the sudden rise of pressure from a new high squeezing up behind. Generally, a good judge of wind strength is to look at the pressure gradients between the two systems; the tighter the gradients, the fiercer the winds.

When the actual low passed overhead, the morning became quiet and rainy, and the sea lost some of its fierceness. Our mood brightened being released from solitary confinement. At last, we could walk our decks. But when we did, to our shock and horror, the powerful seas had ripped off part of our toe rail at the front; that's the timber cap running along the outer edge of the deck. And the strong winds had ripped out an eyelet at a reefing point on our mainsail. Hmm, we think ours a stout ship, plenty of blue water has passed her keel, so we took this as a warning to be even more careful.

Both of us had already had our mishaps. I'd missed my handhold more than once and been sent flying and had seen a few timber edges rush straight at my face. Jude too had bruises violet yellow. A broken hip or smashed arm would be catastrophic, especially now, nearly a thousand kilometres from help. So, we repeatedly reminded each other about being extra careful, taking our time, making sure before leaping into action. I'm probably most at risk, jumping in when perhaps I should wait. But this is an ocean-going ship and things just happen. A line controlling a sail lets go, and unless there's immediate action, the powerful winds could destroy that sail. Middle of a black night, a metal reefing cringle works loose, smashing into one of the cockpit windows again and again. We quickly had to run off the wind or risk shattering the glass. Another time, a huge wave shifted the dinghy then squirted seawater past our aft porthole seals, flooding below. Nothing really serious - just wet, wet, wet, and so cold. Life at sea is 24/7 and never stops.

Following that depression, as we watched a new high-pressure cell approach, it looked perfect for taking us all the way around Tasmania's

South West Cape and beyond to Hobart. Then one morning, that all changed. As the day's weather map arrived line by line, it showed the high splitting into two. One part going north over the mainland, the other moving south. And that was going to be disastrous. By its shape and position, southeast winds were coming, plenty of 'em, strong ones.

In light winds, *Banyandah* can sail 45 degrees off the wind and make headway. In medium winds, it may not be comfortable with the sails pulled in as tightly as they can, but we will still go forward. In strong winds, gale winds, with  sails pulled in tight they'd blow apart, and the head seas would tear bits off our ship. We have to lay off. The stronger the wind, the more *Banyandah* is forced off the wind. Above 40 knots, down here in the southern latitudes where the sea packs a wallop, it's probably wise to run with them if we can. Some boats have to trail warps or sea anchors to slow themselves from such powerful forces. But not our Miss B. She's such a strong, chunky seaworthy ship, she's never needed to do that. Just the once, off Rottnest Island as already mentioned did we encounter such ferocious winds in tight quarters that we lay her ahull; no sail up, letting the wind force the vessel over and waves break over us.

After the south gale set in, we were forced to replot our course to the north of Tasmania and hoped to lay tiny King Island in the middle of Bass Strait. We knew Grassy Harbour to be a safe refuge on the island's east coast. But as the new storm grew in strength, this too proved impossible as

the strong winds just never let up.

Our log is peppered with comments like: *Black, too much wind, squalls to 55 knots (100 kph), Jack says aft cabin all wet, Jude to bed – on floor outside the head, both of us very tired, mainsail down, jib only, wind screeching, waves filling the cockpit.*

And others, just a few: *Lovely sunset through clouds, touched 9.3 knots, bands of clouds with strips of blue sky, hauling up course line, can make Portland. Yippee! Hopefully abeam Cape Nelson at first light.*

The last 24 hours were misty wet with dark low cloud, the wind still from the south, but now a spent force. In the poor conditions, it became even scarier because we'd been blown north into the middle of the shipping channel coming out of Bass Strait. After more than a week of isolation, Jude spotted the red and green nav lights of a cargo vessel coming straight at us. She held on until the last safe moment, and when about to change our course; maybe he saw our lights, maybe his radar picked up our  small target, whatever, he turned and passed a few hundred metres down our side. She felt good knowing that ships were watching too.

First light our tenth day at sea, through misty grey light land became visible. There was no joyous shout of "land ho." Quite simply, we were glad to have survived.

And then as we rounded Cape Nelson, the fierce motion finally began abating. Now that was a great relief. By nine, *Banyandah* was entering Portland. We'd been bound for Tasmania, but ended up in the second largest harbour in Victoria.

Entering between the break walls, our diesel was fired up, the first time since Albany, and I breathed a sigh of thanks. I'd been worried she may have ingested seawater. With elation building, we proceeded directly towards a mass of moored craft. All seemed so glorious. That is until our faithful donk started coughing. Slowing down, she sputtered then stopped. Yep. Right in the middle of a busy harbour.

Bound for Tasmania

Quizzical exchanges between Jude and I marked the last moments of forward motion. Then I made a dash for the anchor praying we had stopped out of harm's way. Diving into the engine room, turning this, prodding that revealed fuel starvation. Never had that happen before. Sometimes that occurs during or after a very rough voyage. Sediment in the tanks gets stirred up, blocking filters, or the fuel outlet line.

And what a mess. Everything in every locker had shifted, crushing spares, spoiling food, even shorting out our electric freshwater pump.

Yes, we had our butts kicked good and proper by the sea. And know what? We're buggered, and sick of being knocked about. But we're also feeling sort of lucky. Lucky to have survived. Lucky not to have broken bones. And lucky to have witnessed the impressive power of Nature and to know we are a team who can still overcome great difficulties.

Will we do it again? Sure. While we can. At our age when something is gone, it's gone forever. And besides, the world has just carried with the same old thing while Jack and Jude have had a grand adventure. And here's the dessert. Jude just worked out that this was our fastest passage - ever! We might have been bound for Tasmania, but where we ended up, we got here super fast! Thirteen hundred nautical miles (2400 km) in less than 10 days. We think that's not bad for a forty-year-old homemade boat and a couple of retirees.

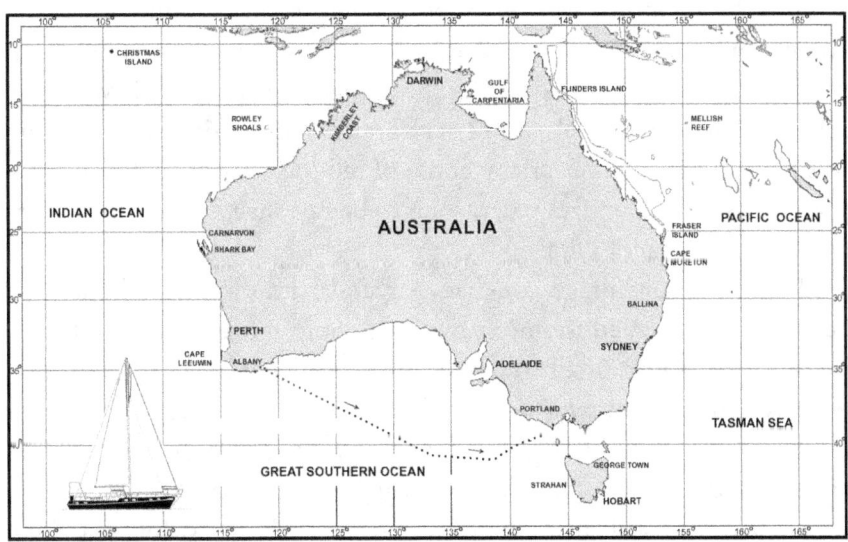

~ Chapter 26 ~

Perfection

COULD IT BE THAT ZEUS SPOKE HARSHLY TO AEGAEON, the god of storms after he had drenched *Banyandah* and given us such a beating on our Southern Ocean crossing? I wonder that because since landing in Victoria, we've had sunshine and calm weather and a feeling of celebration.

It began shortly after going ashore at the Portland Yacht Club where a key to the clubhouse was bestowed upon us by their commodore. Hot, voluminous, lengthy showers were followed by copiously washing out seawater from our bedding and clothes. Then early that April evening of 2011, a romantic candlelit dinner celebrated Judith's 66 years of life on this planet. Add a rather pricey bottle of red to start her next year, well, that put us in bed, on fresh, dry, soon to be hot sheets. Oh la la, the ups and downs of a sailor's life!

From our anchorage, we had a grandstand view of all the port activities that seemed to go on non-stop. Ship movements numbering the second greatest of all Victorian ports involving tugs and line boats were complemented by a bevy of fishing boats steaming in with their catches and being followed by clouds of gulls. Some boats were of a traditional design that compelled us to grab our cameras. Regular visitors were a family of seals marauding around the anchored yachts searching for tucker, and they amused us one morning when they found a tasty cod and began chucking it back and forth as if playing school rugby. Table manners - none - they just seemed to be having fun.

That same weekend, the one before Easter, the Portland Game Fishing Club held their annual tuna fishing contest. Of course, Jude and I didn't partake; we catch only what we can eat straight away. Increasing in numbers each year, over 500 fishing boats targeted tuna, and this year's catch was one of the biggest. This alarmed us when we read a fisheries report stating southern bluefin are overfished around the world, with little likelihood of recovery under current catch levels. Now, we love being hunter-gatherers, it's a right bestowed at birth on planet Earth, so when we hear the human population is set to double in the coming future, that's fewer resources for more people, and that means increased restrictions. There's another reason why reducing the world's population will be beneficial.

We departed Portland on Good Friday with no apology to the followers of Jesus Christ because He would have known the new high-pressure entering The Bight was going to generate the westerly winds we needed for our voyage across Bass Strait to King Island. In the predawn darkness, the harbour lights in the falling drizzle made the weather more suited to a crucifixion than a pleasant crossing of those dreaded narrows. The anchor came up, and straightaway a squall sent me forward to shorten the mainsail. Within an hour of departure, we were hunkered down; leeboards slotted in and us wondering if we were going to get slugged yet again. However, this time Poseidon and Zeus seemed to be keeping an eye on our tiny craft as we began to race across one of the world's most dangerous shipping channels.

Thanks to the gods, the sea only splashed *Banyandah's* decks a few times, never wetting her cockpit while albatross and golden head gannets frequently eyed our fishing lure. Clever creatures, they did not dive-bomb it.

Late in the day when the wind finally eased to under twenty knots (36 kph), a passing rain shower created a rainbow that landed a pot of gold right on our cabin top. No gold coins were left behind just a night sky so crisp and clear we could have reached up and touched the stars. On my watch, *Banyandah* slowed to a walking pace while I admired Orion's Belt sinking toward the western horizon. So different from Jude's time in command, she always attracts the wind.

Maybe Zephyrus has a crush on my lady, or she has a secret allure that calls to him whenever she's on watch? Soon after midnight, he came to her and raised the tempo beyond my previous best. After twenty-two hours of sailing with still another two hours of darkness, Judith recorded seeing the Cape Wickham Lighthouse winking at her from the north tip of King Island. Then as the morning star went to bed, I got up and there abeam stood the white stone structure surrounded by those rolling green hills that make this island so famous. The light structure, quite unique in the southern hemisphere for being the tallest at 48 metres, was constructed in 1861 after Australia's worst maritime disaster with the wrecking of the *Cataraqui* and loss of more than four hundred lives.

The treacherous waters surrounding King Island are notorious for strong currents and being strewn with sharp rocks well off its coast. They have claimed hundreds of ships and far more than a thousand lives.

That morning, to those dangers was added a strengthening gusty wind that lifted the sea into clouds of wet spray. Thankfully we had timed our journey to perfection. Just as it started getting boisterous, we were slipping behind the island's lee with Jude declaring, "How good is this!" Now racing with the wind off the land, tucked close along the black rocky shore, we loved every moment flying past vacant green hills, working *Banyandah*, feeling the power in the gusts.

That night, sheltered close under the cliffs at Naracoopa, our first visit to what is just a sleepy enclave halfway down King Island's east coast, we were rocked to sleep hearing the west wind moan.

Next morning, a rather lazy slow start saw us eventually motor without much wind ten miles further south to Grassy Harbour. The swell becoming so surprisingly big, we had to time our entry or risk a disaster. But that just made it all the more exciting, Jude driving the boat, me watching astern and having her ease the throttle when being lifted by a nearly breaking big one that we rode into the former scheelite mine port.

The previous year, when stopping here en-route to South Australia, we met several fine Islanders. One couple we became good friends with, John and Lyn, own a beef farm as well as a Westsail sloop. They were off-island when we arrived, but like all good mates, they arranged for the use of their Land Rover. On our first day gadabout, Jude packed a picnic, and we went off to tour their beautiful island. South first to Seal Rocks overlooking the island's southwest. The wind had long evaporated, leaving a smooth blue sea gently lining the many jagged rocks in white. There was not a soul in sight when Jude and I stretched upon the grassy hillside to let the sun warm our weary bones. Propped on our elbows looking back towards the horizon we had just come from, of our many thoughts we pondered the long miles just sailed and felt very privileged to have done so.

Gosh, we're so fortunate. Still fit and well-balanced, which is so important, and with a will and desire to continue exploring this magical Earth. And blessed with a growing family, who might think we're a tad mad, but support our crazy notions anyways.

We toured the island from bottom to top until John and Lyn flew in, then presto. We changed into party hats.

On that same morning, Judith had rowed over to purchase a scale-fish from a fisherman just in, and he'd given her a weather-beaten smile then dipped his hand in his fish box ready for shore, and handed across a rather large, red crayfish missing a few legs.

Later that night John cooked it Thai style. Yum! This was our first feast. The next night we filled up on Island beef. Except for Jude. She and Lyn had raided the garden, and Jude was feasting on the harvest.

Such a rollicking time was had that we were delighted when John and Lyn accepted our invitation to sail with us to the Three Hummocks Island, and beyond to George Town where they could catch a return flight. It would be Lyn's first sail ever. It's a fact that at our very first meeting, John had whispered into our ears, "You'd do me a great favour if you can think of ways to enthuse Lyn to sail with me…"

Well, we just had. Picking them up from the dock as the morning sun began pouring liquid gold upon the eastern horizon before Lyn could have a change of heart, we quickly raised sail and ran towards that fast-rising orb.

As I said to her, "You'll find the passage rather bumpy." That's because, between King and Tasmania, fast currents meet the rather huge Southern Ocean swell. But Lyn handled it well, almost like a duck to water. Fortunately, the sea was kind, and all too soon, after a rather romantic cruise of forty-five miles for those two, we had the anchor down in front of the Hummocks homestead

Three Hummocks lies in the lee of Hunter Island and the anchorage off the homestead at Chimney Corner was mirror smooth with reflections of a rather quaint rust streaked jetty fronting a windmill that formed a perfect setting for the period house up the rise.

For many centuries, this island was the summer hunting ground of the North West Aborigines who reached it by swimming five kilometres of open water from nearby Hunter Island.

Farming took place from the late 1800s. But in 1976, the majority of the 7,400 hectares were declared a Nature Reserve, with about 40 hectares staying a pastoral lease.

The following morning we rowed ashore to explore what we thought were abandoned buildings. We yahooed when reaching the rather nicely restored period building, but heard not a peep. Wandering on and rounding a line of scrub, an extensive flat of finely manicured grass spread before us, stopping us dead in our tracks.

Upwards of a hundred Cape Barren Geese, not the least disturbed by our sudden presence, dotted the smooth green. In fact, many of them facing another just kept bobbing their heads in courtship while our video camera whirled and digitals clicked. Jude and I were reminded of our travels through the Galapagos Islands,  where the wild creatures have no fear of man and carried on their normal life in our presence. More humans should have these experiences. It would help change the way we view the wild kingdom.

Having had our Nature slug for the day, we soon discovered a hen house full of chooks. Hmm, someone must be around. So we approached a second building, yahooing again after noticing a large telescope dominating the picture window facing *Banyandah* and the view across the gap to Hunter Island. This time, a gruff, "just a minute," answered our calls.

Looks passed between us as we made our way around the back where we bumped into a well-tanned outdoorsman, a beefy hardworking type sporting a very welcoming grin.

"Sorry. The wife's still in bed. Not so well this morning after staying up all night watching the royal wedding," he said with a shake of his head.

Well, that was just the start of one of those fabulous meetings in far-flung out of the way places. The sounds of shuffling feet, Bev quick out of bed, and far from looking ill, was smiling ear to ear and straightaway fussing over us before taking Jude and Lyn to her collection of island wonders. While, in true Aussie style, the boys hung back in the kitchen where Bev's husband John made tea while we yarned about a wide range of subjects. For example, the caretakers' predecessors: The Nichols family, Bill and Amelia (Ma) who had leased the island from 1933 until 1950, grazing cattle and sheep; followed by the Alliston family. After our cuppa, we got the full tour through each and every building, heard all the stories and got all the goss.

John was a wealth of knowledge and a man of many skills. He had rebuilt several of the old buildings for the two businessmen who now owned the lease and were developing it for tourism. More than that, he and Bev had created one of the finest gardens we'd ever seen using goose dung, kangaroo droppings, and several other naturally occurring ingredients including ground-up bull kelp that they harvested off the beach. Their half-acre garden had to be fully enclosed, or the roos would eat it clean. So much information, no wonder I had to wander off and sit quietly for a half-hour. Nodding off, I heard Bev suggest seeing the island by Land Rover and quickly jumped up to join the rest.

Our ride bumped through scrub forests to the island's airfield then up to the highest point, South Hummock, 237 M above sea level. A geodetic point was established there in 1943 when an Australian copper penny was glued to the highest rock on the island.

According to caretaker/resort manager John, who'd been a woodturner in another life, much of the island is composed of dense scrub dominated by *Leptospermum scoparium*, *Melaleuca ericifolia* and *Banksia marginata*, while 25% of the area is covered by *Eucalyptus nitida* woodland.

This is one of the purest environments on the planet. Crystal clear water, white sandy beaches, inland lakes, and forests largely untouched, while twenty kilometres away, a Baseline Air Pollution Station consistently measures the air as the cleanest in the world. That's quite a place to live. All this, absolutely free if you're onboard the good ship *Banyandah*.

Next morning the wind turned south, making Chimney Corner a lee shore, so we sought sanctuary across the channel at Shepherd's Cove on Hunter Island. Here we played Robinson Crusoe, fishing for our dinner, wandering the rocks looking for molluscs, setting traps for  one or more of the spiny crabs whose shells we found dotting the sandy shore. Crumbed kelpies ended up filling our dinner plates, a delicacy flown live to Asia, but heck, we didn't have to pay that exorbitant price.

Day three of our wonderful cruise found the Fun Four, as we now called ourselves, sailing back to Three Hummocks and into Coulomb Bay, the large bay facing north-west where we'd been the year before. Hallelujah! This time when we walked the uninhabited beach that sprouted huge granite monoliths. While exploring the Nature Reserve,

Cape Barren Geese honked from the tussocks, and Forester grey kangaroos stretched tall then froze as if statues and gazed. When we reached Ranger Point, Lyn's John bared all to dive under the waves, and he brought back that yummy delicacy - blacklip abalone. Quite comical seeing him stagger out. Oh, so brave. It must have been very cold in just his undies that now bulged with much more than his manhood!

During our stay, the winds were light and contrary, nothing useful for completing our last hop of a hundred miles to George Town on the Tamar River. That would require an overnight run. I'd kept an eye on the weather, watching a cold front approach, and planned to use its westerly wind to complete our passage to mainland Tasmania. Each day as the front came closer, my plan solidified for a Tuesday afternoon departure.

That last morning we investigated several more bays on Three Hummocks northern shore, caught and ate some delicious fish thanks to Lyn's prowess, before packing our clobber and cinching down all loose items.

Right from the very start, this passage became one we'll always cherish. Now sailing in the lee of Hunter and Three Hummocks, those big nasty swells from Antarctica were blocked, and we slipped nearly silently through an aqua sea until the western sky melted and cooled to deep red. Under a clear frosty night ablaze with stars, the Fun Four were mesmerized watching our sails cleave a path across the heavens. Seemed a perfect setting to reminisce our perfect cruise; the fine food, good friendship, and Natural wonders. Isn't this how life on Earth is supposed to be? To explore and learn, to wonder and help one another, and not be jealous, or what's so detrimental, greedy.

Much later, when the horizon ahead cracked open to show a slender slash of yellow light, to its right winked the Low Head light just as it had the year before, and for more than a century before that. As the sun rose further, the north shore of Tasmania became rolling green; and to seaward, I spied a ship heading our way. Then in front, a white and yellow pilot vessel was spotted speeding out to sea sending spray skywards that caught the yellow rays, turning them into rainbows.

"There's a race on here," I said to John and Lyn sipping morning cuppas under the protection of our dodger. Lyn ventured a look, and the breeze whisked her hair in front of her eyes. Pulling it away, she enquired, "What do you mean, a race?"

"Well. That ship's going into the Tamar, up to Bell Bay, and the channel's pretty narrow."

"So what will you do?"

I scrunched up my shoulders. "Keep carrying sail. See who gets there first, hey."

And so, adding to the spectacle of a new day rising over such glorious scenery, we now kept our eyes darting to sea, checking the bearing to that container ship. It stayed steady as we closed the gap to the first marker.

I felt the tempo of my heart rise a notch and could see the others peeking forward and then to the ship gaining in size. The wind never faltered; crisp and fresh off the land, filled with the delightful aroma of grassy fields and scant forests.

To save a bit of time, I directed *Banyandah* inside Hebe Reef. Ahead, less than two miles stood the first entrance marker at Yellow Rock, and still, we carried the twenty-five-knot breeze aft of our beam, sending our ship at maximum speed through the slight seas.

John slid up behind Lyn, where she stood leaning against the dodger top and embraced her as I have embraced my own woman so many times in our life together. Loins touching, feeling each other's heat, they craned forward in search of the green entrance marker then looked sideways to the looming ship.

Jude sang out from the sounder, "Bottom's coming up! Thirty feet."

"Cool baby, we're way ahead of that fella. Just hope he doesn't pass us in the narrow channel." I was mentally trying to calculate whether we were losing or gaining ground on his boiling bow wave. Jumping down aft to read the GPS, Jude came with me, and together we recited the order of markers and buoys.

"Green first on our right then either side of the east cardinal mark. There's water inshore if that ship's on top of us. After that, it's dead south down Sea Reach, which we may have to motor."

Back topsides, the first marker whizzed past so close Lyn reached out jokingly trying to touch it. That brought giggles and even bigger smiles all round. Although we now heard him coming and could see into his bridge, the ship was losing the race when we zipped close to the east cardinal mark. At the wheel, Jude turned at the last second to pass it on the channel side, saying she didn't like losing any depth of water.

In the end, magic happened. We raced ahead of that ship and didn't lose the fair wind until zipping around Patterson's Monument commemorating the lieutenant's first landing in 1804. Seconds later, we were dropping sails before slipping into historic York Cove surrounded by George Town, the quaint third settlement of Australia.

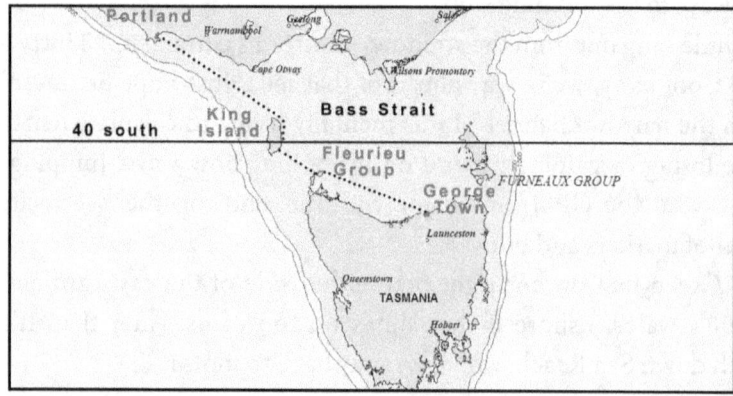

Perfection

Lynette had gotten her baptism of sail. She had crossed the thorny passage and explored isolated islands before her final challenge of sailing through an inky black night. She even raced a ship in the Roaring Forties. Did she enjoy being miles offshore upon an icy cold sea? Had she felt fear?

Here's what Lyn wrote in our guest book on May 5, 2011:

> "Thanks, Jack and Jude for a most fantastic first sailing experience. I had a brilliant time, loved Judith's amazing cooking, our time on Hunter, Three Hummocks, walking isolated beaches, meeting John and Bev, catching fish, and seeing the sun rise at sea. The overnight sail was great. Thank you for sharing your boat. You are obviously such in tune sailors, wonderful seeing you work together. Enjoyed the last six days immensely."

John added this footnote:

> "A great way to introduce my bride to sailing. A special gift. Thanks, Jack and Jude."

SELECT BIBLIOGRAPHY

Hordern, Marsden, King of the Australian Coast, The Miegunyah Press, 1997

Hill, Ernestine, My Love Must Wait. The Story of Matthew Flinders. Angus and Robertson

Forester, Elaine, Black Jack Anderson, Penguin Books, 2008

Brettingham-Moore, Maritime Tasmania – A cruising guide with historical notes, 1988

Laws, Steve, Fremantle Sailing Club, Western Australian cruising, 2nd edition, 1998

Flood, Josephine, The Original Australians: story of the Aboriginal people, Allen & Unwin - Reference to Truganini page 87

Online sources:

Flinders, Matthew, A Voyage to Terra Australis, G. and W. Nicol, 1814
http://www.archive.org/download/avoyagetoterraau12929gut/12929-h/12929-h.htm

Scott, Ernest, The Life of Captain Matthew Flinders,
Angus & Robertson, Sydney, 1914
http://www.archive.org/stream/cu31924028661811#page/n7/mode/2up

Flinders' Discovery of Southern Australia
http://gutenberg.net.au/ausdisc/ausdisc1-16.html

The stories behind the Macquarie Harbour region
http://www.parks.tas.gov.au/file.aspx?id=6778

Wild Goose Chase, Landline, Reporter: Tim Lee 7/10/01
http://www.abc.net.au/landline/stories/s379354.htm

St Francis Island, The Register, Adelaide, December 28, 1914
http://trove.nla.gov.au/ndp/del/article/59937139

Brand, Ian, Macquarie Harbour Research, Volume1, Penitentiary New, Department of Primary Industries, Parks, Water & Environment, Hobart
http://www.dpipwe.tas.gov.au/library/catalogues.html

Heeres, J. E., The Part Borne by the Dutch in the Discovery of Australia 1606-1765
http://gutenberg.net.au/ebooks05/0501231.txt

Information on Tasmanian Aborigines, southernmost people during the Pleistocene era.
http://en.wikipedia.org/wiki/Tasmanian_Aborigines

Australian sea lion
http://www.environment.gov.au/coasts/mpa/gab/sea-lion.html

Glossary

Aback: The wind is on the wrong side of the sails. Sometimes done deliberately to slow the speed.

Abeam: At right angles to the boat's centreline.

Aft: Towards or at the stern of the boat.

Antifouling: A specially formulated paint for coating a boat beneath the waterline to prevent growth of weed and barnacles.

Autopilot: An electric steering device that turns the rudder either via the steering wheel or directly.

Athwartships: Across a ship from side to side.

Beat: To sail as close as possible to the wind.

Beating to windward: Means tacking up wind.

Bilge, bilges: The lowest most internal part of the boat's hull used as a sump to drain any water which may have collected in the boat.

Bloke: a man

Bloody: very (bloody hard yakka)

Boom: Spar that runs horizontally to hold out the bottom of the mainsail.

Bow: Towards or at the front of a boat.

Bulkhead: Vertical partition usually installed to divide a vessel into cabins, and/or watertight compartments. Some bulkheads are for rigidity of construction.

Chainplates: Metal fittings on the sides and stern of a boat to which are fastened the standing rigging or shrouds.

Clew: After lower corner of a fore-and-aft sail.

Cockpit: Central lowered area between the forward living area and the aft cabin, where the helm and compass are.

Companionway: Opening and ladder leading from below decks to above decks.

Cooee: Nearby, I was within cooee of landing a big fish when the line broke.

Dodger: The solid structure over the forepart of the cockpit that protects the helmsman and companionway from the weather.

Fit-out: The built in interior of the boat.

Foredeck: The area of deck forward of the cockpit.

Forward: The front part of a vessel, at or near the bow.

Forestay: Rigging stay which runs from the stemhead on the bow to high on the mast. The headsails or jibs are set from the forestay.

Furling Headsail: Headsail set on an aluminium (foil) tube. This tube encases the forestay and the sail is stowed by rolling it around the foil.

Gooseneck fitting: Metal fitting at the forward end of the boom that attaches it to the mast, allowing the boom to turn in any direction.

Gybe: Turning a sailing vessel so that the wind passes from one side to the other across the stern.

Halyard: A rope, wire or wire-rope combination used for hoisting and lowering sails and flags on a mast.

Head: Toilet area in a vessel.

Keel: The for-and-aft protruding fin under a vessel. The keel provides stability and stops sideways drift.

Knockdown A knockdown is the term used when a yacht is rolled over with her masts and sails in the water – usually in violent squalls or huge breaking seas.

Lead: The direction taken by a rope or sheet. Lead blocks are used to alter the direction.

Log: Ship's journal in which all references to weather, navigation, and daily happenings aboard are recorded. Also a short version of 'sumlog': the device for measuring a boat's speed and distance travelled.

Loom: To appear in view indistinctly. Loom in the clouds is light reflected from a source below.

Luff: Forward edge if a fore-and-aft sail. The luff of the mainsail is the leading edge that runs up the mast.

On the nose: The wind comes from the direction in which one wants to sail. Beating to windward when the wind is on the nose.

Portholes: The windows in a vessel.

Reach: To sail on all points of the wind except running square.

Reef: To reduce sail area by folding (slab), rolling or lashing up sections of the sails. *Banyandah* has a roller-reefing headsail on the furling foil, and a slab reefing mainsail.

Rhumb line: A direct line between two points.

Roller furler: Rotating foil and drum, usually over a forestay, for the headsail to roll and furl around.

Rudderpost or stock: Shaft to which the rudder is attached.

Running square: Sailing with the wind directly from behind.

Running rigging: The ropes used to control the sails.

Sextant: Navigation instrument that measures the angles of heavenly bodies in relation to the horizon.

Sheets: Lines or ropes attached to and used to trim or control the sails.

Sheila: A woman

Skeg: Metal or timber support for a rudderpost.

Slipped: To slip a vessel is to haul it out of the water for repairs, modification, or antifouling treatment.

Sole: Floor of the cabin in a yacht.

Stem: The stem is the curved part of the boat at the bow into which the side parts of the boat run. The stemhead is the top of this structure at deck level.

Stern: Furthest aft part of a vessel.

Stern gland: Gland where the propeller shaft runs through the hull. The stern gland is usually packed with greasy hemp so that the shaft can turn but water cannot enter the hull.

Standing rigging: The wires supporting the masts.

Sumlog: Device to measure a vessel's speed and distance travelled.

Swages: Metal bands or collars that are slipped over two wires and then crimped with a special tool so that the wires are joined together.

Tacking: To bring vessel into wind then take wind on the other side.

Tinny: Small aluminium boat

Top End: Far north of Australia

Transom: The back of the hull, running across the stern.

Ute: Utility vehicle, pickup truck

Windvane: A mechanical device that steers a yacht in a direction in relationship to the wind. *Banyandah* has its own small rudder (servo) attached by lines to the steering tiller.

Yakka: Work (noun), as in hard yakka

www.ingramcontent.com/pod-product-compliance
Lightning Source LLC
Chambersburg PA
CBHW050631300426
44112CB00012B/1749